Jerzy Skolimowski

Jerzy Skolimowski

The Cinema of a Nonconformist

Ewa Mazierska

berghahn
NEW YORK · OXFORD
www.berghahnbooks.com

First published in 2010 by
Berghahn Books
www.berghahnbooks.com

©2010, 2013 Ewa Mazierska
First paperback edition published in 2013

Library of Congress Cataloging-in-Publication Data
Mazierska, Ewa.
Jerzy Skolimowski : the cinema of a nonconformist / Ewa Mazierska.
    p. cm.
Includes bibliographical references and index.
ISBN 978-1-84545-677-1 (hardback) -- ISBN 978-1-78238-055-9 (paperback)
-- ISBN 978-1-78238-056-6 (retail ebook)
1. Skolimowski, Jerzy--Criticism and interpretation. I. Title.
PN1998.3.S585M39 2010
791.43023'3092--dc22

                                        2009047791

British Library Cataloguing in Publication Data
A catalogue record for this book is available from the British Library

Printed in the United States on acid-free paper

ISBN 978-1-78238-055-9 paperback ISBN 978-1-78238-056-6 retail ebook

Contents

List of Illustrations

Acknowledgements

I wish to express my gratitude to Iwona Kurz, Jonathan Owen and Iwona Sowińska for reading the whole or parts of this manuscript and their insightful comments.

I am also indebted to Jacek Cegiełka, Aleksandra and Janusz Gazda, Sebastian Jakub Konefał, Iwona Kurz, Krzysztof Loska, Małgorzata Mazierska, Michał Oleszczyk, Grażyna Grabowska, Waldemar Piątek and Adam Wyżyński, who helped me to find the films, journals, books and stills. I am also grateful to Janusz Gazda for providing me through correspondence with a wealth of useful information about the Polish film industry in the 1960s.

My special thanks goes to Jerzy Skolimowski and his wife, Ewa Piaskowska, who provided me with the vast majority of stills used in the book and granted the permission to use them, as well as inviting me to their home, which allowed me to interview them and see *Four Nights with Anna*, which was at that time not available to the general public. Without their generosity and help, this book would contain many more mistakes than it has now and would have lacked some vital information.

Introduction

Outsider, Nonconformist, a Man In-between

Jerzy Skolimowski is one of the most original Polish directors and one of only a handful who have gained genuine recognition abroad. This position is evidenced by awards Skolimowski has received at international festivals, favourable opinions from the most influential European critics and fellow film makers, including Jean-Luc Godard, and the willingness of stars such as Jean-Pierre Léaud, Alan Bates, John Hurt and Jeremy Irons to appear in his films. Yet unlike Roman Polański, Krzysztof Kieślowski and Andrzej Wajda, Skolimowski enjoys a cult following rather than worldwide popularity. This is largely due to the fact that his films, many of which are practically inaccessible, are regarded as elitist and difficult to comprehend. For most of his career Skolimowski has rejected the rules of cinematic genres and oscillated between realism and non-realism, mainstream and avant-garde. Moreover, he does not comfortably fit any label capturing national allegiance. Both Western and Eastern critics are unsure whether they should call him a 'Polish director' or an 'international director of Polish origin', not to mention using descriptions such as 'British director' or 'American director'. There are even problems classifying the nationality of his individual films. For example, in Poland *Moonlighting* and *Success Is the Best Revenge* are regarded as Skolimowski's non-Polish films and treated separately from the films he made in Poland in the 1960s. Bruce Hodsdon, on the other hand, lists them as belonging to Skolimowski's 'Polish sextet' (see Hodsdon 2003). Skolimowski's own pronouncements, in which he stresses both his patriotism and interest in Polish affairs, while simultaneously expressing his desire to conquer foreign markets and for this purpose to shoot in English, do not help to pigeonhole him. Furthermore, unlike Polański, who updated his directing skills by making at least two films in each decade and produced some genuinely popular films in the later part of his career, Skolimowski's best years as a film director coincide with his youth. After the 1980s he made only two films, including the rather unsuccessful *Ferdydurke*. Consequently, he appears to belong to the by-gone age of the rebellious 1960s and early 1970s, which poignantly contrast with the conformist, materialistic

1980s, 1990s and the new millennium.[1] This position is compounded by a perception, which the director confirms in interviews, that in the last decade or so he lost interest in cinema, wholly dedicating himself to painting (see Popiel 2006). As a result of these factors, there are no books either in Polish or in English devoted to his career, although the number of individual articles, published in many European languages, matches those about Wajda or Kieślowski.

To confirm the opinion of his non-belonging, in the majority of works devoted to Skolimowski, especially those published in Poland, he is described as an outsider (see, for example, Lubelski 1989; Uszyński 1989: 4–5; Sobolewski 1996; Klejsa 2004: 92; Kurz 2005: 74–116) or in similar terms, such as a lonely artist (see Helman 1974) or monad (see Chyła 1992). Typically this opinion is supported by the claim that neither Skolimowski nor his characters, who function as his alter ego, like mixing with the crowd but instead remain detached, and that they would rather give up on any advantages society offers them and accept loneliness and suffering, than betray their views and values. As these examples suggest, it is possible to construct a persuasive argument about Skolimowski's life and artistic persona as an outsider, yet in this book I resist calling him by this term for a number of reasons.

Firstly, I do not regard his protagonists as detached from society, as are the 'classic' outsiders, such as Roquentin from Jean-Paul Sartre's *La Nausée* or Meursault from Albert Camus's *L'Etranger*. True, they do not accept uncritically any opinion people around them offer and try to interact with society on their own terms, but they want to interact nevertheless. One is even struck by the easiness with which they divert from their itinerary and stop on their road in order to meet somebody (who might be an old friend or a complete stranger), engage in conversation and enter into activities in which their peers indulge. This is because, as I will argue in the following chapters, the urge to play and test themselves is stronger in them than the desire to preserve their integrity and distance.

As for Skolimowski himself, his cinematic career comes across not as a solitary pursuit, but rather as a model example of collaboration. He collaborated on the scripts of other directors, such as Andrzej Wajda and Roman Polański, invited friends and colleagues, such as Andrzej Kostenko and Jerzy Gruza, to work on scripts for films he directed, and allowed his actors and other collaborators, such as Kostenko, the composer Krzysztof Komeda, the actors Tadeusz Łomnicki and Jane Asher, to provide input into his films that exceeded a normal job description. Skolimowski also played a significant role in the cultural and artistic life of the 1960s. He travelled with the Komeda Sextet, making lighting for their concerts, and was linked to the students' satirical theatre, STS, befriending the leading figures of this movement, such as Agnieszka Osiecka, Zbigniew Cybulski and Bogumił Kobiela. The main actress of his early films and his then partner, Elżbieta Czyżewska, also belonged to STS. One even gets the impression that the way Skolimowski created his films reflects a certain 'club' lifestyle or mentality.[2] The films arose from encounters with his friends and members of his family and served to immortalise, sublimate and extend their discussions. It is worth emphasising that the perception of Skolimowski's cinema as originating from, registering and fostering the spirit of camaraderie is not limited to his Polish period, as demonstrated by the Prologue added by the director in 1981 to his banned film, *Hands Up!* Part of the Prologue includes Skolimowski surrounded by his friends, including his favourite actors, Alan Bates and Jane Asher, and Polish-British painter, Feliks Topolski. There is another facet to Skolimowski's career, writing poetry and painting, which lends itself to analysis more in terms of solipsistic pursuits, but this will be of little concern to this book.

Secondly, I find it paradoxical, even misleading, to call somebody an outsider who in the mid 1960s was heralded as the voice of his generation[3] and the principal creator of Polish 'third cinema' or the 'third wave of Polish cinema', alongside Henryk Kluba and Janusz Majewski – the cinema of those who were brought up in the People's Poland and addressed their films to their contemporaries (see Płażewski 1965; Gazda 1967a, 1967b, 1968; Hauschild 2007).[4] Skolimowski's position as the voice of young people was not only recognised in Poland, but also abroad, as demonstrated by his participation in the portmanteau film, *Dialóg 20–40–60*, along with Czech Zbyněk Brynych and Slovak Peter Solan. Made in Czechoslovakia, *Dialóg 20–40–60* was meant to reflect the differences in attitudes to love of people representing different generations, those in their twenties, forties and sixties. Significantly, Skolimowski who by the time *Dialóg 20–40–60* was completed, reached the age of thirty, took responsibility for depicting the youngest generation.

I also regard Skolimowski as an insider rather than an outsider because he perfectly embodies the desire to belong to transnational cinema: cinema that 'arises in the interstices between the local and the global' and has a 'singular capacity to foster bonds of recognition between different groups' (Ezra and Rowden 2006: 4), especially those based on the commonality of generational experience, as opposed to sharing the same national history and culture. Equally, Skolimowski was transnational in his ambitions, wanting to make films of European quality. It is worth citing Jan Nowicki here, the actor playing the main part in *Barrier*, who claims that before the Bergamo festival in 1966, where this film received the Grand Prix, Skolimowski conveyed his hope for the main award in these words: 'I am only scared of Visconti. The rest of the competitors do not matter'.

The last reason that I resist the label 'outsider' is the director's reluctance to be treated as such. In an interview conducted by Jerzy Uszyński and published in 1989, Skolimowski describes his life in Poland in such a way: 'I cannot say that I felt hounded or rejected, because I did not try to belong either to an official organisation or to any unofficial grouping ... However, I would not call myself an outsider because I could take from my environment everything I wanted' (Uszyński 1989: 4). This statement can be contradicted by other pronouncements, in which Skolimowski uses the term 'outsider' to describe his attitude and position (see Yakir 1982; Popiel 2006). Even when talking with Uszyński, he agrees that he was an outsider according to the journalist's definition. However, it appears to me that he started to identify with this label only when it was imposed on him, so to speak, by his exegetes, rather than taking to it naturally.

I suggest calling Skolimowski and many of his characters 'nonconformists' rather than 'outsiders'. The problem for them is not belonging but conforming: accepting what is on offer wholeheartedly and uncritically. This term also excellently captures the choices the director has made at various moments in his career. His first professional decision, to use pieces of reels allocated to him in the Łódź Film School for making a full-length feature film, *Identification Marks: None*, rather than for shooting various prescribed 'school exercises', can be perceived as the typical action of a nonconformist. By choosing to make his film in this way, he revealed astonishing inventiveness, perseverance and courage, jeopardising his chance of getting good marks and even risking complete failure. Several years later, Skolimowski decided to emigrate when the political authorities shelved his fourth film, made in Poland, *Hands Up!*, pledging that he would not work again in his native land till it could be exhibited. He kept his pledge, although, as he admitted on many occasions, the personal cost of adhering to his word was very high. These actions testify to Skolimowski's activism and self-confidence rather than withdrawal, which is the main trait of an outsider (see Wilson 1960). Many of his characters, such as Leszczyc in *Identification Marks: None* and *Walkover* or Alex Rodak in *Success Is the Best Revenge*, also at some point in their lives shun the 'easy life' in order to stay true to themselves, even if they are not entirely sure what that means.

Moreover, the director comes across as selective in his approach to various philosophical currents, as well as literary and visual traditions, such as absurdism, surrealism and expressionism. He uses them, but on his own terms. Nonconformism, to a large extent, explains his relative lack of success in the United States, where the ability to adhere to the requirements of producers, or at least to pretend that one accepts them, is at least as important as originality and professionalism.

Both in Polish and Western criticism Skolimowski's artistic persona is contextualised in two principal ways. Firstly, as Roman Polański's 'younger brother',[5] who shared many features with this director, both as a film maker and as a man. Both studied at the Łódź Film School in its heyday of the 1960s and were among the school's most colourful characters; they even became its greatest legends (see Krubski et al. 1998). Likewise, they mixed with the same people, including Komeda and Kostenko. Skolimowski co-wrote the script for Polański's *Knife in the Water* and inspired the character of the Student in this film, who also showed some similarity to Polański. In due course, Skolimowski also followed in the footsteps of the director of *Cul-de-Sac*, choosing life as an emigrant, but one who is happy to return to Poland for work, if he finds a suitable subject and favourable shooting conditions. Skolimowski and Polański both have a gift for seeing the unusual in the ordinary; to capture the absurd and the surreal below the surface of normality. The trajectories of their careers are also similar, as both started with films based on original scripts, full of jazz and lacking any overt moral message, even anarchic, to move gradually to films based on novels written by other authors, more classical in form and conveying distinctive moral messages. Furthermore, both artists combine a directing career with acting.

Secondly, Skolimowski's films, particularly those made in Poland in the 1960s and *Le Départ*, are regarded as a Polish response to the French New Wave (see Jackiewicz 1964: 7; Kałużyński 1965: 8–9; Lachnit-Lubelska 1983: 54). Skolimowski appeared to be especially close to Jean-Luc Godard. When reading

Figure I.1 Jerzy Skolimowski and Roman Polański

some years ago Luc Moullet's account of Godard's early career and persona (see Moullet 1986), I was struck by how much of what the author says about Godard is also true of Skolimowski. Prior to making films, Godard studied ethnology, Skolimowski ethnography. Godard worked in Switzerland as a labourer on the Grand-Dixence dam and he dedicated his first short film, *Opération béton* (1954) to its construction; Skolimowski was a boxer and devoted *Walkover* to this sport, largely drawing on his own experience. Both started their careers making films about young people disfranchised from society,[6] and they avoided traditional psychology. Moreover, Godard and Skolimowski showed remarkable disrespect for the rules of professional film making and succeeded in turning technical flaws into virtues in their films. Both also made their own presence in the film visible: in Skolimowski's case, by playing the main parts in the movies he directed; in Godard, by frequently lending his own voice to the film, as voice-over or by dubbing the actor. In addition, the same principle of alternation governs Godard's and Skolimowski's film making – alternation of realism and non-realism, humour and melancholy, extra- and introvertion. Finally, probably no other directors managed to make a cup of coffee to look as fascinating as they did.[7]

However, at a certain point the paths of these two directors diverged. This point was, in Skolimowski's case, *The Adventures of Gerard*, made in 1970 and based on the novel by Arthur Conan Doyle. In the director's own words, shooting this big budget film made him regret that he did not attend lectures at the film school. If he had, he would have known what 'master shot' meant and, in a larger sense, how to handle such an expensive production (see Uszyński 1990a: 21–3). This admission reveals the crucial difference between Skolimowski and Godard. Skolimowski tacitly assumes that different themes or genres require different approaches from the director, for example, a literary adaptation or superproduction demands employing techniques pertaining to traditional or mainstream cinema. Godard, on the other hand, never shunned from employing 'anti-rules' whenever it suited him. I very much regret that in the later part of their careers the authors of *Identification Marks: None* and *À bout de souffle* made different films from each other, with the exception of *Success Is the Best Revenge* (see Chapter 1), namely that Skolimowski lacked the self-belief and luck Godard enjoyed practically throughout his entire career.

In the following chapters, I will explore in more detail Skolimowski's connections with Polański and Godard by discussing the construction of their characters, visual style and use of music. By no means, however, should the context of Skolimowski's work be limited to what he has in common with these two cinematic giants. There are interesting links with the cinema of other Polish directors, especially Wojciech Jerzy Has, with whom he shared a surrealist sensibility, and Andrzej Wajda, with whom he is linked by his interest in the war and with whom he collaborated on the script of *Innocent Sorcerers*. It is highly symbolic that before Skolimowski began directing his films, he was, in a sense, an apprentice of both Wajda and Polański, the two most successful but also completely different directors to originate from Polish soil, one epitomising Polish national cinema, the other, transnational cinema. Wajda and Polański's careers thus signify the dilemma Skolimowski acutely felt practically all his life and never successfully resolved: to be a Polish or a transnational director. It is worth mentioning that on the cover of the book entitled *Filmówka* (Krubski et al. 1998), which was the popular name given to the Łódź Film School, we see three empty chairs standing in front of the sea with names attached to them. The one on the left belongs to Skolimowski, the one on the right to Polański and one in the middle has 'Andrzej Wajda' attached to it, which positions Skolimowski and Polański as siblings learning from their father, Wajda.

I also regard as important Skolimowski's connection with the work of Czech directors, especially Evald Schorm and Pavel Juráček. This is because the male characters of Schorm's *Každý den odvahu* (*Everyday Courage*, 1964) and *Návrat ztraceného syna* (*Return of the Prodigal Son*, 1966) and Juráček's *Postava k podpírání* (*Josef Kilián*, 1964) and *Případ pro začínajícího kata* (*A Case for the Young Hangman*, 1969) have much in common with Skolimowski's Leszczyc (see Chapters 2 and 3). Equally, in Skolimowski's films we find allegiance to, as well as polemic with, various literary traditions and works by authors such as Stanisław Dygat, Joseph Conrad and Witold Gombrowicz. However, situating Skolimowski's oeuvre on the world map of cinema and literature is not the main aim of this study but rather a means to analyse what is original in his films and to what extent he conformed to certain traditions, genres and ideas.

Skolimowski is the second of the three expatriate Polish directors to whom I would like to devote a monograph. The first was Roman Polański (Mazierska 2007), the third, I hope, will be Walerian Borowczyk. What interests me in their work is their willingness to stretch the borders of realism, which dominated Polish cinema after the Second World War, their preoccupation with absurdism and surrealism, and their ability to make films in postwar Poland that were anything but parochial and yet at the same time carry their Polishness into the 'wide world', making it feel universal. For the same reasons, I also regard them as 'modern' directors. I believe Polish cinema missed having a 'New Wave' of its own, or experienced this phenomenon only in its thwarted version, predominantly because of their emigration.[8]

I was not a witness to Skolimowski's early successes. He belongs to the generation of my parents. I was born in the year when Skolimowski made his feature debut, *Identification Marks: None*, and watched some of his films made in the 1960s later than those from the 1980s. Consequently, I cannot comment first hand on the atmosphere accompanying their release, but I enjoy the benefits of hindsight. Perhaps for this reason, as well as because I am also an emigrant, the division between Skolimowski's Polish films and those made abroad appears to me weaker than to those authors who have previously written about this director, focusing only on one part of his career. On the other hand, Skolimowski, in common with every true auteur, but to an extent which fascinates me, reveals a tendency to repeat and reinforce in his later films narrative and visual motifs introduced in the earlier ones. This might be explained by, on the one hand, his obsession with youth and, on the other, his 'baroque' imagination, making his films burst with symbolic meanings.

Another reason for not dividing Skolimowski's output into 'Polish' and 'foreign' is my conviction that his career was not thwarted, even less killed, by his relocation to the West, which is an opinion I often encounter in Poland. My favourite Skolimowski films come from various parts of his artistic life. Among them are some of his early Polish films, *Identification Marks: None* and *Barrier*, and some of the films he made abroad, *Le Départ*, *Deep End* and *King, Queen, Knave*. On the whole, my favourites are those which best reveal his sensitivity as a 'cinema kid', able to make a film out of anything, and in which the author's urge to explore the potential of the cinematic medium is stronger than his desire to tell a story and convey a moral message. Conversely, I am not a great fan of Skolimowski's favourite 'child', *Hands Up!* Although I am impressed by certain fragments of it, especially the beginning, showing the five main characters at a ball, and the famous sequence of erecting Stalin's image, I find the main part of the film, when the characters discuss their past and present, and lament their lack of ideals, contrived, clichéd and too long for the balance of the film.

My holistic approach to Skolimowski's cinema affects the structure of this book. Chapter 1 is devoted to autobiographical motifs in Skolimowski's films and the way he transmitted them in different chapters of his career. Chapter 2 concerns the characters, narratives and ideologies. It is divided into sections analysing the young characters' search for identity; the relationship between fathers and sons; and relations between men and women. Chapter 3 discusses the visual side of Skolimowski's films, especially their connection with surrealism, romanticism and expressionism, and some persisting visual motifs of his films, such as the house, the road and the sea. Chapter 4 is devoted to Skolimowski's encounters with literature, both in the form of adapting particular literary works and being inspired by certain ideas found in the books of writers such as Joseph Conrad and Witold Gombrowicz. Finally, Chapter 5 examines music in his films, tracing the transition from jazz scores, via pop and 'alternative' youth music, to electronic scores.

In each chapter I search for common traits in Skolimowski's films from different periods and examine whether the features exhibited by his early films were developed in the later ones. Such a method should thus allow an assessment of the continuities and discontinuities in Skolimowski's cinema and account for its richness. The division of material discussed is not sharp. For example, references to the construction of characters will recur in all chapters, as they are central to understanding, for example, the autobiographical effect, the visual style and the use of literature by Skolimowski. Hence the titles of the chapters refer more to the dominant discourse of each chapter than to their overall content. A short biography of Skolimowski is to be found at the end of the book, while an appendix, containing technical details and synopses of Skolimowski's films, allows me to avoid extensive discussion of the content of the films in the analytical chapters.

As previously mentioned, seeing Skolimowski either solely as a Polish director whose career was abruptly disrupted by political circumstances, or as an international director with merely Polish roots, has prevented serious examinations of his oeuvre, both by Polish and non-Polish critics. It appears as if neither East nor West is able to accommodate him, to claim him as its own. However, it does not need to be so forever – the history of cinema is not written once and for all, but can be changed by proposing new insights and creating new discourses. This book is such an attempt in regard to Skolimowski's cinema and, albeit in a small measure, to Polish and world cinema.

That Skolimowski needs to be rediscovered can be seen, for example, from the list of 'hidden gems', published in 2007 by *Sight and Sound*, in which *Deep End* is considered one such gem by David Thompson, who praises Skolimowski's films in these words: 'Skolimowski's direction is extravagant, crude and tender by turns, slapping the audience in the face with its insouciance and weird wit. The energy of a foreigner tackling British territory easily outweighs misjudgements of class accents, and today the soundtrack by Can and Cat Stevens would probably win a high cool rating' (Thompson 2007: 20). I completely agree with this assessment, and would claim that there are more 'hidden gems' in Skolimowski's CV, ready to shine brighter now than at the time they were made.

Notes

1. Such a perception is conveyed, for example, in the recent book by Iwona Kurz (2005), who situates Skolimowski among such legends of Polish culture as Marek Hłasko and Zbigniew Cybulski, all older than Skolimowski and mostly now dead.
2. Andrzej Kostenko describes his experience with collaborating with Skolimowski in this way in one of his television interviews. He also claims that Skolimowski was by no means detached during his stay in the Łódź Film School, but belonged to a group consisting of himself (by all accounts Skolimowski's closest Polish friend and collaborator), Roman Polański and Henryk Kluba. He also claims that a crucial aspect of Skolimowski's work was exchanging ideas and improvisation with fellow collaborators.
3. Maybe this paradox can be explained by the fact that in the 1960s the majority of young people in Poland felt alienated from mainstream society (unlike, perhaps, in the 1970s, where youth culture was encouraged by the authorities). In literature this idea was conveyed by the term 'a man without allocation' (człowiek bez przydziału), coined by Jan Błoński (see Błoński 1961) to describe a man who found for himself no place in society, which, as Iwona Kurz observes, perfectly fits Skolimowski's characters (see Kurz 2005: 82–3). It is worth noting that the term 'a man without allocation' points to the role of the state in allocating to young people their place in the socialist country and, consequently, its responsibility for the conformity and passivity of young people.
4. However, in later discussions of 'third cinema', Skolimowski's name was erased on account of the opinion that his films constitute a separate phenomenon (see Gazda 1968; Hauschild 2007), thus confirming the perception that he was an outsider of Polish cinema.
5. Polański is omitted from the paradigm of 'third cinema' largely because his debut film, *Knife in the Water*, was made several years earlier, and when this term was coined he was already making films abroad. However, the main character in *Knife in the Water*, the Student, is also a man who has no memory of the Second World War and shares other characteristics with the protagonists of the 'third wave'.
6. In the Polish context they were described as 'men without allocation'.
7. Compare Skolimowski's *Identification Marks* with Godard's *Vivre sa vie* (1962), where cups of coffee serve the characters as perfect companions, mirrors, and miniature models of the universe, encouraging reflections about its nature and one's place in the world.
8. The meanings of the term 'Polish New Wave' are discussed in the recent Polish–English publication, meaningfully entitled *Polish New Wave: The History of the Phenomenon which did not Exist* (*Polska Nowa Fala: Historia zjawiska, którego nie było*) (see Ronduda and Piwowarska 2008). Not surprisingly, the cinema of Skolimowski attracted the attention of a number of contributors to this volume.

CHAPTER 1

From Participant to Observer:
Autobiographical Discourse in the Films
of Jerzy Skolimowski

In his native Poland, Skolimowski is regarded as an artist who has conveyed his life and persona on screen more effectively than any other Polish film maker: the ultimate autobiographer in and for Polish cinema. This chapter attempts to establish how Skolimowski managed to convince his viewers that his films are about him, and how his self-portrait evolved over the years. Before I move to discussing Skolimowski's films and his life, it is worth briefly presenting the concept of autobiography I will use. I regard autobiography not so much as a matter of truthful representation of one's persona and life, but of the impression effected by the autobiographer on his reader (see Pascal 1960; Buckley 1984; Lejeune 1989). Accordingly, it is always relative, depending, for example, on the form used by the writer and the moment an autobiography is created and assessed. Lejeune uses the term 'autobiographical pact' but I would prefer to use the term 'autobiographical effect' because 'pact' suggests conscious decisions on the part of writer and reader to write and read a particular work as autobiographical. In reality, 'autobiographical reading' is usually involuntary, almost automatic. Moreover, as I argued elsewhere (see Mazierska and Rascaroli 2004; Mazierska 2007), 'autobiographical effect' is never solely the product of a particular work of art which mirrors somebody's life, but also a product of using one's creative work to shape one's life. As Polish philosopher, Szymon Wróbel, observes, establishing whether a work of art is an autobiography ultimately means matching one partial and subjective representation (autobiography) with another which is also partial and subjective (life). Stuart Hall presents a similar argument, maintaining that 'rather than speaking of identity as a finished thing, we should speak of *identification*, and see it as an on-going process. Identity arises, not so much from the fullness of identity which is already inside us as individuals, but from a *lack* of wholeness which is "filled" from *outside us*, by the ways we imagine ourselves to be seen by *others*' (Hall 1992: 287–88).

Skolimowski – Life and Fiction

Although Hall's and Wróbel's observations are valid in reference to every artist and every man, they ring particularly true in relation to Skolimowski, because in his case the web of life, narration and artistic creativity is extremely complex. I believe that Skolimowski used cinema (which includes, for example, interviews he gave) to create and test his different personas and correct the official version of himself; to share with the public his private life and even, perhaps, to communicate with those closest to him, his family and friends, in a way he could not achieve off-screen. Cinema also *made* Skolimowski, bringing him fame, assuring him the status of a 'cult director' and a major legend of Polish cinema. On the other hand, it severed him from his Polish roots and changed him into a migrant. After projecting on screen a certain image of himself, the director had to live up to this image in his private life, which in later instances affected his films.

To illustrate this mutual relation between life and work I would like to mention three episodes from Skolimowski's biography. The first incident concerns the fate of his fourth full-length feature film made in Poland, *Hands Up!* An important element of its mise-en-scène is a huge portrait of Stalin with two pairs of eyes. The contentious character of this image led to the censors' demand to cut from the film any footage including it. Skolimowski rejected this request, which led to much unpleasantness from the political authorities, including from Zenon Kliszko, the Party official, regarded as the second most important person in Polish politics at the time, after the First Secretary, Władysław Gomułka. The director, however, did not give in and, finally, as he himself confessed in a television interview broadcast many years later, he was offered a passport, which amounted to an invitation to leave Poland. He emigrated, to live life and make films that were without doubt very different from those he previously made in Poland. It is plausible to assume that even if *Hands Up!* had been Skolimowski's first film, he would have acted in the same principled way with the political authorities. It can also be suggested that his reputation as the chief nonconformist of Polish cinema was a factor in his resolute rejection of the offer to compromise. If he had accepted it, he might have saved his film and continued to make films in socialist Poland, even becoming its leading director, but he would have destroyed the rebellious persona he created in his previous films and in this one. When *Hands Up!* was eventually taken from the shelf in 1981, rather than allowing it to be released in its original version Skolimowski added to it a prologue (or rather Prologue with capital P, because it functions almost like a film in its own right), in which he explains the circumstances in which this film was banned in Poland, as well as describing his life concurrent to the period of *Hands Up!*'s belated release. It thus appears as if the director cannot accept any dissonance between his films and his biography – the films always have to be in step with his life.

The second episode concerns Skolimowski's age. According to official documents, he was born in 1936. This date is also 'confirmed' in *Walkover* (1966), in which the main protagonist is about to celebrate his thirtieth birthday. However, in an interview given in *Filmówka*, a book commemorating the history of the famous

Figure 1.1 Jerzy Skolimowski during shooting *Hands Up!*

Łódź Film School, as well as in our talk, Skolimowski presents himself as being two years younger than his birth certificate proclaims. The disparity between his real and official age apparently resulted from his poor physical state after the end of the war. The mother of the future director, wanting to save him, falsified his birth certificate, thanks to which he could go to convalesce in Switzerland (see Krubski et al. 1998: 73). The story of Skolimowski's contentious age can be regarded as trivial, but I find it symbolic of the character and status of Skolimowski's cinema, as well as of his place in Polish culture. Having two dates of birth (official and unofficial but based on personal testimony) seems fitting, given Skolimowski's position as somebody who, thanks to his films, has more than one persona or 'mask', and who can use his power of narration to correct his life. Skolimowski's 'rejuvenation' by subtracting two years from his life, using narration, brings to mind old film stars who wanted to be regarded as younger than they were according to official documents (Pola Negri apparently had several dates of birth). More importantly, it increases the temporal distance between Skolimowski and the war generation. Having been one year old when the war began, the future director was not only excluded from anti-Nazi resistance, but could not even have any significant memory of the war. Not remembering wartime is an important trait of Skolimowski's protagonists in films such as *Identification Marks: None* and *Barrier*, distinguishing them from the generation of war veterans. By presenting himself as somebody who is two years younger, Skolimowski thus increases the similarity between himself and his protagonists. Finally, the story of a wrong date on an official document excellently conveys Skolimowski's distrust of officialdom, especially of any documents produced in socialist Poland. Again, this is also a motif present in many of his films, most importantly in *Identification Marks: None* and *Hands Up!* I must emphasise that I am talking here only about the associations the story of the 'wrong date of birth' has for me, without assessing its authenticity, something I am unable to do.

The third episode refers to the director's relation with Elżbieta Czyżewska, who was perhaps the greatest Polish female star of the 1960s. This actress played in Skolimowski's short films, *Little Hamlet* and *Erotyk*, as well as in *Identification Marks: None* and *Walkover*, where her presence, however, is reduced to a photographic image. These films trace the development of the director's relationship with Czyżewska, from youthful interest in *Little Hamlet*, through erotic fascination in *Erotyk*, to a more complex, multidimensional relationship in *Identification Marks: None* and, finally, separation and her fading away from the director's memory in *Walkover*. They also mirror a certain ambiguity of this relationship, which is lacking from Skolimowski's relationship with Joanna Szczerbic, his later wife, as represented on and off the screen. In particular, we never learn whether Teresa in *Identification Marks: None* is Leszczyc's wife or only plays this role. Similarly, most critics claim that Czyżewska and Skolimowski were married, while in interviews Skolimowski denies this claim and is generally rather taciturn about this chapter of his private life (see Lichocka 1994: 7). Indeed, if the director and the actress never married, then do the critics attribute to him something which they learnt about his cinematic creation, Andrzej Leszczyc? Or, perhaps, it is rather Skolimowski who follows Leszczyc in denying Czyżewska any important role in his life? Again, I do not have answers to these questions and they do not interest me very much. I ask them only to draw attention to the complex mesh of life and fiction in Skolimowski's case.

The presence of autobiographical discourse both links and distinguishes Skolimowski from Roman Polański. The films of both directors lend themselves to autobiographical reading, as both engage with such issues as the condition of an emigrant. Both directors also tended to cast their wives in their films. However, prior to making *The Pianist*, Polański never revealed any desire to make films about his life and vigorously distanced himself from any attempt by the critics to see in his characters his hidden persona. By contrast, Skolimowski consciously and openly created his characters in his own image. Polański is thus a film maker who draws on his life to furnish his characters and stories with authenticity. Skolimowski is a compulsive autobiographer who uses film as a medium to tell different versions of his own story.

Autobiographer as Participant

It is widely agreed that Skolimowski's four early Polish films: *Identification Marks: None*, *Walkover*, *Barrier* and *Hands Up!*, produce the strongest autobiographical effect of all the films he ever made. However, it is worth grouping them together with Wajda's *Innocent Sorcerers* and Polański's *Knife in the Water*, as they project a somehow similar image of the protagonist. As is documented both by Wajda and Skolimowski, Wajda invited Skolimowski to collaborate on his film because it was meant to depict the lives of young people, and by this time the future director of *Barrier* was already regarded as a specialist in this topic (see Wertenstein 1991: 42). Skolimowski fulfilled this expectation by choosing as the main character a young man sharing his interests in jazz, boxing and pretty women, and reserving for himself a small role as a young boxer. Wajda was not content with the overall effect, but not because Skolimowski's vision dominated the film, but because it did not come across more forcefully. He claimed that the effect would have been much better if the central couple were played by Skolimowski himself and Czyżewska, who were the true 'innocent sorcerers' of those times (ibid: 42). Most likely Wajda came to this view retrospectively, by watching films in which his younger colleague played main roles. His reasoning appears to be that Skolimowski's work is by 'its nature' autobiographical; therefore, to make use of his talent one should allow his autobiography to prevail, through using his own body, so to speak. A similar argument is presented by Mariola Jankun-Dopartowa, who claims that *Barrier* is a flawed film because Skolimowski does not play its protagonist (see Jankun-Dopartowa 1997: 100). In common with *Innocent Sorcerers*, Skolimowski joined the team of people writing a script for Polański's *Knife in the Water* and contributed to it immensely (see Polanski 1984: 133) because he knew the idiom of the young generation to which the film's main character belongs – it was his own idiom. Consequently, the Student in *Knife in the Water*, like Skolimowski, has blond hair, and shows no respect for the older generation (see Uszyński 1990a: 8), although he is a 'composite' character, bearing similarity both to Skolimowski and Polański.

The autobiographical effect is much stronger in the films which Skolimowski himself directed. The most obvious reason for that is the director playing the main part in three of them and having the same name in all three – Andrzej Leszczyc. The main character of *Barrier* is played by Jan Nowicki and does not have a name; instead, he is described in the script as the 'Boy'. However, the director offers enough hints within the film's diegesis and off-screen to allow many viewers and critics to regard the Boy as a variation of the character of Leszczyc and *Barrier* as a part of the 'Leszczyc tetralogy'. The most important was his desire to play in this film; he could not because of pressure the political authorities exerted on him not to do so.

Skolimowski explains that he cast himself in *Identification Marks: None* largely because of the unorthodox way the film was made. Assembled from short films he shot during his study at the Łódź Film School as students' exercises, it was made for so long and in such difficult circumstances that it would be next to impossible to employ a professional actor because hardly any actor would agree to play 'on demand' and practically for free (see Krubski et al. 1998: 149). The very difficulty of making *Identification Marks: None* instantly set it apart from the rest of Polish film production. This film was perceived as, in a sense, more than a film – a personal project, even a way of living, and over forty years after its premiere it has not lost any of its uniqueness (see Ronduda 2007). Again, this impression was confirmed by the director, who claimed that if it were not for making *Identification Marks: None*, he would not have persevered with his years as a student in the Łódź Film School (see Ziółkowski 1967: 9). As *Walkover* continued Leszczyc's adventures, it was natural that he again cast himself in the main role. Leszczyc in *Walkover* is older than in *Identification Marks: None* and has already gone through some of the experiences mentioned in the first films, most importantly expulsion from the university where he studied engineering, military service and testing himself in sport. In *Hands Up!*, Leszczyc is even older and, again, he was once expelled from university, although this time from medical school. In *Barrier*, although it was shot after *Walkover*, the main character appears to be younger than Leszczyc in the earlier film, and he is again at university, although about to leave. We see that some details of Leszczyc's life are mutually exclusive, but the general picture in terms of biographical details and character's traits is coherent (see Walker 1970: 39). Most importantly, Leszczyc is partly a rebel, partly a drifter, but neither to an extent which would preclude his future integration to society. It is even possible to construe him as a conformist (see Ronduda 2007).

The cumulative effect of playing a similar character, furnished with the director's physicality, was more important in creating an autobiographical effect than attributing to Leszczyc the adventures and personal traits of the 'real' Skolimowski. Had Skolimowski played Leszczyc only once, the effect would be much weaker, even if his incarnation had more in common with him. Similarly, if in *Identification Marks: None* a different actor was cast, it would be difficult to link this film with the following three, even if Skolimowski played in them. The 'Andrzej Leszczyc effect' can be compared here with the 'Antoine Doinel' effect in the films of François Truffaut, except that the autobiographical effect of the films of the Polish director is stronger because, unlike Truffaut, Skolimowski played his alter ego.

Paradoxically, the impression that we watch the director's autobiography in the 'Leszczyc tetralogy' was also facilitated by a certain sketchiness of the main character. As Konrad Eberhardt observes, Leszczyc is more 'opaque' than his counterparts in the films which Skolimowski only scripted. We know less about him than about the Student from Polański's *Knife in the Water* and Bazyli from *Innocent Sorcerers* (see Eberhardt 1982: 116). Janusz Gazda refers to the same feature, describing Leszczyc as 'abstract' (Gazda 1967b: 3). The consequences of Leszczyc's sketchiness are twofold. Firstly, thanks to being only a 'skeleton', Leszczyc can accommodate different 'bodies': be a somehow disorientated, anti-consumerist and polite man (at least when dealing with officialdom) in *Identification Marks: None*, and a materialist and arrogant Boy in *Barrier*. Secondly, opaqueness and elusiveness set Leszczyc apart from the bulk of the characters of earlier Polish cinema which favoured more 'definite' characters over those who are always in a state of becoming.

In his 'Leszczyc films', as well as in the etudes shot before embarking on *Identification Marks: None*, Skolimowski used his relatives and friends, most importantly, his two girlfriends, Elżbieta Czyżewska and Joanna Szczerbic (who later became his wife), in the roles of girlfriends of the main characters. While watching these four movies we witness the development of the director's involvement with these two women. I have already mentioned the trajectory of Czyżewska's character from the early shorts to *Walkover*. In *Walkover*, Leszczyc looks for a new woman and finds her in Teresa, played by Aleksandra Zawieruszanka, but for a number of reasons their relationship is unsatisfactory. Only in *Barrier* does he appear to find his true match – a young tram driver, played by Szczerbic. The testimony of her importance is the fact that, unlike in previous films, the female character is granted some narrative autonomy (see Kornacki 2004), because for a while the camera leaves Leszczyc and follows the driver. However, as I will argue in the following chapter, this is not matched by her psychological autonomy – she is all for her Boy. In *Hands Up!*, Szczerbic's character, now named Alfa, is friendly not only with Leszczyc, appearing here under the pseudonym of Zastava, but with all four male friends. One can presume that this was the role Szczerbic played at this stage of Skolimowski's life, being not only the director's lover, his guarded secret, but part of his extended social life – the friend of his friends.

Another reason why Skolimowski's early works appear autobiographical is their narrative form, especially in the first two productions, *Identification Marks: None* and *Walkover*, which is that of a 'diary' film. The director himself, in an interview given many years later, compared making films to writing a diary (see Strick 1978: 147). The camera in these works follows the main character for a short period of time, respectively one and one and a half days. It practically never leaves him outside the frame and when it does, the reason is to show what Leszczyc sees or might want to see. It registers events of crucial importance, such as standing in front of the commission, examining draftees in *Identification Marks: None*, and a boxing match in *Walkover*, as well as those which an outsider will regard as meaningless or trivial, such as walking the street and talking to passers-by. Everything seems to be interesting and useful to Skolimowski's camera, as it is for the personal narrative of a diarist (on diary see Heller 1999). There is no hierarchy to the episodes represented: parting with his fiancée has the same status as walking the street. The films are also centred on Leszczyc in the sense that other people exist in their narratives because of him; they belong to his personal story.

The mode of narration is, as Susan Sontag would put it, 'representational' (see Sontag 1994) – we see that something happened, but do not learn why. The lack of conventional psychology is partly compensated for by incorporating in the films various 'texts', such as close-ups of manuscripts, songs, poems and photographs. These 'texts' display the protagonist's personal thoughts and emotions that are easier for him to share with us, the viewers, than with people whom he encounters on his journey. Again, such attitudes parallel that of a diarist who prefers to confess to his diary, rather than share his thoughts with real people. Moreover, Leszczyc looks straight into the camera, as if posing for a portrait, thus breaking a cinematic taboo, according to which the character behaves as if unaware of the presence of the camera. Finally, *Identification Marks: None*, due to being shot over a long period of time, in difficult circumstances, has a sloppy style which bears similarity with home movies.

The saturation with 'texts' and abandoning of conventional plot in favour of loosely joined-up episodes, shot without regard for the rules of professional film making, make Skolimowski's films look similar to those of Jean-Luc Godard. However, if we are to believe the author of *Walkover*, his films were not a response to Godard's cinema, but were made independently – he did not watch any of Godard's films when making his first two feature films. Both Skolimowski's similarity to Godard and his uniqueness were recognised by Aleksander Jackiewicz, who defended the Polish director from the criticism that his films were merely a response to the French New Wave, by writing, 'I will compare him with Godard. Not to question his originality but to underscore that Skolimowski's films are so much his own' (Jackiewicz 1983: 384).

In Poland, the autobiographical nature of Skolimowski's 'Leszczyc films' was augmented by their uniqueness. His whole approach to cinema was different from the vast majority of Polish film makers because he focused on the individual, rather than the whole society or generation, and appraised society from the perspective of a single man. Moreover, he did it in an open, even ostentatious way, without apologising for his protagonist (and by extension, himself) for being self-centred and rejecting the ways of his older and many of his younger colleagues. This feature was excellently captured by the leading Polish film critics of the time, Bolesław Michałek, Konrad Eberhardt, Zygmunt Kałużyński and the previously quoted Aleksander Jackiewicz and Janusz Gazda.

Michałek, in an article published for the first time in 1966, considered the first two movies with Leszczyc in the context of Polish films made by professional writers and scriptwriters, such as Aleksander Ścibor-Rylski, Jerzy Stefan Stawiński, Józef Hen and Tadeusz Konwicki. This comparison is understandable in the light of Skolimowski's earlier literary and scriptwriting career. Michałek observes that, in most cases, the authors whose novels and scripts were the literary source of some of the best Polish postwar films, in their own movies exhibited no more than professionalism and a desire to entertain the viewers, as opposed to any idiosyncratic vision. Against this background the films of Konwicki and Skolimowski were the exception because they revealed a 'personal touch'. About Skolimowski's films the critic wrote:

> We find here something which, except for the work of Konwicki, was missing in Polish cinema and which is a precious attribute of modern literature: personal tone, sincerity, the way of talking which is close to *ich-roman*. I do not mean here an exercise in style, consisting of first-person narration …, but an intellectual approach: searching for one's own truth about the position in society of a man, who is the author's analogue. Thanks to Skolimowski for

the first time a voice was given to the generation that was previously absent from the Polish screen: a generation free from memories of the war, living in the present tense but still having serious problems to adapt to life. (Michałek 1966, quoted in Helman 2002: 145–6)

In a similar vein Konrad Eberhardt argued:

If Skolimowski plays such an important role in Polish cinema, this is because he creates a character who is made up of contradictory elements. This has an immense significance, because Polish postwar cinema conceived a character in one way only: as a product of social and historical processes affecting the whole group. There are very few valuable Polish films in which an ordinary, banal character struggles with reality as perceived by him, rather than having his sensitivity and fate moulded by a group ... Polish cinema does not like 'private topics'. Even in third-class productions we find pretences to describing the 'fate of epoch', the 'tragic fate of the nation'. (Eberhardt 1967, quoted in Eberhardt 1982: 129)

Paradoxically, by choosing a protagonist who speaks only on behalf of himself, Skolimowski captured the attitude of the whole generation of those who had no memory of the war and did not experience any event important enough to furnish them with any distinct collective identity. Inevitably, this generation was more individualistic, even self-centred and consumption-oriented than their predecessors, immortalised in the films of the Polish School. Moreover, these people wanted to live in the present (see Chapter 2).

The autobiographical nature of the early films by Skolimowski changes across the films. The protagonist of *Barrier* is different from Leszczyc in *Identification Marks: None* and *Walkover*. Of course he looks different, having the body of Jan Nowicki, but also conveys a different personality, being self-confident, arrogant and articulate, as opposed to the earlier 'Leszczycs' who came across as lost in the world and unable to express themselves. This difference encouraged Krzysztof Kornacki to exclude *Barrier* from the series, treating it as a trilogy, as opposed to tetralogy (see Kornacki 2004). However, there are also reasons to locate *Hands Up!* outside the 'Leszczyc canon'. This is because, in contrast to *Identification Marks: None*, *Walkover* and *Barrier*, which situate an individual at the centre of the film's discourse, *Hands Up!* does not have any individual protagonist, but a number of characters who one by one take central stage. The man played by Skolimowski does not differ from the rest in the role given to him by the narrative. Moreover, in this film the past, albeit not the war but the Stalinist past, shapes the characters' present. Hence, near the end of the first chapter of his career, Skolimowski moved close to a position which dominated Polish cinema and from which he distanced himself when shooting *Identification Marks: None*.

From the current perspective the early films by Skolimowski come across more as the imaginary biographies of the author than the recordings of his actual life. It feels as if in each film the director chose one stage of his life and one facet of his persona

Figure 1.2 Jan Nowicki as Boy and Joanna Szczerbic as his love interest in *Barrier*

and developed it, at the expense of other stages and facets. *Identification Marks: None* focuses on his experience as a student who has had enough of studying and wants to 'sort out' his life. In *Walkover*, Skolimowski presents himself as a boxer who has had enough of boxing, in *Barrier*, as a man who wants to achieve everything which the older generation achieved, but faster and easier, and without any sense of guilt about compromising himself. In each film the character fails or discovers that he chose a bad path. The 'real' Skolimowski was also once a student and a boxer, but at the time he embarked on film making, he left these 'careers' behind, to concentrate on cinema. By no means was he a drifter who did not know what to do with his life. On the contrary, according to his colleagues from the Łódź Film School, he was a man of extreme resilience and enterprise, perhaps more talented in this respect than Polański.[1] Even the fact that he was able to make a feature film at the school testifies to his focused personality.

Together these four films speculate about what could have happened to Skolimowski, had he not became a film maker. Perhaps he used the stories of Leszczyc as repositories for his anxieties and hopes, including anxiety concerning finding a place for oneself in contemporary Poland or being forced to leave. In a sense, they also foretell Skolimowski's emigration and his ambivalent attitude to this state, namely his ambition to make films abroad and gain worldwide popularity, but also to retain close contact with Poland. The 'premonition' of approaching emigration is alluded to by the motif of a suitcase carried by the protagonist, his interest in 'high style', epitomised by Western cars, and the motif of travel present in them. Moreover, each of the films conveys the character's distrust of and conflict with official structures of power, which also became a feature of the real Skolimowski.

It is not an accident that Skolimowski's films about his alter ego Leszczyc were made in the mid 1960s, rather than the 1940s, 1950s or even early 1960s. In the earlier periods it was difficult to make personal films in Poland. First, socialist realism favoured groups rather than individuals and reduced individuals to the sum of specific political and social circumstances. Moreover, this paradigm was hostile to any form of personal narration, such as a diary or improvisation, which strengthen autobiographical effect. Instead, it favoured a rigid, literary script, producing the effect of an objective, impersonal narration. The paradigm that followed, the Polish School, although it allowed individuals to express their own views, also presented them as products of history, especially the Second World War. Again, such a concept of a Pole did not lend itself comfortably to the 'freewheeling' narrative style favoured by Skolimowski. By the early 1960s both socialist realism and the Polish School were exhausted and a space appeared for testing new characters and types of narratives. This period also coincides in European cinema and literature with interest in young people as unique individuals and use of personal narrations. In the works of film makers such as Ken Loach, Jean-Luc Godard and Věra Chytilová we find characters talking straight to the camera or off-screen explaining their positions. Even if Skolimowski did not know these films, it could be suggested that he breathed the same atmosphere from which they arose.

From Participant to Observer, from Patriot to the Citizen of the World

After Skolimowski left Poland, following the shelving of *Hands Up!*, he construed himself in his interviews in two ways. One is as a cosmopolitan at ease with many cultures and able to take advantage of what they have to offer, without accepting anything wholeheartedly and keeping a safe distance from them (see Boniecka 1983: 8). The other is of an exile, who was forced into a nomadic life by the cruel communist authorities and his own pride and obstinacy, and who in artistic terms did not achieve as much as he could and would have done, had he remained in Poland (see Pogorzelska 2001: 23). The first image likens him to Roman Polański, who never regretted (at least in public) leaving Poland, regarding himself as a model citizen of the world. In the second image Skolimowski projects himself as a kind of new Andrzej Wajda. I will not regard these two projections as contradictory because it is plausible to assume that different positions pertain to different stages of Skolimowski's life as an emigrant. Moreover, people are often glad to be somewhere while simultaneously regretting not being in a different place or being unhappy where they are, while unwilling to change their place of living. However, there is a tension between Skolimowski's acceptance and rejection of his status as an emigrant, which his émigré films reflect, particularly those made in Britain.

Following his emigration, Skolimowski continued to play in his films, but only in episodic roles. He appears in such roles in *Deep End*, *Moonlighting*, *Torrents of Spring* and *Ferdydurke*, as well as in *Skid*, for which he only wrote a script. An exception is the Prologue to *Hands Up!*, shot in 1981, in which he is the main character. What connects all these films from the perspective of autobiography, including *Hands Up!*, is that in them Skolimowski functions as an observer, looking at the events unfolding in front of his eyes from a position which gives him an insight which their participants are lacking. In *Deep End*, it is the position of a Polish emigrant or tourist observing Mike and Susan quarrelling on a train. The fact that he probably does not understand their words (he reads a Polish newspaper) and only draws conclusions from their manner of speaking and body language underscores how Mike, in his infatuation with Susan, is oblivious to the outside world. In *Moonlighting*, Skolimowski plays the mysterious 'Boss' who gains access to the adventures of a group of Polish workers

Figure 1.3 Jerzy Skolimowski as a schoolmaster in *Ferdydurke*

renovating his house while himself living in Poland. In *Torrents of Spring*, the director created for himself a part that does not exist in Turgenev's novel, of Victor Victorovich, the drunkard friend of Maria, who keeps meeting her in the crucial moments of her affair with Sanin. Again, in *Ferdydurke*, Skolimowski plays a character that does not exist in Gombrowicz's novel – that of a schoolmaster.

Skolimowski's taking the position of a disinterested observer in *Deep End*, *Moonlighting* and *Torrents of Spring* parallels and reflects his lack of engagement in the affairs of the countries and people where he lived after he left Poland, to which he has confessed in interviews. It also pertains to his position as the narrator of these films, of somebody who makes sense of the events he is watching and, as is the case in *Moonlighting* and *Ferdydurke*, also provokes them. On most occasions the director makes us aware that his access to events unfolding in front of our eyes is privileged. For example, in *Ferdydurke*, the headmaster observes all his teachers thanks to installing in his office a contraption allowing him to open the door of the teachers' office without leaving his desk. In *Torrents of Spring* and possibly in *Deep End*, his privileged access results from his unimportance, even invisibility, to the main participants in the action. They ignore him, therefore he is able to see them when they are most exposed, revealing their passions and shortcomings.

Skolimowski's presence in the Prologue to *Hands Up!* fulfils a number of functions. The most obvious is explaining to the viewer the background to shelving his film and the context of the ending of this ban. The director tells about his dealings with the secret police which demanded his self-censorship of the film, his uncompromising reaction to this demand, and reveals how this chain of events affected his subsequent life and career. More importantly, the Prologue offers Skolimowski an opportunity to look at *Hands Up!*, film making, and his condition as a director and exiled Pole from a distance dividing the two versions of the film. He even claims that the new version became his diary, a recording of his life fourteen years after shooting the first version of the film.

In this diary the 'old' *Hands Up!* is just one of the many elements filling the artist's life, along with travelling, exhibiting paintings in his flat, meeting friends and realising new cinematic projects. Hence, the forty-something Skolimowski of the Prologue appropriates the position of the creator, the 'father' of his younger self in the main part of the film, if not that of a God, looking at his old film from a different reality. This position is underscored by the camera showing him in profile, gazing, often through windows or portholes, at historical events or their artistic staging. He looks at the old film with sympathy, perhaps even love, but also with a sense of helplessness – his 'child' is no longer truly his, the long separation has changed it into a stranger. In one episode of the Prologue Skolimowski appears as an actor too, but this time in a film shot by another director, Volker Schlöndorff's *Die Fälschung* (*Circle of Deceit*, 1981). This sequence, apart from revealing what happened to the director at the time his film was meant to be released, allows Skolimowski to draw comparisons between film making and other types of artistic creativity, principally plastic arts. He claims that film making is an arena of illusion, rather than of truthful reflection of reality. In a later scene he elaborates this opinion by suggesting that

Figure 1.4 Jerzy Skolimowski in the Prologue to *Hands Up!*

painting is a superior art, most likely because it is more private: painters do not face censors in the way film makers do.

Playing in Schlöndorff's film also gave Skolimowski an opportunity to situate Poland of 1981 on his private political map of the world. He sees it somehow between peaceful (albeit highly bureaucratised and tightly policed) London, where he lived at the time, and war-ridden Beirut. Poland represented in this way has a realistic chance for a prosperous existence and democracy, but is also in danger of slipping into bloody conflict and chaos. This observation, although politically rather banal, is important from the perspective of Skolimowski's discourse on Poland and Polishness, as it implies that he has stopped seeing the country where he was born as a unique place and instead perceives it now as one of many countries, moderately important for European politics and culture. This marginalisation of Poland and, consequently, of himself as a Polish exile, is further conveyed in the scenes of a manifestation in support of Solidarity in London. The director draws attention to the small scale of the event, the fact that largely Poles take part in it, and their tight control by the police. Equally, Skolimowski shows himself speaking about Polish affairs in Hyde Park's Speakers' Corner, where anybody is allowed to say anything and all types of self-proclaimed prophets and madmen perform.[2] The perceived lack of importance of Poland and Skolimowski's own marginal position, provide an interesting counterpoint to the story of the original version of *Hands Up!*, also told in this film (as well as conveyed in its legend), in which he comes across as a very important figure for both the political and artistic life of his country.

Although the prevailing impression Skolimowski conveys in the Prologue to *Hands Up!* is that of an observer, even a tourist, there are also moments where we see him as a participant, as in a footage of himself taking part in a pro-Solidarity demonstration. This fragment of the film plays a triple role. Firstly, in common with the scene shot in Beirut, it tells what the director did when the ban on his film was released. Secondly, it connects the young Skolimowski, who directed the first version of *Hands Up!*, with the one in 1981 by representing both as politically oppositional film makers, in their films taking a stance against the Polish political system. The third function of this scene is to introduce the theme of a Polish political artist in London who from a distance tries to make something for his country.

This last theme is developed or even, as the director himself admitted, overdeveloped, in *Success Is the Best Revenge* (see Combs 1986: 134). Although in this film Skolimowski does not play the main role, which is given to Michael York, critics tend to see in the theatre director named Alex Rodak the emigrant version of Skolimowski (see Klejsa 2006). Perhaps the reason that Skolimowski chose not to play Rodak was to avoid too strong an identification between Rodak and himself. At the same time, in this film Skolimowski, unlike in *Deep End*, *Torrents of Spring* or *Ferdydurke*, does not play any supporting role. This lack of Skolimowski's physical presence strengthens the impression that Rodak is indeed his porte-parole. Off-screen the director pointed to both similarity and difference between himself and Rodak. In conversation with Richard Combs, he has confessed that he created Rodak as his own caricature: an exaggeration of his anxieties and vices (see Combs 1986: 133–34). Skolimowski thus conjured this character in order not to become like him in real life, in a similar way he previously created Leszczyc. Talking with Jerzy Uszyński, on the other hand, he claimed Rodak offers more a portrait of an average Polish artist living in exile than any particular personage, including himself (see Uszyński 1990a: 12–13).

Success Is the Best Revenge appears to be autobiographical for a number of reasons. One is its sheer packing with information, objects and people pertaining to Skolimowski's life and cinematic interests. Secondly, it is his most personal project, in the sense of diverging from the rules of mainstream, realistic cinema. Its focus on home and border crossing, and the 'epistolary' narration (the events unfolded on screen are commented by Alex's son, Adam, in a letter to his father) links it to 'accented cinema' as defined by Hamid Naficy: the cinema produced by emigrants who use film as a tool to convey their yearning for their lost fatherland (see Naficy 2001). *Success Is the Best Revenge* also bears similarity with the films Jean-Luc Godard made in the 1980s. The most obvious comparison is *Passion* (1982), which also puts at the centre of discourse a Polish director on foreign soil, finding it difficult to complete his project. The third reason for *Success Is the Best Revenge*'s strong autobiographical character is its effect on Skolimowski's subsequent life and career. It changed the director's life dramatically, making him literally and metaphorically homeless. Being the film's producer, he mortgaged his London house to finance this project, became bankrupt and lost his house. This incident also put him off England (see Uszyński 1990b: 7) and some years later he moved to the United States.

Alex Rodak is presented as somebody who was educated in a boarding school in Czechoslovakia – the only public school in Eastern Europe. Likewise, Skolimowski attended such a school, where he met such later eminent figures in Czech culture as Václav Havel, Miloš Forman and Ivan Passer. Even the anecdote about how the government planted a pretty girl in the school as a means to corrupt the pupils, which Rodak tells in the restaurant, comes from Skolimowski's own life (see Uszyński 1990a: 4). The fact that Alex's work is celebrated in France, where he accepts the Légion d'honneur, the highest cultural honour in the country, as one of the best European theatre directors, can be regarded as a reference to the appreciation of Skolimowski's work in France, particularly in the 1960s.

The film is largely based on a diary of the director's son, Michał Skolimowski (aka Michael Lyndon), which Skolimowski found by chance. In the roles of Alex's wife, Alicja, and their sons, Skolimowski cast his own wife, Joanna Szczerbic, and their sons, Michael and Jerry. Another major role, that of Mr Gienio, a leader of the Polish extras, was given to Eugeniusz Haczkiewicz, a Polish man who once lived in the director's house, helped him to renovate it and played in Skolimowski's previous film, *Moonlighting*. Moreover, the Rodaks live in the director's real house at the time. Ironically, as I previously mentioned, Skolimowski lost his London property as a result of making *Success Is the Best Revenge*. This story perfectly illustrates the famous phrase by Susan Sontag, 'One cannot use the life to interpret the work. But one can use the work to interpret the life' (Sontag 1983: 111).

In *Success Is the Best Revenge*, the contrast between participant and observer is accompanied by the dichotomy between the citizen of the world and the man attached to one country.[3] The fact that Rodak's work is celebrated in France makes him, if not a model citizen of the world, then at least a citizen of Europe. However, while Rodak's biography points to his cosmopolitanism, his obsessive interest in Polish affairs, as revealed by his ambitious theatrical project of staging in London an avant-garde play about Polish martial law, suggests that deep down he remains a Pole through and through, as conveyed by his name, Rodak (the Countryman). This project can be seen as very idealistic, but bringing it into existence forces Rodak to abandon basic moral principles, including entering into shabby deals with a rich pornographer, Dino Montecurva (Kurwa is Polish for whore).[4]

The complex relations of Rodak with Polishness are reflected in the relationships with his family, other Poles, as well as in his theatrical work. For two years Alex lived away from his wife and sons because he could not leave martial-law Poland, while they stayed in London. Rodak's wife, Alicja, not only struggles to conform to the British and cosmopolitan culture in which Alex is immersed, but even has problems with learning English and feels isolated from all the events in which Alex is involved. Her identity is distinctly Polish; she is weary of Alex's theatrical project that would

Figure 1.5 Michael York as Alex Rodak and Joanna Szczerbic as his wife in *Success Is the Best Revenge*

make them enemies of the Polish authorities and bar them from returning to their country. Moreover, she objects to her sons following in their father's footsteps as conveyed by her addressing them 'You cosmopolitan idiots'. On the other hand, Rodak is exasperated by his wife's provinciality and narrow-mindedness and whenever possible, avoids her. Alex feels close to his older son, Adam, but as I will argue in the next chapter, their relationship is troubled by their competition for the love of their country.

Rodak interacts even more reluctantly with other Poles. He gets in contact with them, plays football with them, appeals to their patriotism, but only to use them as extras in his show, which should appear as their spontaneous performance. Polish emigrants, as portrayed by Skolimowski, come across as a materially and culturally impoverished herd, easily excited and manipulated. The only member of this crowd whom Skolimowski endows with an individual identity, the leader of the Polish extras, Mr Gienio, is reduced to an animal-like existence. He is practically homeless, camping in the back of a restaurant, deprived of basic facilities and privacy.

The lack of interest and empathy with the manual workers differentiates Skolimowski's film from Godard's *Passion*, in which the Polish director Jerzy (Jerzy Radziwiłowicz) enters into a complex relationship, which includes erotic interest, with the factory worker, Isabelle (Isabelle Huppert). Unlike Mr Edzio, who is depicted as if he does not possess any consciousness, class or otherwise, Isabelle, despite her stutter (which might signify the difficulty for working class people of expressing themselves), is able to fight for her rights and comes across as a complex and spiritual person.[5] For the Western viewer Rodak's and, by extension, Skolimowski's, disinterest in, even contempt, for the working class, as conveyed in *Success* (in the film reciprocated by the workers) might be difficult to reconcile with his unequivocal support of Solidarity, which was, predominantly, a workers' movement. However, this paradox can be explained by the anti-communist character of the Solidarity opposition, which made it possible for a large section of Polish intelligentsia to support it, without subscribing to its pro-worker character. Skolimowski's negative view of the working people, as devoid of dignity and agency, can be seen as the consequence of living under communism, where in the official discourses the working class was regarded as a leading force of society, the nation's elite, at the expense of the intelligentsia. The director's mother was a victim of this approach, as her career in diplomacy was cut short due to her not belonging to the Party. It can be also linked to the legacy of his father who was very right wing (see Uszyński 1989: 5).

The staging of Alex's play, which has the same title as Skolimowski's film, *Success Is the Best Revenge*, excellently reveals the tension between patriotism and cosmopolitism in the life and work of Rodak (and Skolimowski). The form of this play is distinctively cosmopolitan. A 'play' is not even the right word to describe Rodak's work, as he synthesises elements of different media, periods, and different discursive regimes, as well as multiplying the locations and breaking the divisions between stage and audience, performers and spectators, art and life. The scenes from Polish streets during martial law are reenacted by Polish non-actors, mostly emigrants working illegally in London. They represent encounters between police and workers, but it is also possible that, rather than acting, the emigrants, enraged by not being paid for their 'spontaneous' performance, really do fight with each other. The scenes on the stage are accompanied by showing a football match between Poland and England on multiple screens, followed by the voice of the speaker (possibly Rodak) commenting on Polish history while presenting pictures of events from the Yalta conference by Feliks Topolski, part of his *Chronicle*. The commentary to these shows suggests that Rodak's project is not so much about martial law as about British and Western indifference to the Polish plight. This multimedia and multi-layered performance is viewed by spectators driven in buses. In this way, they see the performance from many different angles, which can be compared to the position of the disengaged flâneur rather than a nationalistic participant. In addition, Rodak's performance is open in the sense of crossing the boundaries between theatre and non-theatre. It is impossible to detect whether some scenes, such as the discussions between Montecurva and the Polish performers, belong to the performance or are extraneous, as Skolimowski shoots them in such a way that they appear as an integral part of the play. The use of the same title for Rodak's and Skolimowski's project not only strengthens the autobiographical effect of the film, but adds to the openness of the film and the play. We do not learn what happens to Alex after the premiere of his work and to the remaining members of his family. The lives of the Rodaks might go either way.

There is a striking similarity between Rodak's *Success Is the Best Revenge* and the theatrical experiments of Allan Kaprow, the pioneer of performance art and one of the most cosmopolitan artist of the twentieth century. However, while Kaprow's performances were successes, Rodak's show is a failure. The main reason seems to be the obsolescence of Rodak's project. Kaprow's performances felt fresh and genuine in the 1950s; by the mid 1980s *Success Is the Best Revenge* comes across as outdated. Moreover, as Konrad Klejsa observes, the elements Rodak uses in his spectacle (a coffin, covered with black and red flowers, candles, a figure of Holy Mary) after martial law became clichéd and treated with mistrust by the public (see Klejsa 2006: 155). Rodak's failure thus suggests that being successfully cosmopolitan means being ahead of one's times, embracing what is new in different cultures. However, his failure should not be equated with Skolimowski's failure because it could be argued that the director aimed at ridiculing patriotic art *a la polacca* (a project in which his fellow émigré artist, Witold Gomrowicz, excelled), and in this he succeeded.

Success Is the Best Revenge comes across not only as the most autobiographical endeavour in Skolimowski's career, but also as one that is most difficult to comprehend. Even a viewer who knows the national and personal background to this film (to which I return in the following chapters), is used to Skolimowski's trademark thematic shiftiness, gaps in the narrative, disrespect for psychological explanations and internal contradictions in the protagonists, finds it difficult to make sense of it. The idiosyncratic character of *Success* is the consequence of its autobiographical character: building it from what the director regarded as important for him personally (such as his son's thoughts), without attempting to censor it or harness it by any form. In a sense, the film is like life itself: contradictory, even illogical, open, painful to make and painful to watch. In *Success Is the Best Revenge*, Skolimowski reached and, for the bulk of viewers, even crossed, the border when cinematic autobiography ceases being intersubjective and becomes not even a diary, but a kind of stream of consciousness or a polyphonic inner monologue, accessible only to the monologist himself. As Richard Combs aptly puts it, 'This incorporation of the "real" is more than realism would stand … And it is with such intense concentration on the real that surrealism begins' (Combs 1984: 390).

The director also crossed the border where cinematic autobiography is viable as a commercial project. Not surprisingly, after *Success Is the Best Revenge* Skolimowski resisted the temptation to place himself in the centre of the film and instead opted for the more subdued presence of an observer. Yet, despite being both a failure as an act of communication between the film author and the viewers and a commercial flop, *Success Is the Best Revenge* is a remarkable film precisely because it is so courageous in venturing into a territory where few film makers dared to go.

Notes

1. There are anecdotes about Skolimowski's resourcefulness. For example, Leon Niemczyk says, 'Skolimowski was a smart guy. He cast his Wartburg in the etude so that everyday an extra washed it for him at the expense of the taxpayer' (Niemczyk, quoted in Krubski et al. 1998: 164). This anecdote puts in a particular light the on-screen renovating of the director's house in *Moonlighting*: one wonders whether the director made this film to have his house done up for him for free.

2. Nanni Moretti also chose this place to talk about Italy in his *Aprile* (1998).

3. A possible reason why this dichotomy gained such prominence in *Success Is the Best Revenge*, as well in Skolimowski's previous film concerning martial law, *Moonlighting*, was the fact that around this time hundreds of thousands of Poles faced a dilemma: emigrate or stay in Poland. Martial law thus added currency to the discussion (always ongoing in Poland) about how best to serve one's country and who be a true patriot. In addition, the mass emigration drew attention to the options open to Polish emigrants; their chances to contribute to the material, social and cultural lives of their host countries and to preserve their Polish identity.

4. The idea that the artist must prostitute himself in order to find funds for his idealistic projects likens *Success Is the Best Revenge* with some films of Godard, especially *Tout va bien* (1972).

5. This is a consequence of her being modelled on Simone Weil, who in the 1930s gave up a job teaching philosophy in order to work in the Renault factories of Billancourt (see Morrey 2005: 142).

CHAPTER 2

About a Boy: Characters, Narratives and Ideologies in Skolimowski's Films

Polish films by Skolimowski are monothematic: they are always stories about big children – from teenagers to thirty-year-old men. In those films which Skolimowski made abroad the situation is not very different. Only the characters are more consumption-oriented.

(Aleksander Jackiewicz 1977: 173)

Skolimowski can be described as a male director in more senses than one. Men are at the centre of his narratives while women are treated as minor characters, defined through their relation to men, typically as the objects of male erotic pursuits. In many films the man's relationship with other men is far more important than his relationship with women. Moreover, a number of Skolimowski's films are narrated by men and in this way inculcate the viewer's identification with male protagonists. By contrast, a woman does not narrate any of Skolimowski's stories. Another constant element of his films is their focus on young people. Again, they play the main parts and the viewer identifies with them. Yet privileging men and young people does not amount to the wholehearted celebration of manliness and youth, because his young men are lost, psychologically damaged and unsuccessful. In Skolimowski's own words, conveyed in his early poem, later repeated in an essay by Konrad Eberhardt, they 'suffer an injury' (Eberhardt 1982: 112).

Skolimowski's narratives revolve around several motifs: the search for one's place in the world, the competition and reconciliation between father or father figure and his son, and the difficulty in finding and sustaining love. Accordingly, Skolimowski situates his young male protagonists in three types of scenarios. One concerns the relationship of the central character with himself, his peers and the ideologies that surround him; the second with older men; the third with women. These scenarios are not mutually exclusive; often all these types of relationship are present in one film, as in *Barrier*. However, if this happens, one type of relation predominates. These three types of narrative can be mapped onto Skolimowski's career. The first type pertains to his early films, made in the 1960s and the early 1970s, the majority of which were shot in Poland. The second dominates his émigré period, especially the films from the 1980s. The third type can be found in films from both periods, although it plays a more important role in the films made abroad and his latest work, *Four Nights with Anna*.

In this chapter I will examine the main types of characters and narratives Skolimowski uses in his films, trying to establish what connects his heroes and heroines from different periods of his career. My other objective is to discover to what extent we should regard them as 'children of their time' and the cultures that surround them, and to what extent they fulfil certain transcultural or even archetypal scenarios. I believe that the construction of characters and narratives is never ideologically neutral, therefore an additional product of my analysis should be assessing Skolimowski's attitudes to such ideologies as patriotism, state socialism, patriarchy, consumerism and Christianity.

In Search of Identity

Unlike other animals who become independent shortly after birth, humans are born almost entirely helpless and depend for their survival on the care of more mature members of society. 'We are all born "prematurely"', claims Terry Eagleton (Eagleton 1997: 132). Szymon Wróbel, in an essay entitled 'Polityka temporalna' (Temporal Politics), proposes a similar idea, but develops it by assessing the length of human youth not only in relation to other animals but also in relation to the remaining stages of human life. He claims that people develop very slowly, while their ageing is fast. This slowness has crucial consequences for the nature of youth and the character of relations between people of different generations. 'Youth is an empty place to be filled. It does not know what to do with itself. Even if it is full of energy, it is empty energy. If it has initiative, it is blind initiative. If it has intellect, it is devoid of reason' and it is 'frightened by the plenitude of the world' (Wróbel 2005: 266). Consequently, youth, which from the perspective of an older person appears to be the best part of his or her life, is experienced by young people as a period of anxiety, restlessness, even unhappiness and trauma.

Skolimowski perceives youth in a similar way to Wróbel – as dragging on purposelessly and obscenely, leaving its 'user' too much time to fill. His young characters or, more precisely, young men, are childish, although one feels they should already be adult. Waldemar Piątek describes their state as 'intensified childhood' (Piątek 1983: 33). Sometimes they are engaged in activities which do not suit their age, such as Leszczyc in *Walkover*, who is still fighting in boxing's 'first steps', a competition geared to amateurs, although he is almost thirty years old. At other times, they act childishly or lack the nerve to complete their assignment. On such occasions their companions must pretend that the men are younger than they really are to save them embarrassment. Take the episode in *Le Départ*, in which Marc's girlfriend Michèle, after he abandoned the car he stole from a petrol station, phones the station to apologise on behalf of 'her little brother who made a stupid joke'.

In yet other films male protagonists are caricatured versions of young people or exaggerated impersonations of youth itself. This feature is underscored by the choice of actors, especially John Moulder–Brown, cast as the male lead in *Deep End* and *King, Queen, Knave*, who comes across as a child imprisoned in the body of a young man. Not only does he have delicate features, but is extremely clumsy (a trait only partly explained in *King, Queen, Knave* by his myopia), with limbs appearing too long for his torso, shy, absent-minded and inarticulate. The immaturity of Skolimowski's characters is also conveyed by the very surname of his most famous character – Leszczyc, as it awakens association with 'leszcz' and 'szczyl', both contemptuous descriptions of children or immature people. While young men in Skolimowski's films are younger than they should be, old people are withered, disabled or senile. Sometimes, for example in *Identification Marks: None* and *Barrier*, they are like characters from bad dreams or from the 'other side of life' – death. Not surprisingly, the young characters run away from them, as if they want to forget about them and their own fate.

The danger of a long youth is that some people get used to this state and do not want or are unable to leave it. In *Identification Marks: None*, Leszczyc refuses to grow up by evading adult responsibilities. He avoids finishing university and getting a job by not picking up the subject of his master's thesis. He evades family responsibilities by living with Teresa without marriage but pretends that they are married. He also avoids any responsibility towards his dog and does not vaccinate him against rabies (see Jocher 1967: 25; Jankun-Dopartowa 1997: 99–100). As a result of all these evasions, one can say, 'walkovers', he loses respectively the chance to get a degree, the woman who supports him financially and his dog. Leszczyc also attempts to avoid the compulsory three-month-long military training, but he pays for this evasion by going to the army for two years, the period young men without a university education had to fulfil in communist Poland. Using (somewhat jokingly) psychoanalytical language, we can say that on this occasion the 'reality principle' overrides the 'pleasure principle': in the Poland of state socialism, the army is the ultimate reality and its principles apply to everybody.

Skolimowski's predilection for immature characters is also revealed in the choice of protagonist for his early short, *Hamleś*. The title is normally translated into *Little Hamlet*, although *Hamleś* is a Polish diminutive of Hamlet, to emphasise that he is an un-grown (as well as Polish) Hamlet (see Chapter 5). Much later this predilection was literalised in Skolimowski's adaptation of Witold Gombrowicz's *Ferdydurke*, where Józio, a thirty-year-old man wakes up one night to find his old teacher, Professor Pimko, in his room. Pimko pretends (or sincerely believes) that Józio is still of school age and forces him to return to his old school and to become a boarder in the home of the Młodziaks. Although Józio protests against such infantilisation, he follows Pimko and does all the things schoolboys do: sits in a classroom, plays football with his peers and falls in love with Zuta, the daughter of his landlord.

Unlike in Gombrowicz's book, where Józio is depicted as significantly older than other schoolboys, in Skolimowski's *Ferdydurke*, he comes across as being roughly the same age as them. This is because the director casts in the roles of Józio's colleagues actors of a similar age to Iain Glen, who was thirty when he played Józio. A consequence of such casting is the impression that the whole school is full of men who avoided growing up. Not only the appearance but also the behaviour of these 'boys' points to their obscenely long youth. They indulge in silly games, the most childish of which is a face-pulling competition. One boy, Miętus, specialises in naughty and vulgar faces; another, nicknamed Syfon, in soulful and angelic faces. Both types of expression respond to the way adult people conjure up small boys: as naughty or angelic. By making faces, Skolimowski's characters, following those created by Gombrowicz, attempt to overcome the patterns or forms adults use to mould the younger generation, by showing the forms' artificiality. Yet at the same time, they underscore how pervasive and powerful the forms or masks are. By contrast to the young men, who look old but behave as if infantile, Zuta, a schoolgirl, with whom Józio and his school pals fall in love, can plausibly be taken for a college pupil. Similarly, her behaviour does not strike one as artificial. It appears as if she has fewer problems than her male counterparts with the form in which the adults want to imprison the younger generation. This difference might be explained by the fact that society is less interested in changing women because it situates them on the side of nature, while men are positioned in culture.

The large void of youth allows and forces Skolimowski's characters to experiment with different identities. This can be done by embarking on a new life project, such as, in *Identification Marks: None*, falling in love or signing up for a course in Spanish, which is promptly abandoned for a new project. At the same time as considering new opportunities, in this film Leszczyc presents himself to the outside world as somebody whom he is not. He tells his mother by phone that he is working on his thesis and has no financial problems (although he has just borrowed money from his friend); he informs the newly met Basia that he works on the railway, and to the man from the radio he provides a false name. Some of these lies serve to make his life easier. One can guess, for example, that the mask of a responsible man is meant to prevent any preaching from Leszczyc's mother, who might be worried that her son has squandered four years at university at her expense. Other deceptions, however, result from a pure desire to become somebody else, to put on a new mask, even if only for a short while (see Dzięglewski 2002; Klejsa 2004). It must be added that at this stage of Leszczyc's life the mask is the man; young people have no 'authentic' identity that can be uncovered through abandoning a play or a form. In *Identification Marks: None*, this emptiness of young life is conveyed by the fact that Leszczyc brings no certificates to show to the draft board and he has no 'identification marks', apart from a small scar from childhood, easily dismissed by the military men. Accordingly, playing with different personalities is a tool to become a person. According to Arthur Schopenhauer, putting on masks is a preserve of young people. The end of life, by contrast, equals the end of masquerade. The old cannot pretend (their face and body betrays them) and have no reasons to fake, as by the time they reach the final stage of their lives their characters and deeds are revealed and nothing can be changed (see Schopenhauer 1923).

In his conviction that there is no personality outside persona, no ultimate sincerity or authenticity to unearth, Skolimowski comes close to existentialist, anti-

Figure 2.1 Elżbieta Czyżewska as Basia and Jerzy Skolimowski as Andrzej Leszczyc in *Identification Marks: None*

essentialist concepts of personality. This is because existentialism proclaims that existence precedes essence; humans define their identity and reality through living in a particular way. Heidegger and Sartre's claim that man is thrown into existence fits well Skolimowski's narratives, in which his characters behave as if they found themselves in a particular place by chance, as if thrown there from a speeding train. (This idea is even literalised by extensively featuring trains, from and to which his characters jump, when searching for a place to live or only a temporarily stay). In his concept of identity as lacking any essence and always in a state of flux, Skolimowski is also close to postmodernism.

Putting on a mask might also be a means to create a distance from an identity which is already fixed, but which one cannot sincerely accept. This is the case of Marc in *Le Départ* who deeply dislikes his job as an apprentice in a ladies hairdressing salon. For this reason he does not behave naturally at work, but applies the pose of a humble servant, lowering his voice, and bowing and smiling to the female customers. We see how artificial this pose is when Marc leaves the main part of the salon and moves to the staff room. There he transforms, becoming loud and frantic, the opposite of his earlier self. To avoid any doubt that he might identify with his job, he also invites his girlfriend to the salon and there he parodies his usual behaviour, exaggerating his humble gestures and manner of speaking and saying to her: 'This is my role; my coat is my stage costume.'

However, the continuous testing of new possibilities, new roles and 'masks' is difficult, even traumatic. Excessive freedom might disorientate, even paralyse rather than liberate, as shown in *Identification Marks: None*: perhaps because it goes against the human internal striving to fix their identity and be able to say who they are.[1] Another difficulty pertains to pressure the outside world exerts on people to play specific roles in a coherent manner, as shown in *Le Départ*, where Marc risks punishment every time he transgresses from his role of a junior hairdresser. A similar pressure is experienced by the young people in *Deep End* and *King, Queen, Knave*, who have to prove themselves at work. Consequently, Skolimowski's characters follow two contradictory impulses. On the one hand, they try to avoid fixation or, as Alicja Helman puts it, always say 'no' (*są na nie*) (Helman 1974: 12) and, on the other, they try to find a stable place in the world.

The search for identity is never easy, but for Skolimowski's young characters in his four Polish films it is especially difficult, because the vast majority of 'signposts' they encounter prove unsatisfactory. Old people can hardly serve them as models because they have lost contact with current reality and spend their times on rituals. Rituals can fulfil a positive role in rooting a young individual in a community, giving him a sense of belonging and of order in the surrounding world, but to achieve this, they cannot be overused and must be refreshed. Yet the rituals which Skolimowski depicts do not fulfil these conditions. Unlike the games in which his young characters indulge, which are always fresh and genuine (there is an element of inventiveness and unpredictability in them), they do not take their participants to new places or new times, but freeze them in the past. Moreover, they are fake or empty, because distanced from the events that they are commemorating. Those who engage in them do not remember or know what they refer to, as shown in *Barrier*, where a group of war veterans (or men who pose as war veterans) sing a war song in complete dissynchrony and some seem not even to know the song at all. All these features, together with the fact that most of the rituals included in these films are connected with death, make their participants look like zombies, a fate from which young people want to escape. The ritualistic character also pertains to some acts whose main function is to solve something in the present, such as the cross-examination by the military commission, to which Leszczyc is subjected in *Identification Marks: None*, and by the communist youth organisation (ZMP) in *Hands Up!*, as each commission repeats the questions and statements uttered many times before. The latter interrogation especially feels ritualistic, bringing to mind such Stalinist show trials as that of Slánsky in Czechoslovakia. By rendering these interrogations as if they were rituals, staged and predictable, Skolimowski denies them credibility. By extension, he denies credibility to the whole political process in a Poland of state socialism.

The second 'signpost' Skolimowski's young characters, especially Leszczyc, reject, is that of the ideologies which surround them. They cannot accept them because of the gap between the values on which these ideologies are based, and the behaviour of people who purport to believe in them and promulgate them. Polish romantic values, such as patriotism, the desire to give their lives to save others, are questioned by Leszczyc when he sees people who falsely boast about their war achievements. Examples are a war veteran in *Identification Marks: None*, who tries to impress Leszczyc by the story of his war bravery but his narrative does not add up, exposing him as a fantasist, and, more absurdly, the man in *Barrier* who claims to be blind and to have been shot at an execution, although he can see and, of course, is alive.

Skolimowski also points to the simple fact that some values which are crucial in the time of military conflict cannot be realised in the time of peace. A man with a sabre looked noble during a nineteenth century uprising; in 1966 he looks bizarre, even grotesque. On the whole, Skolimowski shows that the generation of Polish 'fathers' is unable to offer the young any direction.

Another ideology denounced by Skolimowski is that of socialism, tackled in *Walkover* and *Hands Up!* People who preach it, proclaiming the superiority of the common good over individual welfare, do not live up to their words. As Leszczyc's friend says in *Barrier*, those driving expensive cars in the 1960s are recorded in old chronicles shouting Stalinist slogans, if not taking part in purges and show trials. Moreover, socialism is criticised by the film's author as intolerant to any transgression (in *Walkover* Leszczys is expelled from the university for being different) and using twisted language (see Chapter 3) – in short, for being totalitarian.

In common with attacking socialism and Polish-style militarism and patriotism, Skolimowski places a question mark over religion. The priest whom Leszczyc encounters in *Walkover* is fake – in reality he used the cassock to save his life during the war and became so used to this costume that he continued to play the role of a priest after the war. As if he had learnt his lesson about fake priests, in *Barrier* Leszczyc, in a night scene, mockingly asks a group of nuns why they stay awake so late. Preaching religion, like exhorting socialism, is also presented as a way to better oneself materially. In *Barrier*, Leszczyc's super-sly friend, Mundek, boasts that he earns his living by selling pictures of Jesus. He does not simply offer them to potential customers but exerts moral pressure on them to buy, suggesting that those who refuse, live godless lives. Again, this tactic is no different to that applied by the ideologues of socialism, who denounce those who refuse to 'buy' anything advertised as 'socialist' as being hostile to socialism itself. Religion is also rendered obsolete by showing its incompatibility with modern life. This aspect is excellently conveyed in *Deep End*, when a group of Christian evangelists try to sell Bibles in Soho; they look ridiculous among people searching for erotic pleasures and, of course, they have severe difficulties in selling any Bibles.

It is worth stressing that Skolimowski's criticism of the aforementioned ideologies is somewhat 'soft', because the director never rejects any ideology on the grounds of it being false, but only deals with their distorted versions and the people who dishonestly take advantage of them. To put it differently, he does not criticise motherland, God and Marx, but only fake heroes, priests and communists. However, at the same time he does not show us genuine communists, priests or patriots, rendering represented reality absurd.

The ideological and axiological 'fog' in which Skolimowski's characters, especially Leszczyc, move, affects them immensely. Leszczyc comes across as a man who simultaneously scorns certain values and attitudes and flirts with them, or, as put by the reviewer of *Barrier*, wants to have everything both ways (see Wilson 1967: 183). The symbol of his attitude is, again, the sabre, with which he plays in a rather inappropriate way, but which he, nevertheless, does not want to get rid of or even sell at a profit. Łukasz Ronduda even brands Leszczyc a mendacious conformist, unable to reject the status quo (see Ronduda 2007). Although I agree that there is less of a rebel or anti-hero in this character than critics initially tended to see, I reject Ronduda's harsh assessment because he assumes that Leszczyc is a mature personality, while he is still in a state of becoming and, like a child, follows his instinct and his desire to play, rather than acting in a premeditated manner.

The search for identity is also difficult for Skolimowski's characters because they lack any distinctive experiences that would bring them close to people of their own age and establish them as a separate formation, in line with the rule that common experiences, rather than simply having a similar age, constitute a generation (see Bauman 2005: 186–87). Of course, for their parents the Second World War was such an experience. The war was so important because, as Kath Woodward observes, 'Times of threat are not moments that can tolerate fragmentation and diversity' (Woodward 2002: xi) or, indeed, any doubts about who we are. War thus furnishes people with a strong collective identity. Conversely, during the time of peace, this identity tends to crumble, although, once gained, might survive in a diluted form thanks to the power of memory. The previously mentioned image of war veterans singing together, but in dissynchrony, reflects this collective identity twenty or so years after the event constituting this collective.

Upon experiencing the discomfort of disorientation and disillusionment with the various 'signposts' standing on their way to maturity, Skolimowski's characters look for strategies to keep at least some of the freedom they enjoy due to their immaturity while finding some direction in their lives. The first three parts of the Leszczyc tetralogy provide several such strategies: some real, some imaginary. The first one is revealed by the protagonist in an interview given to a radio interviewer in *Identification Marks: None*. Asked if he would like to travel to the moon, he says 'yes' and confesses that he will be equally happy to drive large lorries. What attracts him to these pursuits is that they face him with the inevitable and impose on him specific goals and directions, but at the same time permit certain inventiveness and allow for chance. Equally, he succumbs so easily to the prospect of joining the army because he believes that it will be, if not exactly like going to the moon, at least like driving a lorry. Hence, paradoxically, the army, which in postwar Poland was widely regarded as a pro-regime institution similar to prison, is viewed by Leszczyc positively, as a framework within which he can test himself (which, of course, further undermines his position as a political outsider or nonconformist) and preserve some freedom. In *Identification Marks: None*, the army somehow wins over other life projects Leszczyc considers, such as getting a new girlfriend or learning Spanish. The greatest attractiveness of the army for Leszczyc lies in its inevitability. It is more difficult to leave a compulsory, two-year military service than abandon a woman or a foreign language course. Judging from the next instalment of the Leszczyc 'saga', *Walkover*, the army fulfilled the role of providing him a structure – during his military service Leszczyc learnt boxing and driving cars. However, upon re-entering civilian life, he again reveals a lack of direction. It is worth adding that Antoine Doinel, the character bearing similarity with Leszczyc, in François Truffaut's *Baisers volés* (*Stolen Kisses*, 1968) also leaves the army and is forced to start an adult life, to which, like Leszczyc, he is unprepared. However, for Doinel military service was a complete waste of time; Leszczyc, as mentioned, learnt in the army a couple of useful things.

Another way of dealing with one's lack of identity, as well as with the openness of the world, is to excel in sport. The main charm of sport lies in it perfectly reconciling the needs for freedom and order, which Skolimowski's characters

Figure 2.2 Jerzy Skolimowski as Andrzej Leszczyc in *Walkover*

frequently express. For example, someone driving a sports car can be faster than any vehicle moving on the earth, hence in a sense he is as free as a man can be. At the same time, to reach and sustain such speed, and preserve one's life, one has to be precise and methodical, because cars tend to disobey bad drivers. Achievements in sport, unlike in literature or art, are easy to measure. The champion almost immediately becomes somebody – he stands out from the crowd and his merit is widely recognised, even by those who themselves have nothing to do with the sport. Moreover, unlike intellectual pursuits which require a multitude of skills, sport demands single-mindedness. Furthermore, it is a preserve of youngsters; there are few middle-aged people engaging in competitive sport. This is largely to do with the weaker muscles of older people, but also with the indifference to one's life and health that older people rarely exhibit because they have to save them in order to bring up their children. This aspect of sport is captured in *Identification Marks: None*, when some men call Leszczyc with derision 'a sportsman', when he tries to jump onto a moving tram. Sport is not only for young people, but also largely for men. At least the disciplines in which Skolimowski's protagonists engage, boxing in *Walkover* and racing in *Le Départ*, have been till recently a male preserve. Participation in them thus also confirms the characters' superior masculine identity. The strictly masculine character of boxing is underscored by the relationship between Leszczyc and Teresa in *Walkover*. He makes her realise that she does not know about boxing and cannot even use the proper terminology, as she says 'to beat', rather 'to fight'. The attractiveness of the disciplines chosen by Skolimowski's characters also lies in the fact that, as opposed to football or basketball, they boast their individual identity.

In socialist Poland, sport had specific connotations. It was popular both among the masses and the elites. Authorities used sport as a tool to educate young people in the spirit of socialism, build national unity and win on the international stage when other methods to prove one's superiority, such as excelling in economic development and reaching a high standard of living, were unavailable. In this way, sport helped to validate other (fake or modest) successes of socialist Poland. The importance of sport in official life in *Walkover* is conveyed by the director of the plant, who first offers Leszczyc a job, saying 'We believe in sportsmen', and later attends the match where Leszczyc wins by a walkover, repeating his offer of employment to the boxer. The tacit assumption of his offer is that those who are good at sport must be good in everything, as well as politically sound.

Sport in postwar Poland was also a substitute for real fighting in wars and uprisings. As Iwona Kurz observes, achievements in boxing and other fighting sports, such as fencing, were particularly important for postwar authorities because of their link with masculine and nationalist mythologies (see Kurz 2005: 112).[2] Boxing was further elevated as a noble pursuit thanks to the successes of the 'Polish school of boxing' under Feliks Stamm (who appeared in Skolimowski's early film, *Boxing*), which emphasised technique and intelligence, as opposed to purely physical strength (ibid.). By insisting that Teresa call boxing 'fighting', Leszczyc demands recognition of the dignity of his work, and the director identifies with this demand. By drawing comparison between boxing and fighting Skolimowski also tacitly compares Leszczyc with the earlier 'true fighters' of Polish cinema, most importantly Maciek Chełmicki from Andrzej Wajda's *Popiół i diament* (*Ashes and Diamonds*, 1958).[3] Similarly, Leszczyc's ultimate rejection of the walkover, both as a strategy in sport and as an attitude to life as a whole, reminds us of the life stance taken by the doomed heroes of Wajda's films, especially Maciek. And yet Leszczyc lacks the tragedy and dignity of Maciek, partly because in his fights he risks less than his predecessor and partly because unlike fighting in the war, sport, as depicted by Skolimowski, is associated with consumerism. Those who excel in sport are financially rewarded (Leszczyc sells watches and radios he wins to make his living) and, on the other hand, some sports disciplines are available only to the rich.

The connection between sport and consumerism is now taken for granted, but at the time when Skolimowski began his film-making (and sporting) career, it was a new phenomenon. This phenomenon was observed especially in the West, an example being the footballer George Best, mentioned in *Deep End*, whose high living eventually became the subject of tabloid interest. In the socialist East sportsmen also lived above the national norm.[4] However, the high living of sportsmen was much more socially acceptable than that of politicians and managers, because of the transparency of their successes and because those who became sporting champions were not required by their ideology to remain immune to life's pleasures, as were socialist politicians and priests.

In the Polish reality of the 1960s, the highly competitive character of sport and the perks attached to winning in competition, encouraged abuses. In *Walkover*, we find a trainer who knows that some participants of 'first step' boxing should not take part in the tournament, but he allows them to enter, even abets such dishonest competition. The boxer whom Leszczyc eventually beats through a walkover allows him to do so as part of an arrangement, according to which he wins without a fight but will share his winnings with his absent competitor. There is also a motif of scales to measure the boxers' weight, in order to place them in a particular category. It is suggested that the scales might be faulty, pointing to the wider corruption of sport in a socialist country. A journalist of the Polish magazine *Sport* situated *Walkover* alongside a number of Polish films of the late 1960s, such as *Jutro Meksyk* (*Tomorrow Mexico*, 1965), directed by Aleksander Ścibor-Rylski and *Jowita* (1967), directed by Janusz Morgenstern, which presented Polish sport as an arena of corruption, nepotism and mental cruelty (see Salecki 1970). Corrupted sport can also be seen as a metonym of corrupted society. As Michael Walker observes, 'One gets the impression in the film that the scales used for weighing the boxers are always "in pawn". The clerk in the left luggage office is most emphatic: "I wouldn't give the scales to the Minister of Justice!" Does this mean that justice in Poland can only be obtained by paying hard cash?' (Walker 1970: 47).

Walkover can be compared to *The Loneliness of the Long Distance Runner* (1962), directed by Tony Richardson, because both films expose the socially divisive potential of sport and its proneness to ideological manipulation by those in positions of power (on Richardson's film see Hughson 2005). However, Richardson's protagonist, who observes these manipulations, rejects becoming a champion and sentences himself to life in a borstal and, generally, to an existence on the margins of society. By contrast to him, Leszczyc in *Walkover* wants to win. His desire to be a successful boxer suggests that he is oblivious to sport's openness to corruption and ideological appropriation. He even uses the dishonesty of sport 'Polish style' to his own advantage. Consequently, it confirms the opinion that he is less of a rebel against the dominant ideologies than might otherwise appear.

In *Le Départ*, sport is less prone to political manipulation than in *Walkover*. This does not mean, however, that everybody who has talent and is willing to work hard has the same chance of winning. This is because participation in sport, at least in some disciplines, such as car racing, is determined by the initial financial position of a participant. To put it crudely: no money, no car, no victory.

Despite their enthusiasm, inventiveness and lack of concern for the ideological entanglement of sport, Skolimowski's sportsmen, Leszczyc in *Walkover* and Marc in *Le Départ*, lose before they even properly start. Yet their failure does not come across as a tragedy, because they are still young, and therefore have time to fulfil their dreams or abandon them and start afresh, chasing different goals. By contrast, those young people who have achieved relative success or are reconciled with their lot, such as Mundek in *Identification Marks: None*, Teresa in *Walkover*, or Marc's friend and fellow hairdressing apprentice, turn out prematurely old and unappealing.

I would like now to return to consumerism, because Skolimowski discusses it not only in relation to specific ideologies, such as religion, communism or sport, but also as an issue in its own right. His characters often define themselves in relation to material goods, especially those regarded as luxurious. From this perspective they have also changed significantly over the years. In *Identification Marks: None*, Leszczyc is ardently anti-consumerist, as demonstrated by his reproaching Teresa for having a wardrobe full of clothes. He throws them violently to the floor, boasting that he wears jumpers with holes in the elbows. His whole behaviour in this film testifies to his lack of concern for material goods. For example, he borrows money from Mundek, only to spend it irrationally on a Spanish course. His follower in *Walkover* is a somewhat different case. He still has few belonging and does not care about what he possesses or how he looks, but carries more things than his younger incarnation, including a transistor radio, one of the symbols of modernity and youth culture in Poland of the 1960s. The protagonist of *Barrier* not only carries more things than Leszczyc in *Identification Marks: None* and *Walkover*, but also expresses a wish to have all the goods his elders have at their disposal, especially cars and girls. As mentioned earlier, this wish is partly a consequence of his Schadenfreude towards the hypocritical older generation who enriched themselves by collaborating with the Stalinist authorities. Yet it is also a sign that by this stage Leszczyc internalised a consumerist mindset. His other actions, such as refusing to share money from the piggy bank with his friends, visiting an expensive restaurant and sitting in the car of a woman who hired him to clean her house, enjoying the luxurious ambience, shows him as ideal material for a consumer. Finally, in *Hands Up!*, the characters are already keen consumers, as signified by all of them having cars, including some expensive ones, drinking champagne straight from the bottle and admitting enjoying travelling abroad. Consumption, however, does not make them happy. They feel empty and ashamed of what they have achieved. This is partly because, as in the earlier film, affluence is associated with joining the Party, selfishness and a low standard of work and philistinism. An additional factor in their condemnation is the widespread conviction that a good man cannot be rich, which in Poland can be treated as a legacy of both Christianity and communism.

Skolimowski's attack on consumption was regarded with great interest by Polish critics. Bolesław Michałek and Frank Turaj have noted that:

> Skolimowski's anti-philistine message had its sincere doubters. An attack upon the get-rich-quick mentality and materialism in favour of ideals seems appropriate in an affluent society. In the Polish context, it was somewhat questionable. In the 1960s in Poland there was a shortage of consumer goods, with little chance for many to develop a penchant for excessive consumerism. Except perhaps for a handful of the politically favoured, the material ambitions of most people were very modest: a small refrigerator, an old used car, brief holiday. To be sure, greed and materialism can thrive in circumstances of poverty and often do, but an attack on the relatively modest desires of ordinary people can be construed as less than authentic criticism. (Michałek and Turaj 1988: 44)

Skolimowski himself later defended his anti-consumerist message by claiming that it was a means to criticise Polish Stalinism, because an open attack on their leaders and officials would not pass censorship (see Uszyński 1990a: 19). I have no reason to doubt Skolimowski's intentions but would argue that the outcome of his criticism is different and most likely unintended by the director – a defence of socialist ideals.

In Skolimowski's first films made abroad, *Le Départ, Dialóg 20–40–60* and *Deep End*, as I already hinted and as Jackiewicz states openly in the epigraph for this chapter, the characters are even more consumption-oriented than their Polish predecessors. By and large, they define themselves by what they can and cannot consume. For Marc in *Le Départ*, these are expensive sports cars; for Mike in *Deep End*, expensive girls, entry to posh nightclubs, perhaps also a car (although it is only hinted at). They are also well aware that consumption is a complex discursive system; it operates in 'chains'. For example, by driving a Porsche one acquires the right to be treated like a sheikh and visit places off-limits to ordinary mortals. Similarly, in an expensive nightclub one has the chance to meet an attractive, well-bred girl, and with a well-bred girl one is accepted into a good nightclub. In accordance with the theory of Levi Strauss, later criticised by feminists (see Cowie 2000), women appear here as an important part of male consumption.

The Western young men are also resentful of older men, who already earned their Porsches and can afford to buy their girlfriend a diamond ring. The main difference between consumption in the 'Leszczyc tetralogy' on the one hand, and *Le Départ* and *Deep End* on the other, lies in the fact that the characters in Skolimowski's Polish films are aware of other ideas and values, even if they reject them in practice. The protagonists of *Le Départ* and *Deep End*, on the other hand, behave as if they were living in a political, cultural and ideological desert. This difference can be explained by two complementary factors. Firstly, the director, as Michael Walker suggests in reference to *Le Départ*, did not know enough of Belgium to inscribe any deeper cultural or political context into the actions of his protagonist (see Walker 1970: 42). This explanation is somehow confirmed by the director who in interviews frequently admits that he is not interested in the politics and culture of the countries where he lived as an emigrant. The second factor is a conviction that for young Belgians or Englishmen, there is no more to life than work and consumption. Consequently, they are defined by where they work and what they can afford to buy. Such an idea was promulgated in Polish anti-Western propaganda during the postwar period and Skolimowski, perhaps against his will, assimilated it. Again, his interviews, in which he complains that in the West only money matters, confirm this explanation.

Here it is worth drawing attention to the casting of Jean-Pierre Léaud in *Le Départ* and *Dialóg 20–40–60*, where he plays an aspiring musician. Léaud, the 'face' of the French New Wave, perfectly encapsulates the condition of a young person in a capitalist, industrial society, whose life is relatively comfortable, but anonymous and standardised (see Oleksiewicz 1969: 5). In his New Wave Films, as well as in later ones, such as *La Maman et la Putain* (*The Mother and the Whore*, 1973) by Jean Eustache, Léaud's protagonist rebels against his situation, using varied means, such as partaking in political discussions with friends, refusing to work, initiating revolutionary action, even suicide. Off-screen Léaud was also remarkably active in politics.[5] In comparison with the characters in his French films of similar period,

Figure 2.3 Jean-Pierre Léaud in *Dialóg 20–40–60*

Léaud's Marc and the musician in *Dialóg 20–40–60* are less complicated and rebellious. In no sense are they political activists. However, we can read into *Le Départ* and *Dialóg 20–40–60* the meanings Léaud's persona convey and see his search for a Porsche and the good life as signs of a rebellion of sorts. Such a reading is facilitated by the way Skolimowski uses this actor, allowing him to dominate the screen to an even greater extent than he permitted himself in the films about Leszczyc. Consequently, it feels like *Le Départ* and *Dialóg 20–40–60* are less about the specific characters this actor plays, and more about Léaud himself.

Certainly less easy to notice is the on–off screen dialectic between Michèle and Catherine Duport, who played this character in *Le Départ*. However, at one point Michèle talks about her previous modelling career, as if she was talking about Duport, who also gave up on both modelling and acting – *Le Départ* was her last film. Hence both the actress and the character convey a rebellion against the typical scenario offered to a pretty girl in the Western world and against consumerist culture in a wider sense.

If we apply to Skolimowski's protagonists of the 1960s and early 1970s the central concept of psychoanalysis, the Oedipal complex, then we can note a particular trajectory, which Teresa Rutkowska aptly describes as their 'losing innocence' (Rutkowska 2002: 295). Leszczyc in *Identification Marks: None* and, to an extent, in *Walkover*, as well as Marc in *Le Départ*, behave as if they did not want to overcome their Oedipus, preferring to remain immature. Besides, even if they wanted to surmount their Oedipus, it would be difficult, because their fathers are absent, whilst in the process of individualisation, of separation from the mother, the paternal figure is fundamental. The crucial sign of 'young' Leszczyc and Marc's imprisonment in their state of immaturity are their failed relationships with women (which I will discuss in detail later in this chapter). The main character in *Barrier* is somewhat different. Unlike his predecessors, he has a father, although senile, and he openly proclaims that he would like to be a patriarch – have everything that the older generation has acquired: the houses, the cars, the women, and have it sooner than them, preferably now. His decision to leave university can be interpreted not as an attempt to avoid adulthood (which was the case with Leszczyc in *Identification Marks: None*), but to speed up his maturation, reach immediately what his friends expect to achieve in ten years or more. Of course, he does not know how to do it, but this is a secondary issue here. Also in *Barrier*, for the first time, the male character successfully completes an Oedipal trajectory, by finding a woman with whom he appears to be happy. Finally, all the men in *Hands Up!*, including Leszczyc, become patriarchs; they dislodge their own parents from their positions of power and now possess wives (and even lovers), children, houses, cars, careers – everything for which they once envied their fathers.

Post-Freudian, especially Lacanian, psychoanalysis states that the Oedipus complex cannot be taken literally, because it does not refer to the situation of each individual child and the relationship with its parents: to the real fear of castration and penis envy. Instead, it must be understood metaphorically, as relating to the function of the father (the 'Name of the Father'), a means to conceptualise how the child enters the pregiven structure of social and sexual relations which make up society, how he acquires its heritage of ideas and laws (see Lacan 1977). Accordingly, the second reason that Leszczyc in *Identification Marks: None*, *Walkover* and Marc in *Le Départ* prefer to remain in the pre-Oedipal stage is his rejection of everything the Lacanian 'Name of the Father' stands for: the discourses of history, politics, religion, economy and everyday life. Similarly, the characters in *Hands Up!* cannot fully enjoy their completion of the Oedipal trajectory, because mentally they remained detached from the patriarchal order which they have, superficially, accepted. Consequently, they are alienated from themselves. Their mocking attitude to politics and history, and to themselves, conveys this alienation. On the whole, the protagonist of the 'Leszczyc tetralogy' and others of his kind are in a precarious position. If they reject the 'Name of the Father', they remain Peter Pans for ever – wither and die, before growing up. If they accept it, they become self-alienated and equally unhappy, if not more. There is a third possibility – radical change of the social and cultural order, becoming patriarchs on their own terms. Such a possibility was considered and even attempted in some films of the 1960s and early 1970s, for example *La Chinoise* (1967) by Godard, whose young characters plot a revolution. For Skolimowski's early characters, however, rebellion on this scale is not really an option, not least because they are ardent individualists. Even as sportsmen, they shun team games, preferring car races and boxing.

Skolimowski's films, on which I am focusing in this section, can be contextualised in a number of ways. Those made in Poland are perceived, naturally, first and foremost as referring to the Polish reality of the times they were made. This was a period of so-called 'small stabilisation'. This term, derived from the title of Tadeusz Różewicz's play, *Świadkowie albo nasza mała stabilizacja* (*Witnesses Or Our Small Stabilisation*, 1962), captured the stable, but colourless and thwarted decade of the 1960s, when Władysław Gomułka was the Party leader. 'Small stabilisation' followed the Polish October of 1956 and the short political and cultural thaw of the late 1950s, when the citizens hoped that Poland would find its own route to socialism. In common with Czechoslovak 'normalisation' (the term applied to the period following the Czech Spring of 1968), the 'small stabilisation' was about the modesty of material aspirations of Poles, but also about consumption replacing cultural values, about moderate success that had to be paid for by accepting conformity and hypocrisy. On a positive note, during the 'small stabilisation', in contrast to the times of war and Stalinism, Poles were offered an opportunity to be individuals and not to feel guilty about it. Leszczyc is both a creature of 'small stabilisation', by emphasising his individualism, and at the same time rejects this paradigm as offering him too little at too high a price. Tadeusz Sobolewski suggests that the protagonists of Skolimowski's Polish films do not want to grow up because in communist Poland of the time there was nothing which made growing up worthwhile (see Sobolewski 1996: 53). In his intentional and obstinate immaturity the Leszczyc of *Identification Marks: None* and *Walkover* can be compared to a number of characters in slightly earlier Polish films, such as the Boy in *Ostatni dzień lata* (*The Last Day of Summer*, 1958) by Tadeusz Konwicki, Staszek in *Pociąg* (*Night Train*, 1959) by Jerzy Kawalerowicz or the Student in Polański's *Knife in the Water* (see Kurz 2005: 82–83). Their immaturity was underscored by their frequent lack of names (the character in *Barrier* also lacks a name), and the fact that during the course of the film we learn next to nothing about their family, social background, occupation or interests.

Even more specifically, the 'Leszczyc series' can be regarded as a commentary on the situation in the Polish film industry of the 1960s. Janusz Gazda, a renowned critic of this period, claims that at the time when Skolimowski made his feature debut, the 'Father ruled'. For young graduates of the Łódź Film School the road to their full-length feature debut was very difficult because it was expected that they would work first for a number of years as assistant directors and then as 'second directors'. This was in part a conscious strategy of the older directors who were afraid of competition. Similarly, it was easier to make an average, undistinctive film than one that was outstanding, because the mediocre debuts constituted less of a threat to the older film makers and authorities. The idea of 'third cinema', of which Gazda was a chief supporter, was less a description of a new phenomenon, more a project to help the young to 'dig one's way to success' by creating an impression that there was a whole group of the young and talented, the 'new wave' who should be given a chance.[6] Of course, Skolimowski's decision to make a feature film during his studies, using print allocated to him for different purposes was, as the director himself admits, a way to challenge the 'Law of the Father' which sentenced young directors to a long apprenticeship (see Ziółkowski 1967: 9). In this respect the director proved more inventive and lucky than his protagonists, who drifted precariously between the traumatic pre-Oedipal stage and unsatisfactory post-Oedipal period.

The lack of 'identification marks' and unwillingness or inability to grow up, is also a feature of characters of many European films of a similar period, especially in France and Czechoslovakia. Take, for example, the protagonists of *À bout de souffle* (*Breathless*, 1960) and *Pierrot le fou* (*Crazy Pete*, 1965) by Godard, who come from nowhere, find no place for themselves in society and in the end have to escape or are killed, often due to their own actions. In Czech and Slovak films, such as *Černý Petr* (*Black Peter*, 1964) by Miloš Forman and *Return of the Prodigal Son* by Evald Schorm, the young men (from teenagers to men in their thirties), reject the responsibilities of adulthood. This refusal, typically treated with sympathy by the director, can be regarded as a metaphor for their rejection of socialism as an ideology that requires responsibility and maturity even from the youngest members of society (see Liehm 1983: 213). Some of the Czech films, most importantly *Return of the Prodigal Son*, also show the high cost of refusing to leave the pre-Oedipal stage. Schorm's character, who rejects the duties of the father, the husband and the worker, has a mental breakdown and ends up in a psychiatric hospital. *Return of the Prodigal Son* thus shows what could happen to Leszczyc, if after *Walkover* he should continue as a rebellious thirty-something-year-old man. In practically all these films the problem of consumption plays a divisive role, either building a barrier between older and younger generations, or between the young people themselves. In common with the Polish creators of 'third cinema', the French, Czech and Slovak directors of the New Waves also rebelled against their situation as film makers, and their films of this period can be read as metaphorical accounts of their rebellion.

A striking feature of all these films is their sheer masculinism. As Petra Hanáková argues in relation to Czech films, 'the New Wave films – more often than the movies of earlier periods – generalise the man's story as a universal human story' (Hanáková 2005: 63). Certainly this is also true of Skolimowski's films – moral dilemmas and ideological choices only befall his men. Women, as I will argue in the later part of this chapter, are only there to make men realise what they want in life.

The films Skolimowski made in the 1960s conveyed a premonition and offered an excellent build-up to the momentous year of 1968. In this year, young people in various parts of the world, including France, Czechoslovakia and Poland (three countries to which Skolimowski was close during this period), asserted their identity through rebellion against the older generation, their fathers and their 'daddy's politics' (on the conflict between generations in relation to 1968 see Roszak 1995). As I will argue in the next section, in Skolimowski's later films his young characters change. They start to talk to their fathers, as opposed to only revolting against them. Similarly, fathers in Skolimowski's post-1968 films seek their sons' attention, involve them in their lives and decisions, even flatter and bribe them.

The concept of youth as shapeless, directionless and fragmented not only excellently captures the content of Skolimowski's early films, but also their form. The openness of his narratives, the inclusion of many episodes unconnected with the main thread of the narrative, parallel the abundance and amorphism of young life as perceived by Skolimowski. It appears as if the director wants to avoid form in the same way his characters want to avoid any prescription of their lives (see Eberhardt 1982: 122). Moreover, the short period in which his early films are set, never exceeding two days, reflect the nature of youth, when every day seems to last for ever and every meeting might dramatically change the course of one's life. Furthermore, the images which begin some of these films, presenting the figure of a young male with his head hidden and only gradually becoming revealed, can be seen as a metaphor for a man's search of identity. On the other hand, such an image awakens association with death. Together, from these images we can derive the concept of a human as situated between nothingness, abruptly thrown into life and violently taken from it.

Sons, Fathers and Motherlands

Although the relationship between the younger and older generation played an important part in Skolimowski's early films, it was typically represented as impersonal. Older people communicated with the younger through the intermediary of symbols, rituals, narratives, institutions and only in specific circumstances, such as when the young were subjected to a special 'commission' assessing their behaviour. In the rare situations when the characters approached their real parents, the contact was limited, because, as in *Identification Marks: None*, they were talking by phone or, in *Barrier*, the father was detached from the son by senility. Most of the time Skolimowski's protagonists were left to their own devices or were even parentless, especially fatherless. Yet the lack of parents, although not without significance, because it confirmed the young characters' lack of roots, never amounted to a tragedy. They were too old for that, being twenty-something or even thirty years old. Their position of parentless children mirrored the situation of the director himself, who lost his father in early childhood and later, in a sense, his mother, who was so busy with her work as a teacher and then as a cultural attaché in Czechoslovakia that she left the young Jerzy in a boarding school, thus allowing an institution to replace her in her parental role. It also, in a sense, reflected the fate of many young Polish men who lost their fathers in the war or in its aftermath (on fatherhood in Poland see Mazierska 2008).

However, even in his early films we often find a scene pointing to the son yearning for his father or father for son and their failure to communicate with each other. In *Le Départ*, Marc approaches a man whom he wants to emulate – a famous champion rally driver. Marc asks him how he got a car for his first race and became a champion. The answer the older man gives to the younger is polite but useless. He says that he does not remember his racing beginnings, wishes the young racer success and quickly drives away. In *Hands Up!*, one of the characters, nicknamed Record, asks rhetorically: 'What can I say to my children? What at all can I say?' It is suggested that Record, as well as all the other people taking part in the psychodrama, cannot pass any wisdom on to their children because they have no wisdom and no morality of their own.

The motif of father and father-like figure and son gained currency in the middle part of Skolimowski's career, when he moved to Britain and then to the US. It is central to two films from the 1980s, *Success Is the Best Revenge* and *The Lightship*, made when the director's own sons became teenagers and could play a distinctive role in his father's career. In the first film, as I mentioned in the previous chapter, his older son, Michał, under the pseudonym Michael Lyndon, plays the role of Adam Rodak, the son of the protagonist, and Skolimowski's younger son, Jerzy, is cast as his younger brother, Tony. Michał/Michael is again cast in *Lightship* in the part of the son. In Skolimowski's own words, this film was offered to him by a producer who previously saw *Success Is the Best Revenge*. The producer claimed that he had an interesting story about father and son, and suggested that the father could be played by Klaus Maria Brandauer who was physically similar to Skolimowski, and the son by Michael (see Uszyński 1990a: 39).

Off-screen the director pictures himself as, if not failed, at least an inadequate father who left his sons for long periods when shooting films in different parts of the world. Moreover, he admits that even when he was at home he did not pay them much attention (see Mirska 1994: 54). His behaviour thus to a large extent repeated that of his own parents. However, while for his parents such neglect was natural, for the adult Skolimowski it was a source of qualms of conscience. He claims that his wife's utter devotion to their children made him realise that parenthood might look different to what he himself experienced (ibid.). Finding a diary belonging to his son, who depicted his unhappiness living in London, later used as a basis for the script of *Success Is the Best Revenge*, was another cause of his remorse. I believe that

Skolimowski's self-discomfort also had much to do with the changing approaches to parenthood the director must have witnessed in his life. These changes, marked by the publishing of Dr Spock's book advocating permissive child rearing, or *Iron John* by Robert Bly, emphasising the role of fathers in bringing up their sons, as well as the growing standard of living which allowed each new generation of children to be more materially pampered than their fathers, first affected people living in the West, but in due course reached Poland, even if only in a diluted form. Poles of Skolimowski's generation, especially the middle classes, assimilated the new attitudes. Most likely, they were taken for granted when the director moved abroad.

The films that Skolimowski shot with Michael, as well as his involvement in his sons' film, *Motyw cienia* (*The Hollow Men*, 1993), can be regarded as a way to mend their relationship before it became too late, when the sons reached adulthood and went their own ways. Such an interpretation is facilitated by the topic of *Success Is the Best Revenge* and *The Lightship*, which is also a father's attempt to repair his relationship with his teenage son. The father appears to follow Robert Bly's idea that in order to build a good relationship with his son, the father must teach him his craft, be his son's master or at least somebody able to awaken admiration in his offspring. By no means should he allow himself to appear a thwarted male, pushed around by his wife or hiding in the corner of the house watching television. However, the question arises as to how to become one's sons' master, especially the counter-culturally educated sons who learnt to treat their elders with utmost scepticism, begrudging them even for giving them a good education and good pocket money.

Alex Rodak from *Success Is the Best Revenge*, who is a renowned theatre director, has not seen his teenage sons for two years. They reunite when Alex is allowed to travel to France, to be decorated with the Légion d'honneur for his contribution to European theatre. Alex is thus given a perfect opportunity to impress his family as a man of talent and virtue. His sons, however, are not too keen to participate in this event. They demonstrate their lack of enthusiasm, as well as their sense of mischief, by disconnecting the cables for the microphones and in this way switching off the sound, which makes the speeches in honour of Rodak and his response impossible to transmit on television. The boys' act can be compared to the familiar situation when the children switch off mentally, when other people, usually from the generation of their fathers, start to praise their parents. They might do it because they were exposed

Figure 2.4 Michał Skolimowski/Michael Lyndon as Adam Rodak in *Success Is the Best Revenge*

to such adulation many times before and are simply bored by it, or because they do not believe it, knowing their fathers from a perspective that the adulators do not know. On the other hand, praising fathers in the presence of their sons might make the sons realise how much they are still behind them, which is a daunting thought.

The trip to France allows Rodak to move to London and there devote himself to two projects: getting to know his older son, Adam, better, and staging a play about Polish martial law. It is worth mentioning that while Adam is of utmost concern to Alex, his younger son, Tony, does not feature in his plans. We see practically no interaction between the youngest and the oldest Rodak, most likely because Tony is still a child and has some years before he goes his way.

At the same time as Alex attempts to get closer to Adam, his son decides to leave his father and return to Poland. Although it is never spelt out that Alex's return is the reason for the son's departure, such an explanation, although paradoxical, is convincing. We can assume that when Alex was in Poland, for his family he stood for the 'real Poland'. His coming to London reveals that his relationship with Poland is less genuine or it has become so now, when he uses martial law as an 'artistic project' or, perhaps, even a tool for fulfilling his ambition to become some kind of national poet-prophet, in the vein of Adam Mickiewicz. The very project looks suspicious to Adam. Brought up on music by David Bowie (whose poster decorates his room), he finds his father's political art outdated. His suspicions grow when he sees how Adam goes about his business. He is disgusted by his father's attempt to find Polish volunteers to work as extras in his play by organising a football match in Hyde Park, in which they play against a team of Englishmen. Moreover, this match shows that his father is not such a good sportsman as the boy believed. He is equally dismayed by Alex's willingness to enter into some shady business deal with a pornographer and fellow countryman (perhaps of Jewish origin), Dino Montecurva, to get funds for his play. Before Alex's play has its premiere, Adam flies to Warsaw. To pay for his ticket he uses money from pawning the video camera he received from his father for his sixteenth birthday.

This expensive present and Adam's reaction to it points to the father's desire to repay any debt he might have towards his son by a material gift, which is a typical strategy of the 'age of affluence' (see Roszak 1995: xix). However, Rodak is not really affluent and he pays for the camera from money borrowed from the bank. The gift thus signifies either the father's martyrdom or, more likely, his recklessness. Although material gifts do not need to reveal a parent's failure to communicate with their children directly, on this occasion it seems to be the case. For Alex it is easier to pamper his son with gifts than to talk to him. The video camera can also be regarded (especially if we assume that Alex stands for Skolimowski) as an expression of the father's desire to mould his son to his own likeness, by making him a director. Conversely, the son's nonchalant exchange of the gift suggests his rejection of his father's plans. It is worth noting that Adam prefers this option to returning the camera to his father and earning his own money for the trip.

For those viewers who know the 'Leszczyc films', the similarity between father and son is also underscored by the fact that Adam's activities before he leaves London mirror Leszczyc's peregrinations, as reflected in *Identification Marks: None* and *Barrier*. Adam walks the streets of his town, finding it foreign and hostile and one by one breaks his bonds with people, institutions, places and objects that provided his 'identification marks'. He gets rid of his school books and school suit, fights with his school colleague, has sex with a pretty girl he fancied, says farewell to his dog, takes out his mother's best photo from her old passport and, as previously mentioned, pawns the camera he received from his father. The last act can be compared to breaking the sabre Leszczyc received from his father in *Barrier*. Yet, paradoxically, Leszczyc showed more respect for this paternal gift than Adam; he carried it with him and did not want to sell it. Finally, on the plane to Warsaw Adam paints his hair and face red.

Adam's return to Poland, as Richard Combs notes, appears hopelessly romantic; it is as theatrical a gesture as his father's staging the performance (see Combs 1984: 390). Even more than his father's, it betrays Adam's lack of originality (in his red 'mask' he resembles British punks), his naïve concept of revolt as looking different and lack of knowledge of his old country. It can also be compared to Leszczyc's joining the army, as at the outset Adam is told by the border guard to relinquish his passport and wash his face. Thus his rebellion does not help him to sustain his individuality, but forces him to abandon it and stop showing any sign of revolt.

In *Success Is the Best Revenge*, the main point of identification of the director and the viewer is the son. To facilitate the viewer's sympathy, Skolimowski endows Adam with the voice-over, in which the son derides his father. At the same time he prevents the audience from feeling sympathy for Alex by constructing him as a caricature of an émigré Polish artist. Yet these devices do not conceal Adam's immaturity and self-pity. On the contrary, they act as perfect vehicles to reveal the boy's weaknesses[7] and his position as his father's follower, the shadow of his father's persona.

Success Is the Best Revenge can be regarded as an Oedipal story, although not a conventional one because there are no women involved in the father–son competition. Adam's mother, as I will argue in due course, does not mean much to either the son or the father. She is on the periphery of their relationship; her only involvement is as a 'messenger', delivering a letter the son wrote to his father. However, father and son compete for a different kind of 'mother': their motherland, Poland. This 'mother', as Maria Janion argues, for Polish romantics, of which Alex and Adam are successors, constituted the highest value, and it was not a gentle and merciful goddess but a ruthless and demonic entity that did not allow a man to have any other objects of affection (see Janion 1989: 10). Alex tries to recreate or, as Combs puts it, 'reimagine Poland on foreign soil' (Combs 1984: 390). Adam does not believe this is possible and regards his father's love of Poland as fake. Similarly, he tries to convince himself, his father and the viewers, that he will be Poland's 'true lover'. In his last inner monologue he says: 'No more substitutes. I want real enemies. I want to play for Poland and help her win'. Perhaps the Rodaks are the last contemporary characters in films made by a Polish director who adulate their country so much.

In *The Lightship*, the second film with Michał Skolimowski playing the main role, again the father and his teenage son meet after a long separation, on this

Figure 2.5 Klaus Maria Brandauer as Captain Miller and Michał Skolimowski/Michael Lyndon as Alex in *The Lightship*

occasion caused by the father's work as the captain of a lightship that hardly allowed him any time ashore. In common with young Adam in *Success Is the Best Revenge*, Alex is a rebel and has even had trouble with the police. Although Captain Miller cannot impress his son with any recently won trophies, he wears a uniform when taking his son to the lightship, which points to the dignity of his office. However, the costume does not impress Alex; he only finds it odd and questions his father's motives for 'dressing up'. The whole narrative unfolds like a series of father's decisions that his son finds strange and rejects, until he finally understands them, but by then it is too late to mend their relationship.

Captain Miller's method of building a bridge between himself and his son, in common with Alex Rodak's, is through involving his son in his daily activities. Also, as with Alex, it turns out that his situation is more difficult than assumed, on this occasion because the ship is besieged by a group of three armed crooks, looking for shelter. The father is expected to demonstrate his superiority over the leader of the gang, Calvin Caspary, and get rid of the intruders. Both tasks prove difficult because Caspary has many qualities that Miller lacks and attempts to exploit the tension between father and son. Unlike Miller, who after many years of life alone, finds talking very difficult, Caspary has friendly chats with Alex, asking him questions his father is too shy to ask. He also grooms the boy by telling him stories from his adventurous life and sharing with him his fascination for New York. The teenager, who was previously rarely exposed to the pleasures of the high life, finds his interlocutor's dandy style alluring. During his first encounter with Caspary, Alex even refuses to join his father, telling him that he prefers the visitor's company. The gangster also confesses to Alex that the first time he felt free was when his father died. In this way he not so subtly suggests that the boy's interests and those of his father are in conflict, perhaps he even encourages Alex to commit an Oedipal murder. At the same time as grooming the son, the crook attempts to position himself as a kind of a double of Miller and in this way disarm both the son and his father. Yet the features which are meant to link him with Miller are mostly as fake as his title 'Doctor', by which he is addressed by his two companions.

Miller does not give in to his adversary's devious charm, refusing the position of his enemy's doppleganger or competitor for Alex's affection. He remains taciturn and rejects his crew's request to fight the intruders, and demands that his son promises never to use a gun. To shoot and kill, even in a good cause, equals for him putting oneself on the same moral platform as the murderer. Moreover, in his opinion using guns does not guarantee solving any problem; more likely it will create even more trouble. Miller's unwillingness to show resistance, which irritates his son, also results from Miller's professional ethos. As the captain of a lightship, he serves all the other ships which are at risk of losing their way on the sea without the light and could be destroyed by the mines which litter the waters. He puts up with all the excesses of Caspary and his people, as long as they accept the main rule of the lightship – that it must stay anchored. He only reacts when the invaders try to violate this rule. He succeeds, but pays the ultimate price of his own life.

During his stay on the lightship Alex's attitude to his father and Caspary goes through three distinct phases. In the first, he shows his father scorn and gravitates towards the gangster. In the second phase, he gains some distance from both men and limits himself to observing them, as suggested by his own words, 'I cannot understand their game'. In the last stage, he begins to empathise with his father. This happens when Alex is about to shoot one of the invaders, Eddie, but instead allows himself to be disarmed by him. His unwillingness to use a weapon mirrors that of his father. Finally, in the moment of Miller's death, Alex identifies with the captain and accepts his values, as conveyed by admitting that he understands that being on a ship not only means travelling on it, but also serving it. Thus the father becomes part of his son and even achieves some kind of immortality thanks to him. Paradoxically, in his death Miller proves the superior of his chief antagonist, who, without his gun and his entourage of mad henchmen, is a broken man, as shown by his bitter tears at the end of the film, so unfitting to his self-image of a dandy.

Although in the film Miller comes across as a noble and tough character, off-screen Skolimowski judged his character less favourably, even calling him a 'coward' (see Uszyński 1990a: 39). Such a harsh judgement can be attributed to a number of extradiegetic factors. The first is Skolimowski's negative attitude to the actor playing Miller, Klaus Maria Brandauer, and, conversely, his adulation of Robert Duvall who played Caspary. In interviews he describes Brandauer as extremely narcissistic and difficult, demanding more resources for himself than the rest of the cast put together, and trying to steal the limelight from Duvall (see Lichocka 1994: 8). However, these traits of Brandauer's character are not visible on screen. On the contrary, it appears as if it is Duvall who tries to overshadow his opponent and push him out of the frame. Brandauer, like his character, seems to resist this 'game' and underplays rather than overplays his part, as if he was convinced that ultimately his deeds, not his words, would attest to his value.

A second possible reason for Skolimowski's lack of sympathy for Captain Miller is the similarity of this character to his own father whom he often describes as a 'man of principle'. Contrary to what we might expect, such an assessment is more critical than positive as it refers to the fact that an abstract value was more important to his father than the concrete situation, which led to his father's untimely death in a concentration camp and his son's subsequent semi-orphanhood. Skolimowski emphasises that in this respect he is different from his parent, as is Alex from Miller. No doubt the character closest to the director is Alex. Not only is he represented most sympathetically, with all his actions being lucid and honest but, like Adam in *Success Is the Best Revenge*, he is endowed with a voice-over, which further explains his motives, influencing our judgement of the older men. Furthermore, the director frequently uses close-ups to reveal the character's interior. The director's sympathy, however, cannot obscure the fact that Alex is still a child, weak and often lacking perceptiveness. In comparison with him the father is a towering figure. Providing the sons with the voice-over in *Success Is the Best Revenge* and *The Lightship* can be regarded as testimony to Skolimowski's continuous identification with the young generation, hence his inability to 'grow up'. Richard Combs, writing at the time of *The Lightship*'s premiere, not without derision, commented that Skolimowski 'has hung on to the "adolescent" in himself, in his work, more persistently than any other filmmaker (with the possible exception of Arthur Penn, as witness his equally absurdist action picture, *Target*). The fact that, in terms of age, he is now firmly on the other side of the generational divide, makes that sympathy, that magnetic attraction to youthful restlessness, an even more eccentric, switchback current within his films' (Combs 1986a: 132). Again, his feeling for the young, as revealed on screen, has its equivalent in his interviews, where he often shows immense admiration and respect for his sons' talent, commitment and resilience (see Lenarciński 1994: 5; Lichocka 1994: 9; Pogorzelska 2001: 22–23), although objectively they achieved much less than their father in a comparable period and their successes are largely connected with their father's helping hand.[8]

If Miller as a father is distant from Skolimowski, he is similar to him, as well as to the father in *Success*, in that he shares with them the condition of a man without a motherland – an emigrant or at least a stranger. Although he regards himself as an American, he is of German origin and speaks with a foreign accent, which Caspary tries to exploit to his own advantage. Moreover, as a seaman he has no real homeland; his ship is his territory, even his motherland. His obsessive preoccupation with the ship, his refusal to de-anchor her, parallels Alex and Adam's exaggerated patriotism. However, Miller's love of his lightship cannot be shared or even fathomed by his son, therefore there is no real competition between father and son; the competition is between two fathers fighting for the soul of the son. Alex solves his Oedipal complex by losing both fathers, but identifying with only one of them.

A number of films by Skolimowski, although they do not include real fathers, lend themselves to an interpretation as stories about fathers, their sons and motherlands. From this perspective the most complex story is offered in *Moonlighting*, where we find two 'fathers' and two sets of children. One 'father' is the Boss who sends Nowak and his crew to renovate his house in London. Mysterious, distant and elusive, he comes across as a bad father who has only demands and no rewards for his son, and refuses to offer him any help in a moment of crisis, not unlike Katelbach in Polanski's *Cul-de-Sac* (1966), who also abandoned his 'sons' when they were stranded on the island. The Boss in *Moonlighting* is even more cruel than Katelbach as he appears to seduce Nowak's wife in his absence. Nowak, on the other hand, to a large extent mirrors his Boss in his dealings with the group of workers. Again, he has many demands for them and few rewards, shows no understanding for their problems and punishes them for the smallest misdemeanours. Moreover, although Nowak does not seduce their wives or girlfriends (he has no chance to do that, being as physically removed from them as his workers are), he usurps control over their intimate relationships by reading and then burning the letters they send. This behaviour is utterly immoral, but Nowak exonerates himself by claiming that he acts for their welfare – had he not censored the flow of information to which they are exposed, they would be put in much more difficult circumstances. Such an approach was compared to the way the communist authorities acted in Poland because they also forced the citizens to work in difficult conditions, giving them little rewards and harshly punishing any transgressions (see Klejsa 2006: 154–55). Similarly, the relationship between Nowak and his Boss parallels that between Poland and the Soviet Union; both Nowak and the Polish authorities having little power of their own, only following the orders of their superiors. This parallel is the more striking due to setting *Moonlighting* during the time of martial law which was widely regarded as imposed on Poland by its 'Big Brother' or 'Boss' from the East. On the whole, in *Moonlighting*, Skolimowski excellently shows that patriarchy is based on physical and economic force and perpetuates itself using deception. Yet, although patriarchy is disappointing, the 'Law of the Son', as presented by the director, also proves unsatisfactory. Perhaps the ideal would be to eliminate the divide between sons and fathers, but this solution is never fulfilled in this or any other of Skolimowski's films.

'Virgins', 'Broken Lilies', 'Withered Roses', 'Queens' and the Maternal Superego

After discussing Skolimowski's male characters' relationship with themselves, other men and the ideologies that surround and affect them, I shall turn now to their relations with women. Such a treatment practically exhausts the 'women's question' in his films because women, as represented by this director, are merely a part of male stories, typically playing the role of vehicles of a young male's self-discovery. Skolimowski seems to be unable to perceive women as autonomous beings, existing outside male projections. Connected with this narrative marginalisation of women is the fact that they come across as belonging to a specific type, rather than being unique individuals. This feature differentiates them from men, who are one of a kind.[9] Moreover, many of Skolimowski's women define themselves in relation to men; without men their lives would have no purpose.

Skolimowski's women fit into several categories. One is the 'virgin' – a beautiful woman whom the character meets by chance and from whom he soon parts, but whose image he carries with him for a long time, perhaps till the end of his life. She is not necessarily a virgin (although in most cases she is); this description refers more to her spiritual innocence, trust and honesty in her dealings with men than to her

Figure 2.6 Jan Nowicki as Boy and Joanna Szczerbic as a tram driver in *Barrier*

lack of sexual experience. A 'virgin' is prepared to give everything to her beloved man, presuming he is willing to accept this gift. This description fits Basia, the young student of ichthyology whom Leszczyc meets at the university in *Identification Marks: None* and who later comes to the railway station to meet him. We can assume that they will never meet again, but her trusting face returns to him in the moments of crisis in *Walkover*.

In *Barrier*, the virginal Basia is replaced by a pretty tram driver, in the script described simply as a 'Girl'. Leszczyc shows her attention, even pretends to his university colleagues that she is his fiancée, but at some stage he abandons her to follow his other pursuits. Also in common with the female student, the tram driver looks for Leszczyc and finds herself at a students' party, where she becomes an object of ridicule when it turns out that she knows nothing about her suitor. Unlike Leszczyc and Basia, Leszczyc and the tram driver meet again, when he jumps onto her tram, but it is difficult to say whether their meeting is a chance encounter or a consequence of Leszczyc's search for his beautiful companion. Even if the latter is true, we do not see Leszczyc chasing her. Consequently, the impression is given that for these young women men are everything, whilst for the men they are only one of many pursuits.

Gemma in *Torrents of Spring* is perhaps the most virginal of females Skolimowski ever depicted: a perfect virgin. Again, though Sanin falls in love with her, he abandons her, this time because he falls under the spell of an older, more sophisticated and stronger woman, Maria. I will also include Michèle, in *Le Départ*, in the category of 'virgin'. Although she comes across as more worldly than any of the women just mentioned, she is also prepared to give Marc everything he needs: her time, her intelligence and her most precious material possessions. Not so different from her is Pelagia in *Innocent Sorcerers*. Although there is a hint of cynicism about Michèle and Pelagia, it never amounts to bitterness, but rather reflects their desire to 'play the part' and not to come across as too naïve in the 'age of cynicism'. Interestingly, although these women are roughly the same age or are even younger than the men with whom they fall in love, they typically give the impression of being older than their partners. About Michèle, played by Catherine Duport, Michael Walker comments that she has the 'slightly "older and wiser" demeanour of the Skolimowski heroine' (Walker 1970: 57). Their maturity might be connected with the director's conviction that women mature earlier than men. As I will argue in due course, this also has an impact on the manner in which he represents older women.

The second type of Skolimowski heroine I describe as a 'broken lily'. It is a woman who was once a 'virgin', but her experience with men has made her bitter and sometimes cunning. Leszczyc's wife in *Identifications Marks: None* is such a broken lily and, even more so, Susan in *Deep End*. The latter, we can guess, was once the innocent pupil of the womanising PE teacher. He seduced her, while teaching her to swim. In both areas, lovemaking and swimming, Susan persevered, becoming a swimming pool attendant and a classy call girl. She also remained her ex-teacher's lover, although at the end of the film she breaks with him, denouncing him as a pathetic Casanova who only debauches young girls because older women would discover his erotic inadequacies. Although Susan is cynical about men and does not love any man, she is unable to detach herself from them because men have power she cannot gain independently. They manage the public baths where she works, have cars, buy her diamond rings and pay her for sexual services. The only way she can 'cheat' them and the whole patriarchal system in which she operates, is by making sure that she does not do anything for them for free. Her final break-up with the PE teacher is a testimony that she has fully learnt her lesson about men.

Although Susan tries to be independent, as much as a woman of her class, age and social position can be, she is not independent within the narrative. We always see her through the eyes of Mike, who falls for her but cannot reach her, being himself too poor, young and inexperienced. Because Mike, with whom Skolimowski makes us identify, lacks Susan's cynicism and genuinely loves her (even if his love is no more than sexual attraction), her rejection of him is painful to watch. Accordingly, when Mike kills Susan after she humiliates him, it appears as a just punishment. We feel more sorry for Mike than for Susan, whose dead body floats away in the pool, as if she was a receding image, rather than a human being. Her fate can be regarded as a warning to women who attempt to elude male control and imagination.

I also place Anna in *Four Nights with Anna* in the same category. She is both metaphorically and literally broken, being raped in front of Leon, a man who in due course becomes her shy admirer and domestic helper, visiting her shabby apartment at night. Although plain, overweight, noisy, fun-loving, perhaps even promiscuous, she is construed by Leon as a delicate princess. He even spends his redundancy money on a diamond ring for her, which he leaves in her bedroom during her absence. Anna has even less narrative autonomy than Susan, as she is not only seen

Figure 2.7 Artur Steranko as Leon and Kinga Preis as Anna in *Four Nights with Anna*

through Leon's eyes, but practically has no voice. Leon looks at her from a distance or even from a hiding-place in her room, when the woman is sleeping. Moreover, he gives Anna sleeping pills, so she can remain mute and in this way conform to his image of her. Although Leon acts as a stalker, the director sympathises with him and depicts Anna's final rejection of her suitor as an utter injustice.

I will also regard as 'broken lilies' women played by Skolimowski's wife, Joanna Szczerbic, post-*Barrier*: Alfa in *Hands Up!* and Alicja Rodak in *Success Is the Best Revenge*. In the first film, she appears in two incarnations: as a young student who helped Leszczyc to overcome his crisis, following problems with the four-eyed portrait of Stalin, and a woman ten or so years older, nicknamed Alfa, who by this time is married to another man and is very cynical about her husband and men at large. Like women before her in Skolimowski's films, Alfa is also a tool of male self-discovery, but not for the individual male character, but for the whole group of men. To help them find out who they are or, more exactly, what happened to them, and share their knowledge with their friends, she even gives them special 'truth pills'. It does not matter that these pills do not contain any real medicine because they work, in the same way as a placebo works, making the men open themselves up. At the same time as the men publicly bare themselves, admitting to having lovers, joining the Party and working only for money rather than out of any idealistic reasons, Alfa remains enigmatic. Her pseudonym, although it comes from Alfa Romeo, brings association with Alfa and Omega, the first and last letters in the Greek alphabet, a symbol of total knowledge. Alfa's enigmatic presence, her 'abstract' pseudonym, as well as the fact that she is the only female in the otherwise male company, encourages us to treat her less as a real person, more as a kind of collective soul of the four men, or a mirror in which they see their vices. This interpretation is also strengthened by the fact that ten years earlier she also acted as the men's soul, telling them during interrogation that they should not transfer guilt from one to the other but own up to their acts.

Alicja Rodak, being the wife of an educated man who gained a high social position and fame, can be regarded as an older version of the pretty tram driver. Significantly older than Alfa, she lacks sexual allure and spends her time bringing up her two sons when their father is away, engaged in the political struggle. For this reason Alicja can be compared to the archetypal Polish Mother (on Polish Mother see Ostrowska 1998). Yet, she fills this stereotype with contemporary content, being a reluctant and disappointed Polish Mother. Her husband is bored with her, preferring to flirt with his French female boss, as well as having casual sex with other women. Moreover, paradoxically, he criticises her for her Polishness, although it is his Polish cause that forces them to stay in London. She, on the other hand, feels angry with Alex for leaving her and their children stranded in London when he is playing his 'political games'. If she had a choice, she would rather be a political opportunist and reconcile with the authorities in Poland, for the sake of their safe return. She is also sexually frustrated, as revealed in an episode set in court where she wrongly accuses a young black man (who is probably gay) of touching her breast. In common with marriage, motherhood is also a source of disappointment for her. This is because, like their father, Alicja's sons show her little gratitude and ignore her most of the time, immersed in their own lives. Her main relationship with her children is through food, which she cooks for them. We can gather that for intellectual debates they use their father, if he is around, or school pals. The character of Alicja thus shows the real price Polish women have to pay for adjusting to some apparently noble ideological precepts. We can deduce from her situation that it is not worth being a Polish Mother any more (if it ever was); this role brings women no advantages, only disadvantages.

It should be stressed that after twenty or so years of marriage, Alicja exists somehow outside male projections and therefore comes across as a 'real woman', perhaps more so than any other female character in a Skolimowski's film. However, similar to being marginal in her husband's life, Alicja is peripheral to Skolimowski's narrative, which focuses on the male part of the Rodak family.

Many features which Alicja reveals in the film pertain to the real Joanna Szczerbic. Like Alicja, Szczerbic was the main carer of the couple's two sons and had to look after them when their father was away, sometimes for long periods. The director also suggested in interviews that she was less adjusted to their nomadic life than him. Although at the time of the premiere of *Success Is the Best Revenge*, Skolimowski and Szczerbic were still married and the director praised his wife for her perfect Polish Mother credentials, some years later they divorced, as if to confirm that ultimately this role did not suit her (or both of them).

The third category, which I label the 'withered rose', refers to women who have lost their youthful charm, but not their appetite for sex. This type is prefigured in *Identifications Marks: None*, by the character of 'Janczewska' who, although still looks young, comes across as wretched because she tries to present herself to Leszczyc as more attractive than she really is and unsuccessfully attempts to seduce him. However, for the first time a woman unambiguously belonging to this type appears in *Barrier*. She is an elderly aristocrat, or a lady pretending to be of aristocratic pedigree, who offers Leszczyc a bath in her apartment and switches off the light when he is naked. Her attempt to seduce the young man is resolutely rejected. In *Le Départ*, we find this woman's Western counterpart: a rich lady who tries to buy Marc's erotic services, luring him by offering access to a sports car. Although Marc is better disposed to her than Leszczyc was to his 'withered rose', simply because he needs her more than his Polish equivalent, he also resists her advances. Finally, in *Deep End*, Skolimowski includes two 'withered roses': a female customer of the public baths who visits the establishment in search of sex with 'toyboys' and makes a pass at Mike, and the middle-aged receptionist working there. Unlike their predecessors, both women are overweight (therefore the term 'withered rose' is rather ironic in reference to them), which adds to the contrast between them and the young man. Especially pathetic is the first woman, played by Diana Dors, who in her youth was famous for her sex appeal, marked by her large breasts and sensual mouth. In *Deep End*, however, which was made over ten years after her greatest successes, with her bleached and unkempt hair and tight clothes accentuating her overblown proportions, she comes across as overripe and unappealing. When she hugs the young would-be lover, she looks as if she might crush him – he virtually disappears under her suffocating body. Not only is her appearance undignified, but also her erotic spectacle; she almost rapes Mike while pretending that it is him who attempts to have sex with her. Ultimately, she experiences her climax alone, as the boy is unable to understand, still less to share, her reaction. Rafał Marszałek, who observed

Figure 2.8 Diana Dors as 'withered rose' in *Deep End*

the growing presence of older women involved with young men in Skolimowski's films, uses the term 'erotic turpism' to describe the episode from *Deep End* (see Marszałek 1971: 44). I find this description very apt and even suggest that older women in Skolimowski's films epitomise death itself; therefore they bewilder and frighten young men.

The lack of dignity of the 'withered roses' is underscored by their comparing themselves to favourite male pastimes – sports cars in *Le Départ* and football in *Deep End*. When Marc washes the hair of his older client, she asks him what he thinks about, and when he says 'my mother', she replies that she prefers if he was thinking about cars when taking care of her hair. The client of the public bath imagines her erotic encounter with Mike as a football match, in which she is a ball chased by the young man. However, this comparison does not work because Mike is neither keen on football nor understands the older woman's erotic 'game'.

The clear message of these films is that older women should stay away from young men; there is no chance that these men would find them attractive. This misogynistic message is reinforced by the way Skolimowski depicts older men in his films, especially the PE teacher in *Deep End*. Although played by Karl Michael Vogler, thirteen years older than Diana Dors, who was forty when appearing in the same film, he comes across as virile and attractive. Certainly his female pupils do not find him repulsive, but giggle with pleasure when he looks down their swimming costumes before pushing them into the pool. Moreover, almost to the very end he can 'have' Susan practically any time he wants and it is suggested that he never needs to pay women for erotic pleasures. He does not even need to try to flatter the girls; his job as a PE teacher is sufficient to convince them that he is youthful and 'cool'.

Women age quickly; men remain young for a long time – we can derive this message from the way Skolimowski depicts both young and older women in his films. Therefore men like to 'update' their female partners if they can afford to, as conveyed by the answers to the questions asked of middle-aged, affluent men in *Hands Up!*: 'Children? Older and older. Wives? Younger and younger?' This message was already proposed in *Identifications Marks: None*, where one actress, Elżbieta Czyżewska, plays all three main female characters: the virginal Basia who belongs to Leszczyc's future, the earthly, disillusioned Teresa, who marks his present, and the wretched 'Janczewska', who is his memory. Looking at these women we can conclude that experiences, more than the sheer passing of years, make women age.

The final and most interesting category of Skolimowski's women is the 'queen' – a woman with 'regal' ambition to be man's equal, if not his superior. In this category I list Krystyna in *Knife in the Water*, Teresa in *Walkover*, the theatre director, Monique des Fontaines and the bank employee in *Success Is the Best Revenge*, Maria in *Torrents of Spring* and, of course, Martha, the eponymous queen in *King, Queen, Knave*. Some of Skolimowski's 'broken lilies' also have an ambition to rule, most importantly Susan. Similarly, it is not excluded that in other cases, especially Martha's and Maria's, this ambition is the result of relocation of their interest from erotic to material. Yet, unlike young men (the 'knaves'), who have no ambition to reign and prefer to spend their time playing (which is their method of avoiding growing up), and older men (the 'kings'), who take their position of power for granted, Skolimowski's women must fight to fulfil them. Take, for example, Teresa in *Walkover*, who in order to become somebody in the factory, has to impress the director and defend her university project on her own, brushing off the criticism of her unsympathetic new colleagues.

Frequently the 'queens' gain or reinforce their power by setting a younger man against the older one or vice versa. This power game is presented in *King, Queen, Knave*, where Martha tries to use Frank to get rid of her husband and get full control of his fortune; in *Knife in the Water*, where Teresa seduces the Student to humiliate her husband; in *Torrents of Spring*, where Maria's behaviour leads to a duel between her old and prospective lovers and, in a sense, in *Deep End*, where Susan, albeit unwittingly, makes Mike jealous by sleeping with older men. Yet the position as an intermediary between men makes the woman's life unstable and insecure. In *King, Queen, Knave* and *Deep End*, the 'queens' lose their lives when they are literally and symbolically placed between their 'knaves' and 'kings'.

The 'queens' in Skolimowski's films often epitomise official or dominant ideology which the male character rejects. From this perspective Teresa in *Walkover*, the bank official, played by Jane Asher, in *Success Is the Best Revenge*, and the theatre director in the same film are particularly worthy of attention. As a Stalinist with a convent education, Teresa encapsulates two dominant institutions in postwar Poland: state socialism or, more specifically, Stalinism, and Catholicism. Both institutions are depicted by Skolimowski as hypocritical and overbearing, but also seductive, and so is Teresa, who caused Leszczyc's expulsion from the university. The character played by Asher stands for the power of money; in her dealings with Rodak she is rational, exact and merciless. She can also be seen (as Skolimowski himself confirmed) as an impersonation of Margaret Thatcher, who was British Prime Minister at the time he made *Success*. Her attitude to Alex Rodak mirrors that of Thatcher to emigrants and artists; she welcomes them, but only as long as they enrich Britain economically and conform to the English way of life. Although cold and with an aura of superiority, she is not devoid of sex appeal. However, to seduce her, as Rodak learns, is practically impossible. Skolimowski reveals a similar attitude to Monique des Fontaines, the theatre producer. Although, as a person representing culture, she is more sympathetic to Rodak's ideas, ultimately she does not agree to finance them, arguing that theatre, although it belongs to the realm of culture, is also an industry.

The regality of Skolimowski's 'queens' is conveyed by their confident manner of speaking and their alluring appearance. They are the most attractive women in Skolimowski's films, surpassing the beauty of the virgins. Their attractiveness is also underscored by their 'power dresses'. Made from heavy materials in shiny colours, they make their wearers stand out from the crowd. Take, for example Susan's yellow raincoat, the bank clerk's dark blue suit or Maria's red dress which she wears on her trip to the theatre. Sat in the lodge, its owner looks like a real queen greeting her subjects from her window. The dress code suggests that their owners want to have sex, but only on their own terms.

A 'queen' is also a character from a pack of cards; as such, she does not function as a real person, but only as an image – as an ideal or eternal woman (see Chapter 3). Again, this motif is used in *King, Queen, Knave*, where the central plot around Frank and Martha's cheating on Charles is accompanied by a subplot of Charles' commissioning a mannequin, operated by remote control and made of material perfectly imitating human flesh, to be sold worldwide. Although the first attempt to create such an ideal woman is unsuccessful, Charles does not give up, but encourages the inventor to carry on, modelling his doll on Frank's lover, who in reality is Martha. Meaningfully, the dummy is completed immediately after Martha's death. In this way the image of a woman replaces the real woman. A somewhat similar scenario is proposed by Skolimowski in *Deep End*, where Mike kills Susan shortly after seizing a full-size cut-out picture of her displayed in front of a sex shop and swimming with it, as if it was the real Susan. After her death in the pool Susan looks similar to her image; she is equally flat and passive. Thus a fetish first replaced the real Susan for Mike, then the body of Susan replaced for him the fetish.

For Skolimowski's men, the 'queen' is an object of greatest desire and, at the same time, of greatest fear. This is because, to use psychoanalytical discourse, she combines the qualities of mother and lover. Her perfect, full, but not overdeveloped body brings memory of the mother's body from the pre-Oedipal phase of the child's development. At the same time, her involvement with older men and her inaccessibility makes her a perfect tool of castration. It is worth mentioning that after killing Susan Mike cries 'Mummy', as if he realised that by killing Susan his severance from his mother's body has been completed.

By representing women in positions of power as utterly unsympathetic, Skolimowski suggests that women have few choices in life. If they save their morality, they end up disempowered, pathetic or bitter. If they reach power, they will lose their morality or even humanity. Men's situation is infinitely better: they can have everything (power, charm and personal integrity), and not once but many times in their lives.

Irrespective of what type of woman is given prominence in Skolimowski's films, for his male characters women appear in a sequence. No woman is truly unique for them; each can be replaced by another woman or her imaginary substitute and each eventually is. This disposable character of women, in psychoanalytical theory results from the fact that the child, who during his development was severed from the mother's body, is unable to attain this precious object in its fullness. He is thus sentenced to continuously looking for its substitutes, what Lacan calls the *objet a* (object little *a*), with which he tries vainly to plug the gap at the very centre of his being (see Lacan 1977: Grosz 1990: 74–77; 131–37; Eagleton 1997: 145–46). Such a reading can be supported by the way Skolimowski depicts in his feature debut Leszczyc's mother. She is never presented to us – Leszczyc only talks with her by phone and even then she is difficult to reach. It transpires that she is a top official in some bureaucratic organisation, therefore her son must pass some secretaries, to be connected to her. In his conversation with the mother the protagonist is ashamed of himself and therefore lies to her, saying that he is doing research for his master's thesis, although by this time he has already been expelled from the university. The fact that he cannot tell her the truth indicates his fear of her and their estrangement. She is thus an absent, but at the same time a towering and controlling figure: the 'maternal superego', bearing resemblance to various controlling mothers (sometimes from behind the grave) in Alfred Hitchcock's films (on mothers in Hitchcock's cinema see Žižek 1991: 99–104). The fact that Leszczyc's relationship with women in *Identification Marks: None* and subsequently in *Walkover* are unsuccessful confirm this diagnosis. It feels like the 'voice of the mother' blocks any lasting relationship Leszczyc might have with a woman.

The way Skolimowski represents women in his films both reflects their place in the eternal order of things, as perceived in psychoanalytical discourse, and the historical 'reality' of women, namely their secondary position in society. Hence, it can be argued that his portrayal is not sexist, but neutral. However, such an argument is largely rejected by feminist authors who claim that cinema is not only reproduction but also production of signs (see, for example, Mulvey 1996; Cowie 2000). Skolimowski's portrayal of women conforms to the typical treatment of women by mainstream cinema, which perpetuates the lamentable, from a feminist perspective, status quo. In particular, the punishment of his heroines perfectly fits the sadistic scenario, described by Laura Mulvey as 're-enactment of the original trauma' (see Mulvey 1996: 42). In *King, Queen, Knave*, the woman's death additionally helps to solve the riddle of how to pass the inheritance from father to son (or son's substitute) in full, in times when women also have rights to succession or even, in a wider sense, how to push women out of history in times when they have a right to be historical agents. Sadism towards women, as portrayed in Skolimowski's films, even surpasses the mainstream average. Few directors have managed to construct their stories, sometimes in opposition to the texts on which they are based, to arouse in the viewer such great pleasure in seeing women punished. At the same time, the director shows that men's and women's lives are closely linked; conquering and punishing women does not make men happy, but forces them to perpetual unfulfilment and wandering.

The categorisation proposed above captures how the majority of Skolimowski's women are situated within his narratives, but fails to account for how female–male relationships have evolved in his films over the years. The more recent his films (and the older their director), the more important are women in the lives of the protagonists. For Skolimowski's first cinematic creation, Bazyli in *Innocent Sorcerers*, whose greatest passions are jazz and sport, relationships with women are like jazz – they are matters of repeating the same theme in different variations without reaching a climax. Moreover, for him love, like jazz, must be cool: one has to avoid pathos and exaggeration, to underplay it rather than overplay. Although underplaying love means missing the opportunity to truly experience it, Bazyli does not care. The same is true about Leszczyc in *Identification Marks: None* and *Walkover* – women are for him only minor pursuits, games or 'identification marks'; they must disappear into the shadows when something appealing to his masculine side appears on the horizon, such as the army or a boxing match. In *Identification Marks: None*, the relative insignificance of women is perhaps most striking because Leszczyc in this film abandons three women, representing three different female types who also correspond to different stages of his life. In *Barrier*, the tram driver proves more important to Leszczyc than young women to the characters in Skolimowski's earlier films and they meet in the end, suggesting that their affair will develop. However, according to an earlier version of the script, their separation was final (see Janicki 1966: 50) and even in the version which was eventually made, Leszczyc leaves the girl whenever he wishes, without telling her where he goes. Moreover, she is initially only an object in his game with his university pals; he needs her to prove that he has a reason to leave the students' lodging and a chance of fulfilling his own life scenario.

The theme of women continuously losing in the competition for male attention with strictly male activities and environments, as presented by Skolimowski, could in a different cultural context be interpreted as a sign of the characters' unrealised homosexuality. Without entirely dismissing this explanation, I suggest that in Poland it should rather be taken as a measure of privileging masculine values in national culture, especially in the romantic tradition, at the expense of those pertaining to private life. Such privileging largely results from Polish history – the loss of statehood at the end of the eighteenth century and the long struggle to regain it, marked by numerous wars and uprisings. It is worth repeating Maria Janion's words that for Polish romantics the motherland is the only goddess (see Janion 1989: 10). Although after the Second World War Poland enjoyed a period of peace and stability, the old values and attitudes in relation to erotic behaviour did not change in step with political changes, as captured by a rude anecdote by Zygmunt Kałużyński, that when a Polish man undoes his fly on film, bullets from a rifle fall to the ground. While, as I argued earlier in this chapter and will argue in the next one, Skolimowski often reveals a mocking attitude to Polish romanticism; he does not reject a romantic model of masculinity, only laments that it is impossible to fulfil in peace time. Leszczyc's rough or contemptuous attitude to women might thus derive from his internalisation of the romantic ethos and conversely, his neglect of women proves to him that deep down he is a romantic man.[10]

In Skolimowski's first film made abroad, *Le Départ*, women also matter to the male character less than his masculine pursuit, a car, and their value consists largely of their usefulness in acquiring a car. However, unlike in *Walkover*, where Leszczyc leaves his female partner in a train in order to take part in a boxing match which he wins, Marc falls asleep in a hotel room with Michèle and oversleeps the race which he wanted to win so badly. However, he does not have sex with Michèle. Ultimately, he is unable to take advantage of either a car or of a woman – he misses both.

In four later films by Skolimowski: *Deep End*, *Torrents of Spring*, *Ferdydurke* and *Four Nights with Anna*, men desire women more than anything else. On each occasion, however, their desire cannot be fulfilled and the men themselves are to blame for not 'living happily ever after' with the ladies of their heart. In *Deep End*, Mike literally kills Susan and in this way brings their relationship to an end. Sanin, in *Torrents of Spring*, destroys his love for Gemma by becoming romantically involved with Maria. Subsequently, he loses Maria by showing his weakness and not being able to break his engagement with Gemma. Józio, in *Ferdydurke*, falls in love with Zuta but he does not even try to seduce her. Instead, he invents an elaborate plot, involving two other men, to overcome his infatuation. It appears as if Józio knows that male desire cannot be fulfilled, either because, as Gombrowicz suggests, it is inauthentic, being the product of cultural pressure or because, if we look at it from a psychoanalytical perspective, it springs from a lack, which is impossible to fill. Finally, Leon is madly in love with Anna, but he has no courage or need to talk to her; instead he invades her space when she is sleeping.

Although women for these men matter more than to their predecessors, they fall in love not with real women, but with their own projections of ideal women. In most

Figure 2.9 Nastassia Kinski as regal Maria in *Torrents of Spring*

cases these projections are culturally constructed, encapsulating the female ideal of their times – the perfect 'modern women'. Mike falls for Susan because she is the ultimate 'Soho semi-bitch' of the 1970s: bright, hedonistic, cheeky, promiscuous and immoral. Casting Jane Asher, who had been Paul McCartney's fiancée at the time when Skolimowski shot his film, and who was strongly identified with the Beatles and the whole 'Swinging London' phenomenon, strengthens the perception that Susan is the ultimate 'modern girl'. Sanin, in *Torrents of Spring*, first falls for Gemma because he pictures her as a perfect southern virgin – demure and full of grace. Yet Maria replaces Gemma in Sanin's mind because she epitomises a new, liberated woman, as demonstrated by the fact that she has affairs despite being married and takes care of her own finances.

Casting Nastassia Kinski, who in 1979 played Tess in Roman Polański's film of the same title, but is ten years older in *Torrents of Spring*, reinforces her modernity. This is because Skolimowski construes her as a 'Tess who learnt her lesson': gave up on her idealism and is now using men to her own advantage. Moreover, Skolimowski (perhaps unconsciously), makes reference to the film of his 'older brother' by including a scene which looks like a reversal of the crucial scene from *Tess*, where the heroine was chased and seduced (or raped) by Alec in a misty forest. In Skolimowski's film, by contrast, Sanin does not chase, seduce or rape Maria, but allows Maria to lead him on her swift horse and be seduced by her. Finally, Józio, in *Ferdydurke*, openly admits that he is attracted by Zuta because she has all the qualities of a 'modern schoolgirl' (from the period between the two world wars, when the film is set), being sporty and sexually liberated.

The lack of interest in women and unwillingness to grant them greater autonomy in his films is a significant weakness of Skolimowski's films. Paradoxically, although Polański has a much worse off-screen reputation with women, as a film maker he revealed more interest in and appreciation of women than his younger countryman. His female characters are men's true partners or adversaries, rather than their mental creations, and he never indulged in 'erotic turpism', in which a woman is a symbol of human decay. This difference between Skolimowski and Polański was already apparent at the beginning of their careers. In particular, *Knife in the Water* is the only film in the Polish chapter of Skolimowski's cinema in which a woman is at least as important as a man within the narrative, and has the upper hand, sowing the seed of self-doubt in the Student and her husband's minds.

Perhaps Skolimowski would have reveal a different attitude to women if his adaptation of *In America* by Susan Sontag, a book about Helena Modrzejewska, a Polish actress who emigrated to the US, had ever materialised. This is because it would have been very difficult to screen this female-centred story as a male fantasy. However, it did not happen and the problems Skolimowski encountered trying to realise this project might be regarded as symbolic of the external and internal barriers the misogynist director has to overcome to move to a pro-female position.

Conclusions

From the perspective of the choice of characters, Skolimowski's cinema has not changed much over the decades, focusing on beautiful, narcissistic 'boys'. What has changed are the relationships through which the young male characters gain knowledge about themselves and establish their place in the world. I regard Skolimowski's concern with the 'boys' as both strength and weakness of his cinema. On the one hand, it furnishes his films with coherence and authorial signature. He is recognised as a specialist in young people, even youth itself. On the other hand, with the passage of time and the director's own ageing, Skolimowski's young men come across as less and less alluring; they irritate rather than fascinate. This lack of interesting men is only partly offset by presence of women, because the director goes to great length to contain the 'female element' in his films, reducing women to vehicles of a male quest for identity.

Notes

1. It could be argued that our desire to fix an identity is culturally constructed, because it is an effect of the various relations in which the child finds himself (see Woodward 2002: 8–9), but it is internal in the sense of being internalised, regarded as one's own.
2. Later football replaced the sports of fighting as a 'national sport'. Skolimowski refers to the special role of football in *Success Is the Best Revenge*, where Poland's victory in a football match is presented as a way to remind England about its existence and where the Polish protagonist compares receiving the Légion d'honneur to scoring for Poland in a football match.
3. Significantly, Zbigniew Cybulski, who played Maciek in Wajda's *Ashes and Diamonds*, in his later roles played sport's instructors, in *Tomorrow Mexico*, directed by Aleksander Ścibor-Rylski and *Jowita*, directed by Janusz Morgenstern.
4. The relatively high standard of living of sportsmen was depicted in *Mąż swojej żony* (*Husband of His Wife*, 1961) by Stanisław Bareja. In this film the director also points to the extra income earned by high class sportsmen thanks to illegal trade with the West.
5. According to the information found on the Imdb website, in 1968, during the military dictatorship in Brazil, he made a political speech for hundreds of students at Brasília University.
6. I took this comment from my correspondence with Janusz Gazda.
7. In this respect Adam's voice-over can be compared to those in some films noir, for example in *Gilda* (1946), directed by Charles Vidor, where it acts against the narrator's intentions.
8. Skolimowski produced his sons' film, *Motyw cienia* (*The Hollow Men*, 1993), which was met with critical reviews in Poland and was not distributed outside that country.
9. 'Uniqueness' was a term voiced especially in relation to Leszczyc (see, for example, Lubelski 1989, Ronduda 2007).
10. Leszczyc's attitude to women can be compared to that of young men in British New Wave films, in which the cruel and contemptuous attitude of a working class lad to a woman was regarded as a sign of his angry rebellion against materialistic society and a litmus test of his remaining working class through and through.

CHAPTER 3

Between Realism and Non-realism: The Artistic Context of Skolimowski's Films and Their Main Visual Motifs

We change socialist realist works into avant-garde.
(Advert for SKOS, the company Skolimowski set up with his friend, Andrzej Kostenko)

Poeticism, Surrealism, (Anti)romanticism, Expressionism

I consider myself a dedicated realist. One of the main objects of my writing is to cut a path through Unreality to Reality.
(Gombrowicz 1973: 31)

The categories of realism and non-realism fail to capture the specificity of Skolimowski's style, because in the majority of his works the unrealistic elements are juxtaposed or intertwined with realistic ones. This feature was identified early on by critics, most notably by Janusz Gazda, who in 1967 described Skolimowski's films as 'poetic cinema' or even 'cinema of a dream', despite the fact that by then no 'proper' dreams were included in his narratives. This poeticism consisted of building a subjective, authorial vision out of elements depicted with naturalistic, even documentary precision. Consequently, the world constructed on screen demanded a non-literal interpretation: searching for metaphors hidden behind the layer of the narrative (see Gazda 1967a; 1967b; Jocher 1967). In a similar vein, but thirty-seven years later, Bruce Hodsdon talks about the 'dialectic between the objective and the subjective, between the naturalistic and the personal-poetic' in Skolimowski's work and quotes the director saying in relation to *Walkover* that his intention was to make the viewer 'open his eyes wider' (Hodsdon 2003).

Other labels evoked by critics to describe Skolimowski's brand of non-realism include surrealism, absurdism and expressionism.[1] The term 'romanticism' is also used, although typically with the stipulation that Skolimowski is a selective or even transgressive romantic (see, for example, Gazda 1966: 7; Jackiewicz 1983: 387). I regard all these terms as relevant, but only with reference to some of Skolimowski's films. The only possible exception is 'poeticism', not least because it is the most imprecise term and therefore safe to use. As mentioned previously, it concerns the multiplicity of meanings offered by Skolimowski's films and, therefore, for the viewer, the opportunity of infinite speculation. 'Surrealism' is a more problematic term, despite embracing artists of different periods, nationalities, as well as political and philosophical positions. As Michael Richardson observes, over decades it has been 'transformed into an evanescent category denoting a strangeness, incongruity or juxtaposition' (Richardson 2006: 2). If we accept such a wide interpretation, then we can label Skolimowski as a 'surrealist' because these features abound in his films. Richardson, however, objects to treating surrealism as such a 'wide church' and proposes to regard as surrealists only those who embraced it as a moral sensibility, engaged in collective surrealist activity or were involved with surrealist ideas (see Richardson 2006: 10). Again, Skolimowski's films are close to surrealism in all these senses. Firstly, he is a reactionary in the proper sense of the term, as someone who rejects or at least is distrustful of the given, be it political order, religion or national ideology, which Richardson identifies as a crucial aspect of surrealist morality. An anarchistic undercurrent is detectable in most of his works, especially in the 'Leszczyc tetralogy' and *Success Is the Best Revenge*. Secondly, although Skolimowski was never a part of a surrealist collective, the Prologue to *Hands Up!*, in which the director introduces his guests to the works of Polish painters he exhibits in his house, demonstrates his affiliation with the surrealist movement. Moreover, contrary to what he says in one of his interviews (given some years after re-working *Hands Up!*), that he never attempted to stylise his films after particular pictures or artistic fashions (see Uszyński 1990a: 14), in this film we observe a deliberate attempt to make the cinematic images look like surrealist paintings. Thirdly, Skolimowski admits that 'surrealist metaphors affected his films' (ibid.: 14). Even if he did not use the term 'surrealist', this sentence would demonstrate his link with surrealism, because metaphor is for surrealists the principal vehicle of meaning, in contrast to mainstream cinema which creates meaning through metonymy. Metaphors are not the same as ideas, but certainly there is an idea behind every metaphor, as every metaphor pronounces a similarity between two objects: the signifier and the signified, which are, essentially, different.

There is also a connection between Skolimowski's cinema and 'surrealism', as it is commonly associated with the aesthetics created by René Magritte, whose work Skolimowski mentions as an important source of inspiration (see Uszyński 1990a: 14), and Salvador Dalí. His films are permeated by strangeness and contain unexpected juxtapositions, non sequiturs and black humour, all regarded as crucial features of surrealist works. In some cases, such as *Success Is the Best Revenge* and *Ferdydurke*, these features amount to such extreme thematic shiftiness that the final product lacks any core and is barely comprehensible (on *Success Is the Best Revenge* see Chapter 1). The director himself, commenting on his working method, admits that it consists of creating options, so that even at the last moment he can jump in a completely new direction, embrace a new theme or idea (see Uszyński 1989: 5). From this pronouncement we can also deduce that Skolimowski is indifferent to the laws of genre.

The director of *Barrier* likes to surprise the viewer by showing him part of an object or situation that awakens a particular association that is frustrated when we later see it in its wholeness. Usually the whole meaning is more innocent than expected, which reveals the director's dark sense of humour. Two scenes are memorable from this perspective as they open Skolimowski's films. *Barrier* begins with images of human hands bound by electric cable and heads leaning forward. As Jerzy Uszyński observes, this scene looks like the preparation for an execution (see Uszyński 1990a: 14). We expect that the executioner will come and cut off the heads of the leaning men, but in reality this episode depicts a game in which the men compete to catch in their mouths a box of matches attached to a mannequin. In another scene of the same film a conductor on a tram is about to hang himself, but in reality he puts his head in the handhold in the shape of a loop. Skolimowski returns to this technique of showing a frightening part of an object in *Four Nights with Anna*, where a hand thrown into an oven turns out to be a limb cut off during an operation and later disposed of in the hospital incinerator. The entire film is about making wrong judgements, based on seeing only part of the picture.

Typically for surrealism, Skolimowski also reveals interest in inanimate objects. Tom Milne's observation that objects in *King, Queen, Knave* acquire autonomy (see Milne 1973) is accurate about many other films by this director, although in this film they are autonomous in the extreme. Among them we find

> the tie which magically knots itself in a florid loop to demonstrate Frank's powers as a salesman; a piece of artificial skin which springs to some weird kind of life under Frank's onanistic bedclothes; the table which seems to rise up in relief when he is interrupted by Ritter's arrival from completing a letter announcing his despairing departure from Munich; the vast crucifix, ambivalent portent of either peace or pain, that blocks the pavement as he hurries home for his first real assignation with Martha. Sometimes benevolent, sometimes malevolent (the mannequin which threatens to take revenge for Martha at the end), and sometimes simply indulging Skolimowski's taste for surrealist imagery (the wonderfully bizarre shot of two girls and two bicycles up a tree as Frank and Ritter, hounding Charles for a decision about the skin, overtake him in a forest where he has an illicit assignation), these objects lend the film a disturbing ambivalence behind its airy façade. (ibid.: 250)

Skolimowski also shows affinity for landscapes without people and people without landscapes. In *Identification Marks; None*, the camera penetrates interiors with nobody inside, as if crimes were committed there. In *Barrier*, the students' room, which is bare except for a model of the human body and X-ray photographs of bones, looks extremely 'unhomely', if not uncanny. In such scenes the familiar becomes unfamiliar: disturbing, even frightening, as if to confirm Pascal Bonitzer's claim that horror 'resides in the blind space' (Bonitzer 1981: 58). These images point to the disharmony between people and nature, which is also a crucial motif in the work of such renowned Eastern European surrealists as Jan Švankmajer and Skolimowski's countrymen, Walerian Borowczyk and Wojciech Has. The most visible is the connection with Has, for example between Has's *Pętla* (*The Noose*, 1961) and Skolimowski short, *Erotyk*, as they both begin with couples looking at their reflection in a mirror, which bewilders and horrifies them, making them realise that they are strangers. Another fruitful comparison is between Has's *Złoto* (*Gold*, 1961) and Skolimowski's *Walkover*, as both films depict young people arriving at new industrial plants which come across as overwhelming, menacing and, despite the precision with which they are represented, dream-like. Yet, the impression of hostility is contradicted by the development of the narrative where the young men find a place for themselves in the new outposts of industrial Poland. Such incongruity between different levels of the work of art or different messages are at the heart of surrealist art.[2] The sense of disharmony between people and nature is also conveyed in *Four Nights with Anna*, especially in the memorable scene of Leon observing a dead cow floating down the river.

The atmosphere of Skolimowski's early Polish films is simultaneously oneiric and dreary, which can be related to the nature of Polish experience during the period of state socialism, especially the 1960s, when they are set (see Chapter 2). In *Identification Marks: None*, the space of action is very limited and, as Iwona Kurz puts it, 'looped', because all events appear to take place on one, ugly street, ironically named Piękna (Beautiful), and the character keeps returning to the same courtyard and the same stairs (see Kurz 2005: 99). Despite that or perhaps because of it, it is difficult to make sense of distances and directions (see Lachnit-Lubelska 1983: 56). As in a labyrinth, a common image in a dream, everything is at the same time close and far away, the movements of the character appear random but also somewhat compulsory. Not surprisingly, Franz Kafka's name is evoked in relation to Skolimowski's early films (see Dzięglewski 2002: 167). The affinity to a looped space also likens Skolimowski to Has, whose early films can be read as pointing to the exitlessness of life under socialism, most importantly in *The Noose*. In *Walkover*, the space which Leszczyc traverses is larger, but it is also looped, as the protagonist keeps returning to the same places and meeting the same people. Moreover, his relationship with them is unclear; they might belong to his past or to his dreams, like Teresa, whom he finds familiar, but we are not sure whether she is familiar because he met her before or because she looks similar to his old girlfriend.

Even more dreamlike and drab is the Warsaw of *Barrier*, which inspired one reviewer to comment: 'Just as Godard made Alphaville out of Paris, so Skolimowski turns Warsaw into an unreal world: buildings looming up menacingly, a mass of unending glass and concrete; streets filled with acres of lighted candles and mesmerised throngs of commuters running round in circles and stopping in mass obedience at a set of fake traffic lights; enormous blood donor posters with a finger pointing out accusingly' (Wilson 1967: 187).

Figure 3.1 Warsaw as a house of mirrors in *Barrier*

To this description we can also add a tramway depot that looks like a descent into hell and a ski-jump, 'surreally' placed in the middle of town. The strangest object included in *Barrier* is the restaurant where Leszczyc has his date with the tram driver. In reality it is 'an architectural monster, a Roman Pantheon with a courtyard like in Wawel Castle [in Cracow], rebuilt in the style of the Palace of Culture, all made of artificial marble' (Janicki 1966: 44). As the action progresses, this restaurant expands into a huge ballroom, with surreal paintings or windows with views of the mountains and the sea, which at one point begins to move, like a real sea. The oneiric character of the place is accentuated by the strange behaviour of the guests and staff. For example, Leszczyc gives the waiter a piggy bank, perhaps to pay for his meal, but later a pig appears on his table, as if it was a proper meal, and Leszczyc uses his sabre to cut it into halves. The war veterans sing patriotic songs adorned in paper hats made from a woman's magazine. In common with the two earlier films by Skolimowski, it is impossible to mentally connect the places the director shows because Warsaw in *Barrier* lacks any familiar landmarks and is highly subjective, distorted by the peculiar way Leszczyc looks at the world, seeing only objects which interest him and ignoring the rest. This effect is achieved by eliminating from the frame anything which is not important for the main character and thus making them appear 'graphic and clean' (ibid.: 45), as well as multiplying and magnifying certain objects by mirrors. Practically all encounters in this film are accidental but also somehow necessary; the characters keep meeting the same people, as in a labyrinth, albeit larger than that conjured up in *Identification Marks: None*.

Another feature that links Skolimowski with surrealism is the incorporation of written text into films. His early shorts, *Little Hamlet* and *Erotyk*, are literally littered with newspapers. The female character in *Erotyk* is locked in a room where the floor and the walls are covered with printed sheets. Newspapers also hang from the ceiling like curtains, obscuring her view and suffocating her. Skolimowski's use of newspapers can be seen as a cheap and effective way to convey the stifling atmosphere of the erotic situation he is showing. It might also be a reference to the assault of texts on Polish citizens which leaves little space for private life. The assemblage of strange figures in *Little Hamlet* first read propagandist newspapers, then trample on them, which can be interpreted as a metaphor of the attitude of Poles to official ideology. In Skolimowski's feature films, the focus is moved from newspapers to more publicly displayed texts. Leszczyc in *Identification Marks: None* and *Barrier* walks through a town decorated with various slogans, announcements, posters and adverts, many of which have a political character. Their inclusion demonstrates that the ideology of socialism is conveyed by texts or even that it is a collection of texts – beyond the texts it does not exist. The peregrination through a town built of signs also points to Leszczyc's desire to decipher his environment and, at the same time, his inability to do so, which sentences him to the position of a perpetual stranger.

In *Barrier*, the sentence 'Niech żyje' (Long Live) is put together out of huge letters, most likely to commemorate some communist dignitary. However, the slogan is not finished and it reads 'Nie żyje' (S/he does not live) which brings reminiscence of the crucifixion of Jesus Christ, not least because the film is set during the Easter period. This episode demonstrates the arbitrary character of language and in a wider sense, the ambiguity and contingency of meaning. Such a contingency was explored by Magritte in his series *Word Paintings*, produced between 1927 and 1930, where he attached to common objects such as a shoe, an egg, a hammer or a pipe, a description which did not correspond to its usual meaning. By showing that 'Niech żyje' includes 'Nie żyje' Skolimowski also points to the opportunities of transgression or even subversion offered by the language; opportunities worth taking advantage of in the political reality where overt rebellion against the state is forbidden. However, in his next film, *Hands Up!*, the director demonstrates that these opportunities cannot be explored without risking political sanctions; polysemic writings and readings are rejected by the ideology of state communism which strives for language that is univocal.

The inclusion of written text into the film was common practice for the creators of the New Waves, such as Jean-Luc Godard and Věra Chytilová. Skolimowski is especially close in this respect to Godard because the French director also inserted public texts into his films, accentuating the severance of his characters from society, and used written texts as a way to display his character's private thoughts. Moreover, Godard also included close-ups of words which looked similar to each other, for example were made of the same letters but had different meanings (see Hayes 2002). Behind the inclusion of written text, in the films of both directors, lay the concept of language as a battleground between its private and public users.

Not only are written texts misleading in Skolimowski's films, but verbal communications are too. For instance, in *Identification Marks: None* and *Walkover*, we hear a poem, recited on the radio, which arrests Leszczyc's attention because it conveys his fear of wasting his life. It turns out that he misapprehends texts which are in reality only adverts for ties and insurance companies. In another scene in *Identification Marks: None*, a shop assistant asks a customer to say something and he says 'something', which is obviously not what the woman wanted to hear. Similarly, when she asks whether he wants white or dark bread, he says that it does not matter because the bread is for a blind person. Perhaps the most poignant example of miscommunication is the conversation Leszczyc has with the military draft board. When he says that he wants to join the army, the board members laugh and comment that this might be a new method to avoid military service – by playing an idiot or an eccentric. Leszczyc's conversation with the board also points to language as the arena of a twisted political struggle, where those who are in positions of power decide the 'correct' meanings of the utterances of their subordinates or adversaries. Even more extreme examples of the manipulation of language are offered in *Hands Up!*, in a sequence of the interrogation of students by the leaders of a youth organisation. Some texts, uttered by the politically minded interrogators, invite laughter, but the laughter is not cheerful, but bitter, making us realise how hypocritical and absurd was the reality of People's Poland (see Dzięglewski 2002: 175).[3]

Some of the surreal effects discernible in Skolimowski's films are a result of the method of their making, especially the modest funds and technical poverty which their author had to endure. For example, the crude transitions from one scene to another in *Identification Marks: None*, that produces the effect of unexpected juxtaposition, result from shooting the film over several years and with a 3:1 shooting ratio, many times lower than on even a small budget film. In *Success Is the Best Revenge*, a similar situation took place – a lack of funds forced the director to join 'disjoined' episodes, neglecting the rules of continuity editing. In *Barrier*, the impression of incongruity and fragmentation results from the lack of a conventional script, which was replaced by the improvisation of the director and actors – the director had to start making the film at such short notice that he had virtually no time to write it. However, these features should not count against Skolimowski's allegiance to surrealism because surrealists appreciated poetry in films that were not technically accomplished (see Short 1997: 97–98). Moreover, Skolimowski's early tendency to improvise links him to the surrealistic principle of automatism.

Many of the features which I have discussed so far, considering them as 'surrealistic', can also be regarded as signs of Skolimowski's allegiance to absurdism. Absurdism is a movement arguably better rooted and more respected in Polish culture than surrealism, which was condemned by eminent writers such as Czesław Miłosz, for frivolous detachment from objective reality (see Janion in conversation with Krzemiński 1991: 17).[4] However, these movements have much in common: both depict and comment on the disharmony in human life; both accept the ambiguity of language and, consequently, the contingency of meaning; both can be regarded as a reaction to certain phenomena brought about by modernity, such as alienation, loneliness and insecurity. Even common parlance demonstrates the closeness of these two styles and ideological positions: 'surreal' is often used interchangeably with 'absurd'. The main difference concerns the medium favoured by adherents of the two movements. Surrealism found its home in visual art, especially painting and cinema; absurdism is associated mostly with literature and theatre. Moreover, surrealists are interested in subjective reality; absurdists focus on the external or intersubjective world. Yet if we agree that surrealism draws not only on the individual unconscious but also, or perhaps even predominantly, on the collective one, and that the objective world, present in absurdists plays, is typically mediated by subjective experience, then we might regard the last division as artificial. Nevertheless, it is worth mentioning absurdism in connection with Skolimowski, because the late 1950s and early 1960s, when he studied at the Łódź Film School, was a period of great success by Polish absurdist poets and playwrights, especially Sławomir Mrożek and Tadeusz Różewicz. Absurdism also spilled into popular forms, such as students' theatre and cabarets. The director himself admits that he was greatly impressed and affected by the famous students' theatre Bim Bom of absurdist pedigree, largely because of 'their abstract black outs, such as the alarm clock ringing on a grave' (Uszyński 1990a: 10).

Skolimowski's unexpected juxtapositions and non sequiturs often concern Polish collective imagery, which is romantic. In this respect his work again parallels that of Magritte who also drew on the surrounding traditions. Being himself middle-class, Magritte built his visions from the iconography of a bourgeois milieu, such as the figure of a man in a dark coat or a bowler hat, but rearranged the familiar elements and altered their scale so that they looked strange. Using the same principle, Skolimowski rearranges elements from Polish romantic vocabulary and situates them in unexpected contexts. A new and surprising arrangement of, as Aleksander Jackiewicz puts it, 'props from the patriotic lumber-room' (Jackiewicz 1977: 171) is offered in *Barrier*. One such prop is a sabre with which Leszczyc gets a sponge to be used in his bath and later attacks a car. Such a use points to the redundancy of this noble weapon in contemporary circumstances or, conversely, to the need to have a war to put sabres to their proper use. In another sequence we find a small girl and an older woman covered in a transparent cloth which makes them look as if they are wearing a veil. In Polish romantic tradition the veil signifies the sacrifice Polish women have to make for their patria, when their husbands leave to fight in the wars and uprisings. Such a veiled bride appeared in Wajda's *Lotna* (1959), a famous Polish School film that laments the end of the noble cavalry tradition destroyed by the advent of the Second World War. However, in *Barrier*, the veil, like the sabre, is an empty signifier; it underscores the absence at the heart of contemporary romantic discourse.

Christianity is an important motif in Polish romantic literature, especially in the works of Adam Mickiewicz and Cyprian Kamil Norwid. Accordingly, as a subversive romantic, Skolimowski uses elements of Christian imagery in unexpected ways. In *Walkover*, an excavator digs out an immense cross. This act of clearing a field to build an industrial plant can be viewed as a reference to the communist persecution of the Catholic religion in Poland or a sign of Leszczyc's inner suffering. In *Barrier*, Leszczyc looks like Christ in a crown of thorns when walking under some branches. The Christian connotation of this scene yields irony to the character, because, with his utter selfishness and appetite for consumer goods, he is everything but a saint, not unlike the Student in *Knife in the Water*, who also in some scenes looks like Christ, but behaves in a very unsaintly fashion. Thus, the Christian symbols, like the 'props from the patriotic lumber-room', point to traditions still celebrated in Polish culture but irrelevant to contemporary lives. Skolimowski does not artificially link surrealism and Romanticism. Their connection is more 'organic', because there is a strong fantastic element in Polish (as well as English) Romanticism (ghosts, demons, vampires), which can be viewed as the content of the human unconscious (see Janion 1989: 33–53).

'Expressionism' is another term capturing the way Skolimowski diverges from realism. In common with surrealism, it is also a highly problematic concept. However, as I lack space to discuss the various definitions, for the purpose of this analysis I will regard it as a quality of expressive emphasis and distortion which may be found in works of any person or period but especially in Germanic art, theatre and film, from the turn of the century to the present day (see Willett 1970: 8).

Skolimowski's link with expressionism is most discernible in his films with a Polish subject: the 'Leszczyc tetralogy', *Success Is the Best Revenge* and, albeit to a smaller extent, *Moonlighting* and *Four Nights with Anna*. This is partly due to similarities between Polish romantic art and expressionism. The Polish School, the cinematic paradigm most influenced by Romanticism, is sometimes labelled the 'Polish Expressionistic School'. Skolimowski's connection with expressionism pertains to all aspects of the mise-en-scène: iconography, camera positions, lighting and make-up. Stairs and candles are his most memorable 'expressionistic props'. In *Identification Marks: None*, Leszczyc walks hundreds of steps, mostly in his tenement block, meeting on his way some strange-looking people, such as a Gypsy woman who appears to know all about his past and future. Stairs appear again in *Barrier*. We find here an enormous ski jump and a strange restaurant where Leszczyc dines with his girlfriend, with stairs, angular lines and galleries. The continuous ascending and descending of the characters in these films mark their restlessness and entrapment, which is also a motif of the Polish School. For example, Jasio Krone, the character in Wajda's *Pokolenie* (*A Generation*, 1955), dies by jumping from the stairs when cornered by Germans.

Similarly, Skolimowski's characters are sometimes modelled on characters from expressionistic cinema and theatre. Typically the intention of such stylisation is to make a joke. However, there is a serious idea behind the joke. The man played by Gustaw Holoubek in *Erotyk* can be taken for a vampire or a hypnotiser. The fear he awakens in the young woman brings to mind the reaction of the heroine of Murnau's *Nosferatu* (1922). Leszczyc in *Identification Marks: None* also bears resemblance to a vampire. He leaves his home at dawn, as if he was sneaking out after committing some menacing act, avoids contact with fellow humans and is equally avoided by them. Like a vampire, he is a tormented soul and a stranger in the city he crosses, and casts an enormous shadow. Leszczyc's vampire-like nature (partly joking, partly serious) is reinforced in *Barrier*, where a man with Skolimowski's face is shown on posters encouraging citizens to become blood donors. Skolimowski also exaggerates repulsive aspects of reality. He often shows cripples and fragile old men, going along in various types of wheelchairs and on crutches, which can be read as an allusion to the period of Polish history which made Poland and Poles look literally expressionistic – the Second World War and its aftermath.

The fact that a large proportion of Leszczyc films are set at night, and that they are shot in black and white, also adds to their expressionistic, ominous effect. Take an episode in *Walkover*, when Leszczyc and Teresa meet a man whom in darkness Teresa takes for a ghost. Darkness requires light for those who cannot sleep at night; hence the abundance of candles in Skolimowski's films. They not only illuminate the night, but also commemorate various metaphorical nights of human and specifically Polish history: the First and Second World Wars in *Barrier, Hands Up!* and *Success Is the Best Revenge*; the death of Jesus Christ in *Barrier* and the martial law of 1981 in *Success Is the Best Revenge*. In other films, red, which is the expressionistic colour par excellence, is given special meaning. Take, for example, the focus on red telephone boxes in *Moonlighting*, red paint in *Deep End*, interiors immersed in red light in *Success* or the fire in a hospital incinerator in *Four Nights with Anna*. Red in these films marks the characters' restlessness, their sense of danger, foreboding and claustrophobia.

Skolimowski often presents places that look like stage sets. An example is the sports hall where the boxing championship takes place, and the restaurant visited by Leszczyc and Teresa, in *Walkover*, and the hall where the veterans celebrate in *Barrier*. A propos the last film, the director talked about 'a certain artificial contrivance in my

Figure 3.2 Expressionistic effect in *Hands Up!*

films which makes people think of theatre' (Skolimowski, quoted in Hodsdon 2003). Most similar to a stage is the interior of a cattle-truck where the main part of *Hands Up!* is set. The effect of the theatre is underscored by the static camera and behaviour of the actors, who look straight into camera, as if addressing the audience, as opposed to cinematic characters disavowing the spectator's presence.

This manner of acting is reinforced in the film credits, when the names of actors playing the main parts accompany their silhouettes, which brings to mind the way actors in theatre enter the stage to greet the audience at the finale.

Like *Barrier*, *Hands Up!* also lacks conventional narrative, has a very theatrical setting and freely juxtaposes various temporal and ontological orders. When the guests leave the party and find themselves on an empty station platform, we feel that they not only travelled in space but also across realities. The impression that the platform and the carriage belong to a different realm altogether is reinforced by the later information that the train did not move at all. The lack of conventional action and the use of dialogues and monologues as the main transmitters of meaning add to the theatrical effect, as does make-up, which renders the characters' faces white and their eyes very dark, resembling vampires. Even the fact that the actors come on stage without make-up, but bring to their cattle-truck bags of lime and put it on their faces to look like actors in a theatre, underscores its artificiality. Expressionistic effect is magnified by reference to specific works, such as the Polish neo-romantic play, *Wesele* (*The Wedding*, 1901) by Stanisław Wyspiański (see Janicka 1985; Kurz 2005). Wyspiański's play used the wedding of his friend, Lucjan Rydel, as an opportunity to criticise contemporary Polish society. He achieved it largely by applying symbolic or fantastic characters as embodiments of Polish national vices. *Hands Up!* also begins at a ball and then moves to a cattle-truck where a kind of psychodrama takes place. Its participants, as did the guests at the ceremony depicted by Wyspiański, represent diseases debilitating Polish society, such as greed, hypocrisy, selfishness and incompetence.

The second important reference made in *Hands Up!* is to Polish School films. The characters compare themselves to their parents, who took part in the war and died in concentration camps. However, having no personal memory of this event, they cannot convincingly even reenact scenes from the war. Instead, they repeat scenes from famous Polish films about the Second World War, most importantly from Wajda's 'war trilogy', comprising *Pokolenie* (*A Generation*, 1955), *Kanał* (*Canal*, 1957) and *Popiół i diament* (*Ashes and Diamonds*, 1958). For example, when the man nicknamed Zastava (Bogumił Kobiela), emerges from a hole in the floor all covered in lime, helped out of the ground by his friends, he looks like a doomed insurrectionist from Wajda's *Kanał*. The numerous candles with which the characters surround themselves and their discussions about how they have changed bring to mind Wajda's *Ashes and Diamonds*. The dramatic scenes of executions resemble scenes from *A Generation* and *Kanał*. The very title of the film, *Hands Up!*, is a well known cry from war films and is recognised by the majority of viewers as such. The reenactment by Skolimowski's characters of these scenes does not really make them similar to those whom they mimic, namely heroes of war films, but underscores the difference between the past and the present and their position as members of a generation which does not have any achievements except for material ones.

In this and other films, Skolimowski also pays homage to Polish expressionists of international renown, most notably Feliks Topolski, whose works appear in *Success Is the Best Revenge* and the Prologue to *Hands Up!*. Topolski realised an artistic programme that was close to Skolimowski's heart, especially in these two films. This programme, best revealed in Topolski's *Chronicle*, fragments of which feature in *Success Is the Best Revenge*, consisted of presenting a large panorama of events, but without losing sight of their individual participants, such as Poland, and his own role in creating and immortalising them. Topolski's work is thus at once autobiographical and epic (see Kilian 1992). Skolimowski, like Topolski, also diverges from realism in order to convey more in the limited space and time than if he had used realistic techniques. Non-realism allows him to be concise and expressive, attacking, so to speak, all the senses and imaginative powers of the spectator. The price which he has to pay is the risk of the viewer misinterpreting his message, reading into it more than is offered or missing important information. However, Skolimowski was always willing to take this risk, in interviews inviting the audience to make their own sense of his films (see Uszyński 1989). Besides, after the famous 'death of the author', as announced by Roland Barthes, the audience is the ultimate creator of artistic texts anyway.

From Realism to Non-realism and Back

So far I have attempted to capture the main features of the form of Skolimowski's films without paying attention to its evolution. Although I argue that practically all of this director's films contain symbolic meanings, some are more concerned with the principle of verisimilitude than others.

Skolimowski began his career with *Identification Marks: None* and *Walkover* that, despite having an oneiric atmosphere, could be interpreted realistically, as stories respectively of one and one and a half days in the life of a young Polish man. These films also mastered some techniques, such as location shooting and long take, which, according to André Bazin, were crucial to making films true to reality, and which themselves were quite new in Polish cinema in the 1960s, significantly adding to the authenticity of Skolimowski's films. The fact that Skolimowski shot *Walkover* in only twenty-nine shots became in due course part of its legend, proof of its artistry and uniqueness, although the director himself regarded it as its minor characteristic (see Oleksiewicz 1965: 11). By contrast to the first two films, *Barrier* and *Hands Up!* do not lend themselves easily to a realistic reading – the lack of causal explanation of events represented, theatrical setting, surrealist deformation of space, gaps in the narrative, the 'poetic dialogue' and the use of music (which will be discussed in a separate chapter) prevent such a reading. In the West, Skolimowski undertook a similar route – *Le Départ*, *Deep End* and *King, Queen, Knave* are awash with symbols and include non-realistic inserts, but can still be read realistically, while in *Success Is the Best Revenge* and *The Shout* non-realism prevails. Similarly, after the classical adaptation of *Torrents of Springs*, came surrealistic *Ferdydurke*, followed by more realistic *Four Nights with Anna*.

Several reasons might explain the first change in style. One of them was the previously mentioned financial and temporal constraints. This might account for the limited setting, the lack of conventional plot, which is replaced by an episodic structure, abrupt transitions from one scene to another, and montage based on intellectual associations rather than continuity; all elements conducive to a non-realistic effect. By this time the director also discovered that using long takes is a difficult and cumbersome practice, the effect of which is overlooked by the average viewer (see Uszyński 1990a: 13). It is thus easier to make a film by editing many shorter shots than by shooting a few long ones. The change in style, noticeable in *Barrier*, might also result from artistic and ideological reasons, namely Skolimowski's disillusionment with realistic means as tools of representing reality or, perhaps, even, his change of opinion as to what constitutes reality worth artistic representation. Hence, while in *Identification Marks: None* and *Walkover*, Skolimowski was preoccupied with a 'slice of the life' of an individual character, Andrzej Leszczyc (albeit against the rich background of contemporary Poland), in *Barrier* and *Hands Up!*, without losing the individual from sight, he embarked on producing a synthetic vision of Poland – Poland made up of signs pertaining to its present, past and its future. This ambition is conveyed subtly in *Barrier*, when the main character, while climbing the stairs, says, 'Lets now look at all of this from the top'. As a consequence of this bird's-eye view approach, Leszczyc in *Barrier* is no longer the chief subject of the director's exploration, but a medium through whom he investigates his physical and cultural surroundings.

An additional sign of the shift from private to cultural landscape is the abandoning of any means that were meant to put us in contact with Leszczyc's inner life, such as fragments of poems or photographs that attract his attention or belong solely to his mental landscape. Unlike the character in *Identification Marks: None* and *Walkover*, the Leszczyc of *Barrier* lives an external life. What belonged previously to his interior is now divided amongst other characters. An interesting example is the poem, containing the words 'Po czymś takim jak młodość lub miłość' ('After such a thing as youth or love'). In the first two films it is presented as belonging to Leszczyc's private world, even if the words are only heard by him on the radio. By contrast, in *Barrier* they belong to a song sung by a cleaning lady, working in a restaurant Leszczyc visits. She sings it with a voice that does not belong to her but to a famous Polish singer, Ewa Demarczyk. However, to cover this dubbing, Skolimowski produces the effect of increased dissynchrony and theatralisation. Not only is the very situation in which a cleaner suddenly rises and sings for the guests artificial, but she sings as if she was a completely different person – a towering figure, a prophet revealing to the dramatis personae their future. Leszczyc is not the only recipient of her words – they appear to capture the condition of many like him, perhaps the whole nation. Moreover, although in *Barrier* Leszczyc is still the main character, he is not continuously on screen. The camera abandons him to show us the daily chores of the tram driver, with whom he becomes romantically involved, and the 'larger picture', as, for example, in a scene at the restaurant when the guests are dancing with paper hats on their heads. In *Hands Up!*, the impulse to present a synthetic vision of Poland, at the expense of painting the story of an individual, appears to be even stronger. The film does not have an individual character and the people represented in the film lack any psychological depth. As previously mentioned, they personify various sins gnawing at Polish society, rather than real people. Moreover, they define themselves chiefly in relation to Polish history and fate.

Skolimowski's disillusionment with realism in the second half of the 1960s did not take place in an artistic void. As Jonathan Owen observes in his discussion of the Czech New Wave, whose development is largely concurrent with the Polish stage of Skolimowski's career, a similar trajectory can be observed in Czech and Slovak films of the 1960s. Artists such as Věra Chytilová and Jaromil Jireš (or even Zbyněk Brynych whom Skolimowski befriended), began their careers with films that focused on individual characters, observed with minute precision. These films commented on contemporary society through the techniques of neo-realism and cinema verité, but in due course moved away from realism, enacting their critiques of reality by using surrealism and absurdism (see Owen 2008). In Skolimowski's case the stylistic shift can also be perceived as a sign of him growing up as a film maker and attempting to enter a dialogue with his older colleagues, particularly the chief romantic of Polish cinema, Andrzej Wajda.

Skolimowski went through a somewhat similar trajectory in his films made outside Poland. *Le Départ* and *Deep End* can be compared to *Identification Marks: None* and *Walkover* as they focus on an individual character against a rich social and cultural background: the upper-class and petit-burgoise milieu in Belgium in the 1960s in *Le Départ* and London's Soho of the 1970s in *Deep End*. Many images and scenes in these films lend themselves to metaphorical interpretation and seem to be included largely because of their visual impact. The montage is often rhythmical, as in the part of the film when Marc tries to contact his rich female patron who is attending a modelling show. Moreover, in *Le Départ*, the flow of narration is often disrupted by poetic inserts such as the one when Marc and Michelle sit in 'their' halves of a car that moves around, displaying them as if they were stars. However, despite their poeticism, the overall effect is of being anchored to one ontological order, rather than floating between many realities.

In contrast to these films, *The Shout* breaks with realism in a radical way. We do not know whether the story told by Crossley, a man locked in a psychiatric asylum, happened in reality or was only invented or dreamt by him. Why did this break with realism occur? In Britain of the 1970s, when Skolimowski made *The Shout*, non-realism was utilised by a number of talented directors, such as John Boorman and Nicholas Roeg. *The Shout* was almost concurrent with Roeg's *The Man Who Fell to Earth* (1976) and Boorman's *Exorcist II: The Heretic* (1977). The script of *The Shout* was first offered by its producer, Jeremy Thomas, to Roeg (see Newman 2007: 6). All these films focus on 'aliens' – people who come from afar and disrupt the lives of ordinary citizens. Their style is also similar; in particular Skolimowski and Roeg tell their stories in a non-linear way. It is very likely that the style of *The Shout* was Skolimowski's own invention, as he never mentions Roeg or Boorman in his interviews. However, together the films exhibit a new approach to cinema.

As I mentioned earlier, in Skolimowski's Polish films the shift from realism to non-realism coincided with the director's wish to provide a wider, synthetic vision of his country. I will suggest that *The Shout* and *Success Is the Best Revenge* arose from the opposite impulse: to depict somebody's (grandiose) vision. Together these films demonstrate Skolimowski's skill in using non-realistic techniques for different purposes.

Surrealist sensibility likens Skolimowski to Roman Polański (on surrealism in Polański's films see Mazierska 2007). Yet there are significant differences between their brands of surrealism. Polański's borrows directly from world-famous surrealists, such as Magritte, and from surrealist film makers, such as Buñuel. For Skolimowski, on the other hand, surrealism is mostly a tool of his take on Polish reality. He 'surrealises' Polish Romanticism or, perhaps, unearths a surrealist core at the heart of this movement. Like Polański, Skolimowski also has an affinity for certain locations and visual motifs, such as mirrors, large areas of water and 'defective' houses, which he uses in both realistic and symbolic ways. In the remaining part of this chapter I will discuss the meanings with which Skolimowski furnishes these motifs.

People and Their Images

There is a striking difference in the way Skolimowski depicts men and women in his films. Men are singular and unique, women multiply. One of the reasons *Identification Marks: None* feels oneiric, is the use of the same actress, Elżbieta Czyżewska, in three different roles: Leszczyc's wife Teresa, the student Basia, whom

Figure 3.3 Czyżewska's face in the mirror in *Identification Marks: None*

he befriends on his last visit to the university, and an older woman, 'Janczewska', with whom he had sex in the past and whom he visits again, possibly to make love. Casting Czyżewska, who at the time was Skolimowski's partner, was, as she herself admitted, a kind of 'budget and convenience' decision. It was cheaper and easier to shoot the film with her than with three different actresses, because she was always available to Skolimowski, sharing a home and bed with him (see Smader and Demidowicz 2004: 106). However, this decision also had important repercussions for the film's meaning, which Skolimowski exploited in his second film, *Walkover*.

Casting the same actress in more than one character or having one character personified by more than one actress is a common practice among directors close to surrealism: examples are *Vertigo* (1958), directed by Alfred Hitchcock, *Cet obscur objet du désir* (*That Obscure Object of Desire*, 1977), directed by Luis Buñuel, *Lost Highway* (1977), directed by David Lynch and *Každý mladý muž* (*Every Young Man*, 1966), directed by Pavel Juráček. In these films, as well as in *Identification Marks: None*, the male character is searching for some kind of lost object. Sometimes this is a woman, sometimes the object of his desire is not clearly defined, although a woman appears to be a key to this desired object. On each occasion, however, the search is not successful. This is because, as I argued in the previous chapter, drawing on Lacanian psychoanalysis, such search is the consequence of the child's separation from the mother's body and his futile attempt to plug the gap in his being which this separation caused. Being unable to attain this precious object in its fullness, he is thus sentenced to continuously looking for its substitutes. Leszczyc's directionless search, his encounters with three women, and the replacement of the wife by a female student and then by 'Janczewska', point to this endless substitution of one object for another in the search for lost plenitude. The three female characters look the same because they all signify the Lacanian *objet petit a* that men locate in women. Moreover, in the last scene in which we see Basia at the station, when she comes to say good bye to Leszczyc, she appears less like a material person, more like a photograph or a mental image: immobile and blurred. We can guess that Leszczyc will take this mental image with him to the army, to quench and to feed his primal desire. Indeed, this happens, as *Walkover* confirms. By then, thirty-year-old Leszczyc still carries with him a photograph of a woman with Czyżewska's face.

During the course of this film another woman commits suicide by throwing herself under a train. We can deduce that it was 'Leszczyc's woman' (perhaps the student he befriended in the first film), but this event is rendered ambiguous. It is possible that Leszczyc used the information about the suicide of some unknown young woman to mentally substitute Czyżewska's character for the woman who was found dead, because it enabled him to preserve the idealised image of a girl whom he once loved. If she continued to live, he would lose control over her image and have to come to terms with her becoming very different to the one he wanted her to be. In *Walkover*, female substitution also takes place when Leszczyc accosts another woman who alights from a train. He calls her different names: Krystyna, Barbara, although in reality her name is Teresa. But for Leszczyc her true name hardly matters. The important thing is that she reminds him of someone from his past. As we learn later, Teresa is a colleague from the university whom he perhaps loved and who betrayed him, as possibly did two women played by Czyżewska in an earlier film. It is also possible that she brings back a memory of the first woman in his life – his mother. Leszczyc has an affair with Teresa, but we are made to believe that their relationship will not last – he will bury her in his memory and continue searching for his 'obscure object of desire'.

Hands Up! is practically all devoted to mourning the changes brought about by time, both to men and to a woman. However, apart from the passage of time that has affected himself, Leszczyc mostly mourns the change that has affected Alfa. A significant aspect of the film refers to comparing her as she looks now and how she was ten years earlier, and catching her previous beauty, innocence and quasi-maternal selflessness. These qualities, however, cannot return, therefore the two old friends and lovers again part. Finally, in *Deep End*, we do not need to guess that a woman with whom the male character has sex reminds him of his mother, as we are told so explicitly by Mike who, after having sex with Susan, tries to make her stay with him and when she leaves, says with a weeping voice 'Oh, Mummy!'

The idea that Skolimowski's male protagonist does not seek any real, unique woman, but only the idealised image of a woman representing his primal desire, is conveyed by the motif of a mirror in which he sees reflections of women. The mirror de-materialises and multiplies the woman, underscoring the rule of eternal substitution. A woman in a mirror appears for the first time in *Erotyk*. In this three-minute-long etude a man pushes a woman (meaningfully played by Czyżewska) towards the mirror, as if he wanted to erase her from the material world. The idea that the woman belongs to the mirror, that this is the place where a man finds her, is confirmed by the song sung by Czyżewska at the end, 'We only meet in the mirror'. Similarly to his predecessor in *Erotyk*, Leszczyc in *Identification Marks: None* prefers to look at the mirror reflection of his wife than directly at her, as if she was only the remnant of the plenty, of true reality that cannot be achieved. Their conversation in front of the mirror, however, confirms that she does not want what he wants her to be, namely a free-floating signifier that can be given any body at his whim, but prefers to be a 'material' woman, identical only to herself. Similarly like Leszczyc, Sanin in *Torrents of Spring* prefers a woman's reflection over her material self, as conveyed by the recurrent motifs of mirror and frame. For example, when Gemma is dancing, Sanin does not look at her, but at her mirror reflection. Later he watches her when she is looking through the window, as if he was contemplating her portrait. Women, however, take revenge on men for reducing them to images. It happens when Sanin goes to Venice searching for his second lover, Maria, but finds only her elusive image and no real Maria, which leaves him devastated.

Mirrors and mirror-like objects also appear in *Four Nights with Anna*. When Leon observes Anna in her room through his window, we get the impression that he watches a screen and she is the star of his private film. Yet Anna rejects being positioned as an object of somebody else's fantasy – she wants to shape her own identity. She forgives Leon for invading her private space, but asks him to leave her in peace and, no doubt, this requests makes him devastated. These episodes show that by reducing women to images men also impoverish and hurt themselves, even shatter their own identity.

The rule of eternal substitution is also conveyed by the motif of an artificial woman: the automatons in *King, Queen, Knave* and the full-size cut-out image of a woman in *Deep End*. The automatons in *King, Queen, Knave* resemble the dolls constructed and photographed by the German associate of surrealists, Hans Bellmer, in the 1930s. Making connections between Skolimowski's automatons and Bellmer's *poupées* is the more justifiable as *King, Queen, Knave* is based on Vladimir Nabokov's novel, which was written in Berlin in the late 1920s, a period almost concurrent with the time Bellmer worked on his creations. Moreover, as I will argue in the following chapter, Nabokov in his novel is largely concerned with 'surrealist stuff': the content of the unconscious, and the drive of sex and death. Skolimowski's automatons not only physically resemble Bellmer's *poupées*, but they also belong to the domain of the uncanny. As Hal Foster observes in relation to Bellmer's creations

> Made of wood, metal, plaster pieces and ball joints, the poupées were manipulated in drastic ways and photographed in different positions. For Bellmer they produce a volatile mixture of 'joy, exaltation and fear', an intense ambivalence that appears fetishistic in nature ... Each new version is a 'construction as dismemberment' that signifies both castration (in the disconnection of body parts) and its fetishistic defense (in the multiplication of these parts as phallic substitutes). (Foster 1993: 102–3)

Foster also compares Bellmer's take on the female body with that of Breton and Bataille. He quotes Bellmer saying: 'The body is like a sentence that invites us to rearrange it' (ibid.: 103), which evokes the Bretonian idea of the shifting of desire, also paramount in Skolimowski's works. In Skolimowski's film the automatons are commissioned by Dreyer from a scientist, an inventor of 'voskin', material perfectly imitating human flesh. They are operated remotely thanks to a complicated electrical system. At some point we see batteries and the whole machinery placed in the mannequin's body, similarly as we see the interiors of Bellmer's *poupées*. However, this only happens when the scientist demonstrates his invention to Dreyer. It is assumed that when the automatons are eventually mass-produced and sold all over the world, their production will be concealed, according to the Marxist account of commodity fetishism operating in capitalism. For their inventor, a lonely man whose only other occupation is spying on Frank making love with Martha, the automatons and even 'voskin' itself play the role of a substitute for sexual contact, and perhaps any other human. The first sets of dolls, as required by Dreyer, are both female and male, but the female ones are more important for Dreyer and on them future mass production is meant to focus. Initially the automatons are not successful as they dismember each other when switched on and set in motion. However, neither Dreyer nor his American business partner is put off by their self-destruction. They ask the inventor to resume his work and out of the remnants of the old mannequins produce a new model, only more 'sexy'. It can even be suggested that the shattering of the dolls is part of the automaton's attraction. This is because as material to be destroyed and reassembled, they convey the male desire to possess, subjugate and destroy the female, and to do it over and over again. The mannequins in *King, Queen, Knave* not only replace each other and substitute some abstract woman whom the inventor and his customers strive for, but also stand for a real woman: Martha. A mannequin looking exactly like her is produced shortly after she is drowned. Martha's death thus allows the men to preserve her ideal image in the dummy or, more exactly, in a series of dummies, as the doll is meant to be produced serially.

While the identity of Skolimowski's women is blurred or even erased by multiplication, men's identity, as often happens in surrealistic paintings, tends to be concealed.[5] I already mentioned the headless men at the beginning of *Barrier*. Similarly, the first image in *Le Départ* shows a man without a head – in reality it is the film's hero, Marc, putting a jumper on. The next image reveals his head, which emerges from the neck of the jumper. Like many surrealists, and Magritte especially, Skolimowski depersonalises the human subject (in his case male) by covering its individualising identifier, the face, with a mask or some masking object. We find examples of such practice in *Erotyk, Barrier, Hands Up!, Torrents of Spring* and *Ferdydurke*. For Skolimowski's characters these objects serve to hide their identity or create a new one. Putting on a mask is also a way of frightening or teasing an adversary because one expects that there is something ugly or unnatural under the mask: a deformed face or a wound. A mask plays such a role in *Hands Up!*, where Leszczyc at a ball gradually reveals his face by uncovering bandages. A mask in this episode might signify the wound he carries from the time he was expelled from university, a desire to be somebody else, as well as his way to cover the passage of time. In the Prologue to the same film, the director himself puts on a gas mask, which can be interpreted as a reference to the communist authorities' attempts to silence him or even make him invisible. Johanna Malt, drawing on Georges Bataille, argues that the image of an *acéphale* (the headless man) is a sign of the surrealists' rejection of rationality and civilisation and glorification of the 'lower functions' of the body (see Malt 2004: 186). Perhaps it will be far-fetched to regard the proliferation of masked men and *acéphales* in Skolimowski's films as testimony to his contempt for civilisation, but certainly the director always presented himself as one who follows intuition rather than any rigid ideas and as hostile to 'cerebral cinema' (see Janicka 1966: 9).

While the images of women feature only in private male fantasies, representations of men constitute a part of public discourses. We see it in *Barrier* and, most importantly, in *Hands Up!* In *Barrier*, the town through which Leszczyc walks is decorated with large posters of a man encouraging citizens to donate blood for their country. The identity of the man is not disclosed but the viewers might know that the poster represents Skolimowski. With his stern facial expression and his finger raised he looks like a severe god – somebody who is physically not 'here', but whose power extends everywhere the posters are displayed and even beyond them. Therefore when Leszczyc takes the poster from the wall and puts it onto his head, his act has a taste of sacrilege.

According to the rule that subsequent films by Skolimowski reinforce themes introduced in earlier ones, the motif of a poster of a stern and powerful man is developed in *Hands Up!* This time it has gigantic proportions and represents Stalin. As does Skolimowski in *Barrier*, only more so, Stalin on the poster looks like a god – huge and severe, which is underscored by his hand up in a gesture of warning or judging. The Soviet leader is an 'absent' personage within the film's narrative. Nobody in the film plays Stalin, knows him first-hand, talks about him or even mentions his name. Nobody knows who the 'real Stalin' is and nobody cares. What matters is not the real politician but the values he embodies within the system of communication between the authorities and citizens. The shyness with which Stalin's image is treated by the members of the youth organisation in the retrospective part of the narrative bears resemblance with the treatment of gods in religions – even saying the name of god without a serious reason is regarded as a sin and severely punished. Yet Stalin in the film, although absent, is also overbearingly present. Firstly, the poster literally thwarts the people who construct it: when the character played by Bogumił Kobiela runs away from it, one is worried that the huge mass of cardboard will crush him. Secondly, the ability to treat the image of Stalin in the 'right' way is the litmus test of the characters' political and moral qualities and thus a determinant of their current position and future success. We are made to believe that the group of medical students volunteered to raise the gigantic billboard, not sparing their time or effort, in order to give the impression of being good communists. Consequently, when they do not rise to the challenge and construct a faulty portrait of Stalin out of the elements provided to them, they are interrogated and their future becomes uncertain. It is paradoxical, yet also very typical for totalitarian systems, that the attitude to representations or signs in a more general sense is treated as more important than the attitude to any real people (see Havel 1985). The very term 'totalitarian' suggests this superior status of abstraction over anything concrete.

The crime committed by the hapless students consists of adding to Stalin's image an extra pair of eyes. They claim that they did so by mistake, because they were very tired; one person even says that he fell asleep while completing his assignment. However, even if this was the case, their behaviour was not insignificant as it could be compared to a Freudian 'slip of the tongue', namely to saying something which one consciously does not want to say, but which the unconscious demands to be revealed.

It is difficult to say whether the extra pair of eyes elevates or diminishes Stalin. On the one hand, four-eyed Stalin looks more powerful and godlike than the real Stalin. On the other hand, the extra pair of eyes might be also interpreted as an allusion to the omnipresence and continuous surveillance of ordinary people by the socialist authorities. Nobody, however, investigates the meaning of the new representation. What matters is not the nature of the transgression but that it took place at all. As was observed on many occasions, for example in *The Power of the Powerless* by Václav Havel (1985), state socialism, and Stalinism especially, was very distrustful of any form of transgression from the set protocol, even if it led to showing the socialist ideology or practice in a more positive light. Conformity was looked on more positively than enthusiasm (ibid.). The portrait of Stalin can also be

Figure 3.4 The poster with four-eyed Stalin in *Hands Up!*

regarded as surrealist because 'many surrealist portraits replace, deform or ridicule the social, public face of the subject' (Levy 1997: 9).

In Skolimowski's films made outside Poland, large figures of people still feature prominently, although typically they are not figures of politicians, but of attractive people, both men and women, used to advertise certain consumer goods, services or attitudes. We find many of them in *Le Départ*, Skolimowski's first film made in the capitalist world, where he was probably more sensitive to this type of image than after many years of living in the West. Take, for example, the large poster of a woman decorating a hairdressing salon or the images of smiling people in cars, simultaneously advertising cars and covering building sites. They are similar to political posters because they function as signifiers divorced from the signified and they are used to sell something, but in socialism they tended to sell ideas, in capitalism consumer goods. Both types of image are dangerous because, as Skolimowski demonstrates with his sharp irony, they diminish and obscure real people and ultimately, disfigure the world. In this observation the director is close to the leading theoreticians of postmodernity, such as Jean Baudrillard, who also lamented the overshadowing of the kingdom of things by the kingdom of images. However, Baudrillard developed his concepts through observing the West, principally the US; Skolimowski built his ideas while moving between East and West.

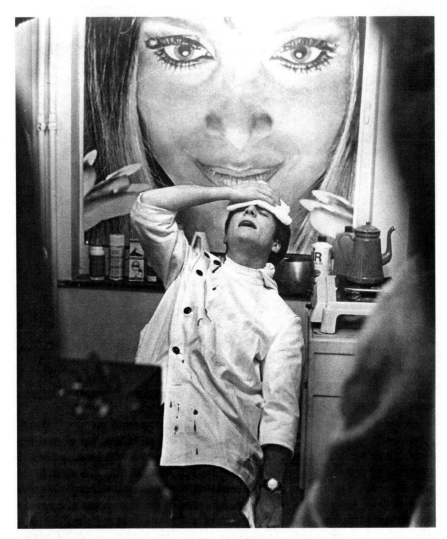

Figure 3.5 The poster decorating a hairdressing salon in *Le Départ*

The House

'I do not really have a home', says Andrzej Leszczyc in *Walkover*. This sentence can be attributed to the majority of Skolimowski's characters because they do have a roof over their head, but the roof might be leaking or belonging to somebody else, or serving the character only for a limited period of time. Consequently, they rarely feel at home when they are in their houses. In *Identification Marks: None* and *Barrier*, the accommodation is inadequate because it is drab and temporary. In the first film this is a loft, rented by Leszczyc with his girlfriend or wife; in *Barrier*, a students' lodging

Figure 3.6 Jerzy Skolimowski as Andrzej Leszczyc entrapped in his loft in *Identification Marks: None*

which he shares with three other men. We can also guess that before Leszczyc began his peregrinations through Poland in *Walkover*, he also lived in a shared room, either with fellow students or with soldiers doing military service. The interiors of these dwellings lack privacy and any personal touch. The rooms are small and with minimal furniture and they are exposed to constant intrusions. In *Identification Marks: None*, Leszczyc has to endure the company of young women who sunbathe on the roof above the loft where he lives and comment on his private life. In *Walkover*, Teresa's apartment, the only place where Leszczyc can spend a night and perhaps stay for longer, is so new that it has no furniture yet, and is visited by other people who work in the industrial plant. At the same time, contrary to cinematic convention which makes ceilings invisible, in *Identification Marks* ceilings are always in the frame when we see Leszczyc in his flat. They point to the entrapment of the protagonist and his desire to escape.[6]

Already in Skolimowski's early films, home is strongly associated with a woman and a stable relationship. Although in *Identification Marks: None*, Leszczyc shares a flat with his girlfriend, by paying the rent she has more rights to their apartment than he. She also feels more at home there, as suggested by the wardrobe full of her clothes, whilst Leszczyc's belongings, as he himself admits, fit into one suitcase. The sign of his fragile connection with the apartment is his eventual departure following his joining the army, without worrying about officially terminating the lease contract. The motif of moving in with a woman who has more rights to an apartment than him is repeated in *Walkover*, where Leszczyc's new girlfriend, also named Teresa, just got the keys to her own flat. The alternative is a place in a workers' hostel because, as the director of the industrial plant informs him, the apartments are only available to people with university degrees and Leszczyc failed to get one. After abandoning the shared room in the students' lodging, in *Barrier*, Leszczyc also joins a woman, a pretty tram driver. Although they never go to 'her' place, one can suspect that this is the most likely scenario. In this film the protagonist also says overtly that he wants to marry because he wants to have a home. Interestingly, after this confession the tram driver slaps his face, as if protesting against using her as a pretext to acquire this precious good. On the whole, Leszczyc's housing options in the first three films are limited to staying in communal accommodation (a room in the students' house, a hostel or barracks) or being a 'kept man'. These choices would be far from ideal for most young men, but for Leszczyc, who is an ardent individualist, they are particularly inadequate.

Leszczyc's near-homelessness can be regarded as the director's commentary on the difficult housing situation in postwar Poland, where an apartment in a faceless block was a luxury and hundreds of thousands of people lived in depersonalised 'workers hotels'. Leszczyc is made to realise that to have anywhere to live is a luxury in the first scene of *Identification Marks: None*, by the concierge boasting that if he wanted, he could rent out their flat to people who would pay for it a year in advance. Similarly, the director of the plant in *Walkover* keeps saying that the housing situation is difficult, suggesting that the workers should be content with any place they are offered.

Leszczyc's lack of a real home can also be seen as symptomatic of a wider condition: the lack of cultural roots, atomisation and alienation, typical for urban and industrial society, where contacts are frequent but brief and insignificant. This interpretation is supported by the way Skolimowski depicts industrial landscapes, such as the sawmill in *Identification Marks: None* and the chemical plant in *Walkover*. Against these backgrounds people appear small and lost. Not surprisingly, some critics compared Skolimowski to Antonioni, the chief painter of industrial deserts (see Czerwiński 1965: 7; Jocher 1967: 25). Leszczyc's lack of a true home can also be seen as symbolic of the loss of homeland experienced by Poles due to their country's loss of its sovereignty following the Second World War. This 'political' homelessness, as I already indicated, is excellently conveyed by language. Leszczyc is rarely 'at home' with language, especially when he talks to bureaucrats and people in positions of authority; he cannot understand them and they misinterpret his words.

Furthermore, his situation can be (psychoanalytically) read as an indicator of a more fundamental homelessness, which follows separation from his mother and childhood. Certainly Leszczyc excellently fits the description of a 'motherless' man. His birth home is never shown on film and, as I mentioned in the previous chapter, he only talks with his mother by phone in *Identification Marks: None*. Leszczyc has difficulty reaching her and their conversation is far from friendly. One gets the impression that Leszczyc's own mother conspires with individuals and institutions that reinforce his metaphorical homelessness, rather than trying to alleviate it.

The house can not only be taken as a metaphor of the wider world but also, somehow in contradiction, as a non-world: a buffer or protection against external influences (see Bachelard 1994: 40–41). Obviously, the more hostile the universe, the more people need houses to hide in. Leszczyc, who feels alienated from the socialist reality, needs a house very much but, as mentioned previously, his houses are too much like the external reality.

Of the three 'houses' Leszczyc inhabits, the most homely, despite its drabness and openness to intrusions, is the loft in *Identification Marks: None*. There Leszczyc cooks (food is associated with homeliness, because mother, the first home of the child, is the one who feeds) and has a dog. Small and fluffy, the dog might be seen as a surrogate child for the childless couple, or even a memory of maternal comfort. Ultimately, it is the dog which makes Teresa and Andrzej's apartment a home. Yet Leszczyc loses the dog when it turns out that the pet was not vaccinated against rabies and might have got this disease. Once the dog is gone, Leszczyc has no reason to stay at home and some hours later he leaves to join the army. The fate of the dog can be viewed as an index of the totalitarian state's interference in the lives of its citizens. It can also be regarded as metaphor of the collapse of Leszczyc's relationship with his wife and a sign of his sadistic attitude to her, his desire to harm her. Such interpretation is encouraged by Skolimowski's earlier film, *Erotyk*, which casts a similar dog in the role of the pet of the central couple. At one point the dog is brutally thrown on the floor by the man and most likely killed, to the horror of the woman. In this act we can see not only cruelty towards the animal but also the man's desire to hurt his partner, as in the action of Leszczyc. However, if taking the dog to the vet in order to put him down is an act of sadism on the part of Leszczyc, it is also not free of masochism – the protagonist appears to be truly heart-broken by losing his pet.

In Skolimowski's films made outside Poland, the houses are also far from being homes. In two films shot in London, in which he represents Poles living abroad, *Moonlighting* and *Success Is the Best Revenge*, the houses are in a state of disrepair. In the first film, the house only provides a roof over one's head and even this cannot be taken for granted as the roof is leaking. Moreover, it does not have even the most basic facilities, such as toilet or kitchen utensils. It is actually the Polish workers who are to repair it, whilst living there at the same time. The house does not belong to them, but to their Polish boss. While living there, the men are thus semi-homeless. They are also metaphorically homeless, because they are separated from their families and their motherland, and have no money to go to the Polish church, which for Polish emigrants is a small island of Polishness in the ocean of otherness. However, even such an imperfect house becomes the centre of the world for the people threatened by constant intrusions and deportation. They are prepared to defend it at all costs, as suggested by barricading the doors and blackening the windows when they feel under attack. On the whole, the house in this film can be read as a metaphor for the condition of the emigrant: a state which is miserable but still difficult to abandon.[7]

In *Success Is the Best Revenge*, the house is also renovated, but this time largely by British workmen employed by its Polish owner, Alex Rodak. Despite the intrusion, the house comes across not only as habitable but quite comfortable and cosy, with wide stairs, pictures decorating the walls and a dog who looks exactly like the potentially rabid one put down in *Identification Marks: None*. However, this time it is a truly 'private' dog and he survives in the film, although everybody around him is in a state of crisis.

Rodak's inability to finish the house betrays his inability to settle in London. It also reflects the Rodaks' marital problems. At one point the roof of the house collapses, while Alex has extra-marital sex, in an episode which brings back memories of *Barrier*, where Leszczyc said that he wants to marry in order to have a house. In common with Poles in *Moonlighting*, the Rodaks also suffer from frequent intrusions, which highlight English xenophobia. For example, the council inspectors pay Rodak a visit to inform him that his alterations to the house do not comply with building regulations, although his neighbour made similar changes without suffering any sanctions. Obviously, the intrusions negatively affect the characters' quality of life, making them feel 'unhomely' in their own homes. On the whole, the situation of Polish emigrants in London is not very different than that of Poles in Poland. Poles thus appear to be sentenced to perpetual homelessness and wandering. This idea is present in Polish romantic work, but Skolimowski enriches it with modern content.

However, even nice and cosy homes, as depicted by Skolimowski, do not guarantee happiness and stability. Take, for example, the house of the Fieldings, in *The Shout*, which becomes virtually a 'haunted house' after Crossley's visit; the house of Gemma's family, in *Torrents of Spring*, which had to be sold due to the bankruptcy of the owners; or the Polish house of the noble family of Józio's aunt and uncle, featured in *Ferdydurke*, which is both a madhouse and a nest of revolutionary ferment among the servants.

Because the houses in Skolimowski's films are so inadequate, his characters search for alternatives, offered by the road: the vehicles, enabling movement from one place to another, the cafés and restaurants, giving temporary respite, hotels and houses of other people where they can stay for the night. To them I devote the next section of this chapter.

The Road

Skolimowski's characters are often travelling, sometimes for work, on other occasions to meet their family and, most often, for no particular reason. Accordingly, iconography pertaining to travelling fills his films. We can list here places where people begin and finish their journeys such as railway stations, airports, tram depots; vehicles which allow them to change location such as trains, trams, planes, bicycles, motorcycles and, most importantly, cars; and the objects they carry, especially suitcases. The suitcase appears so important in the early films of this director that Konrad Eberhardt labelled his protagonist a 'man with a suitcase' (Eberhardt 1967: 14), and this description was later repeated by numerous critics. In *Walkover* and *Barrier*, Leszczyc literally carries a suitcase. In the latter film, the suitcase not only contains his belongings but also fulfils many other functions. Leszczyc sits on it at the edge of the road, slides on it down a slope, even uses it to light his cigarette. Some of these uses show that for him the suitcase can replace the comforts of home. Others, however, point to the homelessness and discomfort of the traveller. Unlike a rucksack or travel bag, a suitcase is a heavy and bulky piece of luggage. It testifies to a large amount of experience and memories, as well as material possessions, from which its owner does not want to part. It is difficult to move freely with a suitcase; a passenger with a suitcase is forced to look for accommodation and preferably he would stay there for more than one night. Leszczyc's suitcase appears especially huge in comparison with the small luggage of some earlier travellers of Polish cinema, such as Maciek Chełmicki in Wajda's *Ashes and Diamonds* and the Student in Polański's *Knife in the Water*. Maciek and the Student carried little because they had little, as well as because they did not want anything to hinder them in their peregrinations. Their most precious possessions were their weapons, respectively a gun and a knife. Leszczyc, on the other hand, does not put any weapon in his suitcase, being a child of peaceful times. He sports a sabre in *Barrier* but this is really an ornament, not a weapon, contrasting with his utterly contemporary demeanour. In *Walkover*, we are privy to some material possessions Leszczyc carries with him: a transistor radio and numerous watches he won in boxing competitions. As typical sporting trophies, they can also be regarded as signs of 'small stabilisation'. Equipped with these gadgets, Leszczyc can be regarded as a living advert of Gomułka's policies. His behaviour, however, suggests that he tries to resist such connotations by selling his trophies and using the proceeds to continue his journey. We do not know what the protagonist of *Barrier* put in his suitcase, but we are informed that he did not leave anything for his pals from the students' lodging, most likely on account of his individualism and

Figure 3.7 Jan Nowicki as Boy sliding on his suitcase in *Barrier*

materialism. On the whole, the suitcase in the 'Leszczyc tetralogy' is a sign of the character's freedom and its limitations. He is as free as a citizen in a socialist country can be: he can move, but slowly and with a considerable effort, and keep to the beaten track, rather than exploring new routes.

Another important element of Skolimowski's iconography is the car. Not only does it feature in his cinema more widely than other modes of transport, but in his 1960s films Skolimowski elaborated a unique way to represent it. There it functions not so much as a vehicle of real travel but as an object of dreams. Skolimowski's characters more often talk about cars and look at them than drive them. Jan Nowicki, who played the main role in *Barrier* and is Skolimowski's contemporary, claims in a programme accompanying transmission of this film on Polish television, that in the 1960s young Poles were so poor in comparison with their Western counterparts that they did not even try matching them in terms of material possessions. It was enough for them to dream about a car; they did not plan to acquire one. If this was indeed the case, I suggest that Skolimowski perfectly captured the state of mind of Polish young people of the 1960s.

The 'dream car' features for the first time in *Identification Marks: None*. Asked by a radio journalist about his dreams, Leszczyc answers that he would like to drive big lorries. This dream links Leszczyc and, by extension, Skolimowski, to Marek Hłasko, one of the greatest legends of Polish postwar literature, who in his semi-autobiographical accounts depicted his experiences as a lorry driver, travelling to some of the most remote and dangerous parts of Poland. However, unlike Hłasko, who managed to be a real driver, Leszczyc in this film does not even have a driving licence. He crosses his town by foot and when he eventually leaves, he goes by train.

Yet by the time Leszczyc returns in *Walkover*, he has become an accomplished driver, having learnt this skill in the army together with boxing. He shows his driving skills when he stops a convertible, driven by an older man with an attractive woman as a passenger, pretending that he is a policeman. He asks them to take the back seat and drives with Teresa to a restaurant. In this sequence Leszczyc literally does what he intended to do metaphorically in *Barrier*: displaces an old man in his luxurious car, stealing the attractive woman from him. Moreover, he does so when he is still young, as opposed to waiting twenty or so years when he will be old himself. The naturalness with which he achieves this goal and the timidity with which the older man allows Leszczyc to appropriate his car, points to the ease with which this goal could be accomplished in socialist Poland. There are more cars in *Walkover* but the majority of them are lorries and vans, used to transport objects needed at the industrial plant. Others, like the white convertible and the black Volga driven by the factory director, are used by the socialist elite: the managers and Party dignitaries. Obviously, Leszczyc at this stage does not belong to this class, neither does Teresa. During the course of the narrative Leszczyc has to rely on the good will of strangers as well as on his own power of persuasion to be picked up and be driven from place to place. His constant waiting for a lift highlights his position as an outsider, somebody who does not have his own place. Although he is constantly on the move, he appears immobile because everybody overtakes him.

Figure 3.8 Leszczyc, Teresa and a car in *Walkover*

In *Barrier*, Leszczyc expresses for the first time a desire to have a car, preferably an Opel Record. In his monologue he links expensive cars with expensive women; he would like to have both. However, he does not do anything to acquire a car or a high-class woman. Instead he befriends a female tram driver who, although pretty, is nothing luxurious, as signified by her heavy boots and sheepskin jacket which keep her warm in the Polish winter. Leszczyc sits in a car only once, in a garage that belongs to a rich woman who hired him as a cleaner. He turns the wipers on and smokes a cigarette but does not drive. As with many other scenes in this film, it is difficult to say whether the car belongs to reality or fantasy. In another episode, Leszczyc attacks a car with a sabre; which is a reference to the history or mythology of the Second World War, when Polish cavalrymen attacked German tanks with sabres. Replacing tanks with cars points to the shift from patriotism to consumerism that took place in Polish culture of the 1960s – a shift which in this scene appears to displease Leszczyc. Although Leszczyc and his university friends have no cars, the director hints that this generation will soon acquire them because, as is mentioned at the ball for war veterans, young men nowadays all have driving licences and from the tram windows we see a large assembly of new cars, waiting to be appropriated by the new elites.

In *Hands Up!*, cars are still talked about rather than used, but the characters do not muse about any abstract automobile, but are able to name the car they possess: Alfa Romeo, Wartburg, Zastava, Opel Record, and appropriate the names of these cars as their nicknames. The cars they possess thus become their 'identification marks'. The owners of these nicknames also compare them to pseudonyms used by resistance fighters during the Second World War which, again, underscores the importance of the cars for their personal identity, while simultaneously pointing to the cultural change which has taken place in postwar Poland. These names are not arbitrary, but capture characters' behaviour and outlook on life. There is an economic division between Alfa, Romeo and Record on the one hand, and Zastava and Wartburg on the other. Members of the first group, owners of Western automobiles, emphasise their affluence and high social status at each step. The owner of the Record even says that money is what he strove for and what he eventually achieved. Romeo (from Alfa Romeo) also connotes affluence and Westernisation, as well as popularity with women. Alfa is also an ardent consumer, as testified by her admitting that her favourite pastime is foreign travels.

By contrast to Alfa, Romeo and Record, who diffuse an air of self-confidence, the owner of the Wartburg comes across as thwarted. We derive from his behaviour that this East German car is the peak of his achievements and he is very anxious not to lose it. Wartburg is played by Bogumił Kobiela, an actor who in the 1960s specialised in the roles of thwarted 'socialist men', who happily settled for the goods offered by Polish 'small stabilisation', such as a small apartment in a block and an Eastern car. He played such a role, for example, in *Człowiek z M-3* (*The Man from M-3*, 1968), directed by Leon Jeannot. The humblest car is the Zastava, which belongs to Leszczyc. Not only is this vehicle the cheapest of all the cars belonging to the group but, as Leszczyc admits, it is old and battered. Leszczyc's choice of Zastava signifies that its owner did not give in to consumerism as much as his friends. Although the characters in *Hands Up!* possess cars, in the course of the film they travel by train. They board their automobiles only in the final scene of the film. This moment also marks the end of their fragile friendship; once in their cars the friends each go their own way. This scene poignantly demonstrates that the car is a tool of the individualistic life.

Only in *Le Départ*, Skolimowski's first film made in the West, does the automobile appear as a truly material object, something the character touches and drives. And touching is what Marc likes most about cars. The first time we see him in contact with the car, he delicately strokes its roof, as if it was animal fur or a woman with whom he is about to have sex. After this initial caress he boards it, which can be compared with sexual penetration, and starts driving it very fast. The suggestion that Marc's attitude to the car is erotic is confirmed on a number of later occasions. For example, the middle-aged customer of a ladies salon, where Marc works, asks him what he is thinking when he is washing her hair, and when he answers first 'my mother' and then 'cars', tells him that she prefers if he thinks about cars. In due course, he has to flatter her to get access to the car so he can drive in a rally. The director of *Le Départ* also compares cars to women, or more exactly, to their sexualised bodies, by showing them as exhibits. Cars are admired at car exhibitions, women at fashion shows, and both events are shown by Skolimowski simultaneously. The cars and female models are even presented in a similar way – both revolve to show that they have no flaws. Moreover, Marc constantly experiences a dilemma: to have 'a girl' or 'a car', as if it would be impossible to have both without betraying one.

During the course of the narrative, Marc drives a number of expensive cars, such as Porsche and Mercedes. It can be suggested that such use of a car is specific to European cinema where cars are 'disposable, transient, temporary and impersonal' (Orr 1993: 132). However, in the case of Marc this is not because he wants them to be transient, but because he has no money to buy a car or even rent one for more than one ride. For this reason, as well as because Marc strives to possess a first-class vehicle, his cars, despite the sensuality of his contact with them, are also, in a sense, dream cars. They are also dream objects because they are related to Marc's master plan of leaving his job as an anonymous, low-paid hairdressing apprentice and becoming somebody rich and famous. The dreamlike nature of the car is best shown when Marc and his girlfriend Michèle visit automobile exhibitions. When the show is closed for the night, they sit in a vehicle that looks as if it was broken into two halves. Marc occupies one part of the car, Michèle the other. They swirl in their halves as on a merry-go-round: young, careless, glamorous, as if they were models, advertising the cars. Skolimowski links cars with youth not only by showing how good young people look in luxurious and fast cars, but also how old people are unsuited to them, most clearly in an episode when an old man faints behind the steering wheel of a vehicle shown at the exhibition.

Whilst Marc dreams about a Porsche, he uses a scooter for his daily errands. He does not like this vehicle and treats it badly, kicking it and abandoning it on the street when it does not start, and eventually pawning it to get money to rent a car. Marc's attitude to the scooter parallels his attitude to his job and his social class – he would be happy to exchange the tangible advantages they offer for the flimsy chance of a higher position. It is worth noting that in Wajda's *Innocent Sorcerers* the scooter played the role of a luxury. Its much lower status in *Le Départ* testifies to the fact that vehicles or any other consumer goods do not have any intrinsic value but are culturally constructed; their worth depends on their place and time, and relations with other goods.

A vehicle can also be an object of aggression and destruction. We see it in *Deep End*, where the car driven by Susan's fiancé crushes the bike Mike uses to go to work. Later on, however, Mike gets his symbolic revenge for this act by puncturing the car tyres of Susan's other lover, the swimming instructor. Consequently, the teacher is stranded and for a long time cannot reach Susan, while Mike, unencumbered by a car, goes with her to the baths and has sex with her there. Similarly, in *Skid*, which Skolimowski scripted (discussed in detail in Chapter 4), the main character first tries to blackmail somebody by accusing him of causing an accident when driving a car and later kills his girlfriend, while driving the car received from the victim of his blackmail.

Numerous authors emphasise the link between the car and cinema. For example, David Laderman maintains:

> Both cars and movies promised to express the idealised uniqueness of the individual consumer. Conceived together, automobiles and films dynamically reflect our culture as it becomes transformed by transportational and representational technologies … The structure of the car, designed both to conform to our bodies' shortcomings and powerfully extend them, has become how we regard the world (through the screen-like, Panavision-shaped lens of the windscreen and, like a miniature movie within a movie, the rear mirror). (Laderman 2002: 3)

This quote captures both the way Skolimowski's films conform to the dominant way of representing the car and the extent to which they diverge from them. Certainly, cars in his films encapsulate the individualism and consumerism of the characters. However, they do not convey their mobility but rather their immobility. Neither does the inclusion of cars add to the dynamism of Skolimowski's films. Their dynamism results chiefly from capturing the movements of the characters' bodies and not their technological 'extensions'. In fact, cars constrain rather than liberating his characters, because they do not 'organically' belong to them, behave capriciously and their symbolic meanings elude control.

Since *Deep End*, the narrative importance and the symbolic significance of the car in Skolimowski's films have diminished. The last time the director draws our attention to a vehicle is in *Success Is the Best Revenge*, in a scene where Rodak unsuccessfully asks the bank official to lend him money to buy an expensive car which, clearly, he wants to use as a status symbol. This diminishing of automobiles can be explained by the fact that, from the 1970s, cars, at least in the West, stopped being a luxury and instead became an object of everyday use. Consequently, it became more difficult to idealise cars and dream about them. Skolimowski already hints at this diminishing of the car's value in *Deep End*, where cars are owned by ordinary people, including the swimming instructor. It appears to be easier for this man to afford a car than an everyday bath.

In the early part of Skolimowski's career a car was also his own 'identification mark'. First it was a humble Zastava (as was the car of Leszczyc in *Hands Up!*). From the royalties for *Le Départ* the director bought a more luxurious Ford Mustang, which he later sold to Czesław Niemen (see Uszyński 1990a: 23), who was one of the greatest pop stars in postwar Poland. A well-known Polish director, Marek Koterski, also recollects Skolimowski's visit to the Łódź Film School, when in his expensive car and fashionable clothes, the director of *Walkover* epitomised what his younger colleagues, including Koterski, aspired to: wealth, international career and, going with them, self-confidence. Clearly, this car became the symbol of his early successes and international career – a sign of his difference from the 'socialist crowd'. Skolimowski's latest car, one in which I had the pleasure to be driven to his house, also distinguishes him from the crowd. It is an old Mercedes, a vehicle that connotes an affinity for comfort and power, but also a yearning for the past, when cars had more style and aged with more grace.

Water

> He did not picture life's ocean, as do poets, all astir with stormy waves. No, he saw it in his mind's eye as smooth, without a ripple, motionless and translucent right down to the dark sea bed. He saw himself sitting in a small unsteady boat, staring at the dark silt of the sea bottom, where he could just discern shapeless monsters, like enormous fish. These were life's hazards – the illnesses, the griefs, madness, poverty, blindness…
>
> (Ivan Turgenev, *Spring Torrents*)

Water is a frequent setting in Skolimowski's films and his films are 'awash' with water metaphors. His characters live on or near water (*The Lightship*, *The Shout*), travel on water (*Ferdydurke*), work with water (*Deep End*), study water life (Leszczyc in *Identification Marks: None*) and like to bathe in it (*Little Hamlet*, *Barrier*, *Deep End*). Moreover, the protagonist of the 'Leszczyc tetralogy' has a name associated with water, as 'leszcz' in Polish means 'bream'. Yet unlike Polański, Skolimowski is not associated with the mise-en-scène of water, most likely because Polański began his career with a distinctive take on water, while Skolimowski elaborated it for a longer time. Large areas of water feature more prominently in his later films, while in his early productions water rather drips than floods. Take his early *Little Hamlet*, in which the Polish Ophelia has a bath in a humble bathtub and most likely drowns there. By contrast, in Polański's cinema vast areas of water already appear in his early shorts and his feature debut, *Knife in the Water*.

Both Polański and Skolimowski represent water as a liminal space – a passage to a different reality. However, in Skolimowski's films water not so much signifies moving to the realm of fantasy (pure fantasy rarely appears in his films), as a transition between different stages of life, including the passage between childhood and maturity, and life and death. The only possible exception is in *Ferdydurke*, where at the end of the film Józio embarks on a boat, escaping everything which he encountered during his peregrinations as a schoolboy. This trip signifies Józio finally leaving the realm of childhood and becoming a man, as well as his parting from

Poland. These associations are suggested by the name of the boat, 'Trans-Atlantyk', which is also the title of a famous, semi-autobiographical novel by Witold Gombrowicz, who left Poland on a ship of this name and landed in Argentina. Leaving Poland, for Gombrowicz and Skolimowski, not only means parting from the geographical location but also from the historical and cultural entity – the prewar Poland of decadent aristocracy and disappearing 'simple peasants'. However, even if we regard the boat in *Ferdydurke* as a vehicle of a metaphysical journey, this journey lacks the suggestiveness of the two men from Polański's *Dwaj ludzie z szafą* (*Two Men and a Wardrobe*, 1958) disappearing in the water. Moreover, the viewer must have some minimal literary knowledge to grasp the meaning of Józio's final trip.

There is no sea or any other large areas of water in Skolimowski's feature debut, *Identification Marks: None*, but the sea is often talked of by the characters. Leszczyc, in tune with his 'fishy' name, studies ichthyology and tells his mother that for his thesis he will go to the sea and the lakes to study the life of fish. This statement is, however, not true, because he will go to the army, although his army unit is based by the sea. In this film, Leszczyc admits that he went to university to study anything, after failing to be accepted by the art school (not unlike Skolimowski, who chose ethnography when he was rejected by the art school), but we can guess that this subject suited his free spirit. By contrast, in the city he feels like a fish 'out of water': lost and suffocated. His colleagues perceive him like that and tease him by putting a heater in a small tank with a fish (perhaps a bream) to cause it suffering and death.

In *Barrier*, water is associated with maturing and falling in love. Suggestive of that is an episode when Leszczyc and the female tram driver sit at the edge of the road, covered in snow. She washes her face with snow while he melts it using the warmth from a cigarette and candles. The melting of snow parallels the melting of any barriers between them, and the proximity of fire underscores, almost too obviously, the fire of love burning in their hearts. Their coming together is reinforced by their tram trip to the other side of the city, across a bridge over the river (in reality the Vistula, although the name is never spelt out in the film). By the time they reach the other bank, they have become a couple. Water in *Barrier* is also associated with seduction, with 'dirty' sex, as in the scene when Leszczyc finds himself in an apartment belonging to a female aristocrat or a woman appropriating such an identity. She invites him to have a bath on the pretext that his face is dirty and then switches off the electricity, so that they can be together in darkness. Leszczyc, however, discovers her plot and refuses her advances, saying that he has a fiancée. Later in the film the connection between an older woman, dirty water and dirty sex is reinforced in a scene in a restaurant where a female cleaner who is moping the floor is asked jokingly by the master of the ceremony to finish her bath and sing. It is worth adding here that the role of the cleaner is taken by Maria Malicka, a star of Polish prewar cinema, who after the war was banned from acting for collaborating with the Nazis. Her 'bath' thus awakens associations with moral cleansing 'Polish style', rendering it highly dubious.

Water in similar contexts appears in Skolimowski's first British film (although shot in Munich), *Deep End*. Again, as in *Barrier*, snow connotes the true passion of young people. However, when the snow is brought indoors to be melted (because it holds a diamond from the ring Susan received from her fiancé), its purity gives way to impurity, both literal and metaphorical, understood as promiscuous sex. Such sex, in *Deep End*, leads to death at the bottom of an empty swimming pool. As in *Barrier*, the bathing environment is also used in *Deep End* by older women as a place to seduce young men. It appears that water can be pure only when it is not contaminated by any human presence. Where it is transported and contained in baths or swimming pools, it starts to resemble dirty human fluids.

In *Torrents of Spring*, the atmospheric phenomenon of torrential rain coincides with Gemma and Sanin's confession of love and their first kiss. This kiss will change their lives forever but not in a way they expect: Sanin will betray Gemma with Maria, Gemma will eventually marry another man. Sanin's crucial encounter with Maria also takes place near water; this time in a swamp which the couple pass on their way to some ruins. Their last meeting also takes place in proximity of water, in Venice, a place that perfectly encapsulates the connection between water, eroticism and death. Here Maria pours a glass of wine on Sanin from the balcony, before disappearing into the crowd of people celebrating carnival. Later we learn that Maria died the same year.

When Skolimowski's characters find themselves on water or even approach water, they risk their lives or those close to them. I have already mentioned the fatal incident in *Deep End*. In *King, Queen, Knave*, Martha invites her husband on a boat where Frank is meant to kill him, but she herself drowns. The gangsters who invade the eponymous lightship from Skolimowski's film cause mayhem there and kill the captain, but they also become decimated. In *The Shout*, on the beaches near the ocean, Crossley checks the power of his deadly shout, causing the death of a man who accidentally happens to be there. Water, death and injustice are again linked in *Four Nights with Anna*. In the memory of Leon, the images of a dead cow are juxtaposed with the scenes of sentencing him for a rape which he did not commit and his prison misery, where fellow prisoners use dirty water to inflict extra suffering on him. The unpredictability of events taking place near water (what actually occurs contradicts the plans of the characters) demonstrate that water is a dangerous and, most importantly, perverse element. It cannot be subjugated by any human being, but should be treated with humility.

Skolimowski focuses, more often than Polański, on silent, dead water – water that does not move or in which a man stands still. We see it in *Lightship, Deep End, Torrents of Spring, Four Nights with Anna* and the Prologue to *Hands Up!* Such water epitomises everything life keeps for people and the time that passes silently, unnoticeably, although eventually transforming everything. When one dies, all one's achievements and unrealised opportunities disappear – death levels everything, as does the water after the sinking of a ship. It is thus not surprising that images of the sea, both photographed and painted, accompany the director's monologue in which he mourns that his last Polish film before emigration, *Hands Up!*, was destroyed by time and cannot be recovered. Similarly, when standing on a small barge and looking into the water, Sanin in *Torrents of Spring* muses on his wasted chance for love. It might appear far-fetched, but I find a premonition of Sanin's gaze in *Identification*

Marks: None, where Leszczyc looks into his cup of coffee as if trying to learn what the future holds for him.

For Skolimowski water is also a perfect *materia prima*, contrasting with the world created by people. This idea is offered in the Prologue to *Hands Up!*, where images of Beirut, destroyed during the war, are juxtaposed with images of a peaceful sea. At the same time as lamenting the demolished houses and wasted human lives, Skolimowski shows admiration for the non-human part of the universe – the ocean which is eternal. Such a description of the ocean also appears in Skolimowski's interviews when he talks about his house in Santa Monica, built on a rock and boasting an excellent view of the ocean. He admits that since moving there, shortly after finishing *The Lightship*, he lost interest in making films and, indeed, any 'human affairs' and prefers to stay at home and admire nature, including the sound of the sea and night calls of the birds. Moving to the seaside appears to have sharpened the director's sense that human lives are mostly trivial, and engaging in worldly affairs will only multiply redundant production (see Uszyński 1990b: 44; Smader and Demidowicz 2004: 107).

Notes

1. I am avoiding capital letters when using these terms, because in most cases I will not consider Skolimowski's films as belonging to particular, historically and geographically delineated movements, but as revealing specific qualities found in works of any artist or period. However, I capitalise 'Romanticism', because I consider it as a distinctive movement in Polish history.
2. It could also be argued that such a discrepancy was the only means to convey criticism of Polish industrialisation (which uncritically followed the Soviet Union model) in a way acceptable to the censors.
3. By drawing attention to the misleading character of Polish language Skolimowski began a series of Polish films which focus on this problem, by parodying typical expressions or official formulas. The best known examples of this strategy are the films of Marek Piwowski, such as *Muchotłuk* (*The Fly Killer*, 1967) and *Rejs* (*The Cruise*, 1970). In the next decades the specialist of parodying official speak became Stanisław Bareja, the author of the cult hit *Miś* (*Teddy Bear*, 1980). It is likely that Skolimowski inspired Bareja in this respect, not least because Bareja's scripts were co-written by Stanisław Tym, who played in Skolimowski's *Walkover* and *Barrier*.
4. Janion in the same interview claims that the lack of assimilation of psychoanalysis is a significant shortcoming of Polish culture.
5. Magritte often blocked any view of the subject's face with a drape, an apple, a hand or a shawl, as in *Les Amants* (*The Lovers*, 1928) and *La Grande Guerre* (*The Great War*, 1964).
6. Ceilings are also visible in *Ashes and Diamonds* where they similarly point to the entrapment of the protagonist, Maciek Chełmicki.
7. The importance of home for emigrants is discussed in a number of essays included in the collection, *Home, Exile, Homeland*, edited by Hamid Naficy (see Naficy 1999). My conclusions regarding the use of home in Skolimowski's films are concurrent with the uses of home discussed in this book.

CHAPTER 4

In the Land of Hamlets and Don Quixotes: Skolimowski's Encounters with Literature

The relationship between literature and Skolimowski's cinema is complex, not least because he is a man of literature: a poet, a playwright and a scriptwriter of films made not only by himself but by other film makers as well. Thus he not only adapts literary works of other authors, but allows cinema, including his own films, to adapt his literature. Particularly interesting is the way he uses and develops his own poetry. Another reason that Skolimowski's relationship with literature is complex is the fact that, as he himself remarked in relation to his screening of Siegfried Lenz's *The Lightship*, his film adaptations often have, figuratively, many scriptwriters (see Combs 1986: 133). This means that in his adaptation of a particular novel or a short story we find strong influences from the works of other authors. Such 'foreign' influences can also be detected in the films based on Skolimowski's original scripts. Moreover, almost all the films he has adapted bear the strong stamp of his artistic persona, which can be appreciated by comparing them with his original work. Hence, we can say that he not only adapts himself to the requirement of a particular literary work, but adapts this work to his own sensibility.

For these reasons, it makes sense to widen the discussion about the place of adaptation in Skolimowski's oeuvre by treating film and literature as equal partners, existing in a complex and unstable web of relationships with other texts. Following the terminology of Gérard Genette, inspired by the work of Mikhail Bakhtin and Julia Kristeva, Robert Stam proposes to treat adaptation as a relation between the 'hypertext' and an anterior text, the 'hypotext', which the hypertext transforms, modifies, elaborates or extends (see Stam 2000: 65–66). At the same time, some hypertexts (films) match their hypotexts (novels) better than others. In due course I will examine in what respects Skolimowski's films match their hypotexts.

Skolimowski's encounters with literature are to a large extent similar to those of Polański. For both, the earlier chapters of their careers were dominated by films based on their own original scripts. These films exhibited traces of various literary influences, but the strongest thread in them was the directors' own presence. Their reputations are still largely based on these films. The second parts of their careers, on the other hand, are dominated by literary adaptations.[1] Such a strong reliance on literature can be explained by external and internal factors. One was the enthusiasm of Skolimowski's producers for particular books and, consequently, the relative ease of financing projects based on literary works, as opposed to original ideas. For Skolimowski, adapting literature was a way to alleviate some of the problems resulting from not knowing the film's milieu. Such an explanation can be supported by the fact that those of his emigrant films that are based on original scripts, *Moonlighting* and *Success Is the Best Revenge*, concern Polish characters. Finally, his reliance on adaptation in the late 1970s and 1980s is a sign of his diminishing confidence in his power to create an utterly original film. Such confidence returned when he moved back to Poland for good in the early 2000s; the making of *Four Nights with Anna* is a sign of that.

As a director screening somebody else's work, Skolimowski appears to be less successful than Polański. Only one of his adaptations, *The Shout*, achieved any significant commercial and artistic success. The lack of recognition for his other films based on literature was often a consequence of extraneous factors, such as untimely distribution. The director's own criticism of some of his films also did not help to prolong their longevity. However, at least one of them, *King, Queen, Knave*, deserves better, both as a work of art in its own right and as an example of a rich, albeit harmonious, dialogue between the writer (as inscribed in his text) and the film maker.

Poetry and Cinema

As was already mentioned, before he started making films Skolimowski was a successful poet. His two published volumes were entitled *Gdzieś blisko siebie* (*Somewhere near Myself*, 1958) and *Siekiera i niebo* (*An Axe and the Sky*, 1959). Reading them almost half a century after their publication, I was surprised how readable they still are, if we take into account the young age of the author and his lack of any formal literary training and, indeed, his rather poor and disrupted education. It is clear that Skolimowski understood perfectly that the essence of poetry is abridgement and ambiguity: conveying maximum meaning in a minimum of words and in a way that leaves the reader's imagination with something to work on. Skolimowski's poems are thus very rich in metaphors. Sometimes their author even tries too hard to dress his thoughts in poetic language: there are too many metaphors and they are too baroque for the subject of the poem and its length. Moreover, some motifs recur too frequently. Meaningfully, these motifs would later be used extensively in Skolimowski's films. As one critic notes, Skolimowski the poet had an obsession for ceilings and ceiling-like objects (see Janicki 1966: 40), such as the sky. The sky is often heavy or covered with stones, which mark the boundary of the protagonist's exploration, his utter entrapment and helplessness. Take these fragments:

Spotyka nowe zdumienie –
człowieka który dźwiga niebo
(*Szyba i kamień* in *Gdzieś blisko siebie*: 5)

He is astonished again –
by a man who carries the sky
(*A Glass and a Stone* in *Somewhere near Myself*: 5)

Z góry zwisa
bezmyślne niebo
(*Rozbudzanie wyobraźni* in *Siekiera i niebo*: 31)

Thoughtless sky
hangs from the peak
(*Awakening of Imagination* in *An Axe and the Sky*: 31)

Odsuwam
te wszystkie
furtki sufity
(*Narcyz* in *Gdzieś blisko siebie*: 17)

I move away
all these gates ceilings
(*Narcissus* in *Somewhere near Myself*: 17)

Another somehow too incessant motif is a mask or other object, which covers or replaces the protagonist's face:

Opadają
ze skrzypieniem
moje pokrowce
z twarzy
(*Narcyz* in *Gdzieś blisko siebie*: 15)

My cases
fall from
my face
with a creak
(*Narcissus* in *Somewhere near Myself*: 15)

This repetitiveness of a limited number of motifs might be attributed to the short period in which Skolimowski's poems were produced, and the lack of a good editor who would suggest to the young author to be more selective and self-critical. The second striking feature of Skolimowski's early verses is that they betray the hand of the future film maker. The author frequently conveys his perceptions as if he were a camera, searching for the best angle and distance to shoot from and registering its surroundings with cool objectivity, or an editor trying to make a whole out of separate frames, or a cinephile who sees the world as if it were a screen. We can find all these perspectives in this passage:

Kiedyś
podchodziłem do okna
był tam kawałek
niemego filmu
co chwila
kończącego się nocą

Po szybie
przemykały twarze
wciąż te same
nieznane
Z profilu z góry
zbliżenia ust i rąk
strzępki gestów
urywki pejżaży
(*Jeszcze ograniczenie* in *Gdzieś blisko siebie*: 14)

In the past
I used to come to the window
I saw there a fragment of
a silent movie
finishing with the night

On the glass
the faces kept passing
always the same
unfamiliar
shown from profile, from above
Close-ups of mouths and hands
fragments of gestures
scraps of landscapes
(*One More Limitation* in *Somewhere near Myself*: 14)

In Skolimowski's poems we also find numerous mirrors and mirror reflections that reveal the hero's future or present him from an unexpected perspective; objects emphasising the contrast between darkness and light; and religious objects such as churches, crosses, confessionals and altars, and religious people, principally nuns; all playing important roles in his films. References to religion betray distrust, even fear of official, institutionalised religion, and at the same time a desire to have a private faith or spirituality, to be able to pray:

Za podwójnym
dnem
mojej świątyńki

pod dywanami
pochwał
i kolumnami
aprobaty
ukryłem
relikwie
swojej wiary
(*Narcyz* in *Gdzieś blisko siebie*: 15)

Behind the double
floor
of my little temple
under the carpet
of praises
and the columns
of approval
I hid
the relics
of my faith
(*Narcissus* in *Somewhere near Myself*: 15)

Skolimowski's second book of verse is distinctly surrealist, as revealed by the titles of the poems, such as *Kawiarnia 'Panopticum'* (*Café 'Panopticum'*) and *Kwartet na żyletkę i trzy odbicia w lustrze* (*A Quartet for a Blade and Three Reflections in the Mirror*), and the images the author constructs in them.

Dlatego odwracam oczy
a moje odbicie zostaje
i spogląda za mną
ze współczuciem
(*Lustro na końcu drogi* in *Gdzieś blisko siebie*: 30)

Therefore I turn my eyes
and my reflection stays behind
and looks at me
with sympathy
(*Mirror at the End of the Road* in *Somewhere near Myself*: 30)

Taken together, these verses construct a portrait of a rebellious, disorientated and lonely young man, whose new incarnation(s) we find in Skolimowski's 'Leszczyc tetralogy'. This young man suffers from inner emptiness. 'Empty field' and similar descriptions abound in his poems; one of them is even entitled *Pustka* (*Emptiness* or *Void*). He does not yet know who he is or he has experienced too little to have a strong sense of identity. At the same time, he would like to be the true author of his life, rather than leaving it to others (his elders) to decide his future. Skolimowski's feature debut, *Identification Marks: None*, can be regarded as the cinematic equivalent or hypertext to a poem which provides the title to Skolimowski's first book of verse, *Somewhere near Myself*, which contains this fragment:

Nie znajduję siebie
w danych statystycznych
że wzrost – kolor włosów
lub numer obuwia
Te symbole
charakteryzują bryłę
skatalogowaną
pod moim nazwiskiem

Więc w lustrze sprawdzam
te bzdury o głębi twarzy
Jej trzeci wymiar
Kończy się jednak na skórze
Potem mięśnie i kości –
to anatomia nie poezja

Tu mnie nie ma ...

Jestem gdzieś blisko siebie
Lecz jaka to bliskość?
Sprawdzana dotykiem –
Czy mierzona latami świetlnymi?
(*Gdzieś blisko siebie* in *Gdzieś blisko siebie*: 52–3)

I cannot find myself
among statistical data
height – colour of hair
or shoe size
These symbols
characterise the figure
classified
under my name

So I'm checking in a mirror
these silly things about the depth of face
Its third dimension
finishes however on my skin
Further down are muscles and bones –
This is anatomy not poetry

I'm not here…

I'm somewhere near myself
But what kind of closeness is it?
One that can be checked by touch –
Or measured in light years?
(*Somewhere near Myself* in *Somewhere near Myself*: 52–53)

Equally, Skolimowski's poems convey the protagonist's fear of old people and ageing, as well as of himself as an old man. As in his films, youth is full of uncertainty, loneliness and trauma, but old age is still worse, as it is very close to irreversible non-existence. Although Skolimowski's poetry arose more from his own emotions and observations of the outside world than from analysing the work of other poets, it did not exist in a cultural void, but reflected concerns typical in the existentialist literature of authors such as Sartre and Camus.

Skolimowski's poetry was also, naturally, in dialogue with his contemporaries, primarily Andrzej Bursa (1932–1957) (see Lubelski 1989: 26; Uszyński 1989: 5; Klejsa 2004: 97–98), as well as with the works of Tadeusz Różewicz. In Bursa's poems, we find such familiar motifs as fear of wasted youth, contemplation of one's death, a mask replacing one's face and a barrier between the older and younger generations of Poles (on Bursa's poems and his myth see Stanuch 1990). Bursa also used 'cinematic metaphors', for example in the poem *Warszawa – Fantom* (*Warsaw – Phantom*), where we find the line 'Błysk kamery filmowej zamiast dziewczyny' (Flesh of cine-camera instead of a girl). Some themes present in the work of Bursa, such as his polemic with romantic tradition, are not developed in Skolimowski's poems, but became significant in his films. Perhaps the closest both to the spirit of Skolimowski's own poems and his films is Bursa's *Rówieśnikom kameleonom* (*To the Peer Chameleon*), in which the author criticises his passive, 'faceless' generation. There is no doubt that Bursa was a better poet than Skolimowski. His works possessed what the majority of Skolimowski's poetic attempts lacked: self-discipline, ability to sustain an idea throughout the whole poem and sparser use of metaphor.

With the benefit of hindsight, Stanisław Janicki maintains that in Skolimowski's case replacing pen with camera was not a dramatic change (see Janicki 1966: 40). Indeed, the type of protagonist, the mood, the images, even the basic ideology survived the transition/translation. Cinema, thanks to its multimedia character, also allowed Skolimowski to solve the problem he encountered in his poetry, namely how to convey more metaphors or more complex metaphors in a single work. As I argued earlier, for this aim he used all the opportunities offered by film, sometimes to the annoyance of critics, who were overwhelmed by his baroque, undisciplined imagination.

The shift from poetry to cinema was also smooth because, as much as possible, the director preserved in films his 'poetic' style of work: shooting very quickly and without a precise script. Not surprisingly, Skolimowski's early films, like his poems, strike us as personal, intuitive and spontaneous. They always have an individual character and apply this character's point of view. Another legacy of poetry in

Skolimowski's films is their thin plot. Except for *Walkover*, not much happens in the 'Leszczyc films' and external events give the impression of being signs of occurrences taking place in the character's soul. Finally, Skolimowski's poetry survived in his films as text. One poem appears in different versions in three films: *Identification Marks: None*, *Walkover* and *Barrier*. In the last film it reads:

Teraz on
Po złych dniach
albo po czymś takim
jak młodość
albo miłość

Z ręką na gardle
chce to naprawić
pragnie znów być
Bóg wie kim.
Z ręką na gardle
chce to naprawić
pragnie znów być
Bóg wie gdzie
i poprawia krawat.

Now he
After bad days
Or after something
Like youth
Or love

With a hand on his throat
He wants to make up for lost opportunities
He wants to be again
God knows whom.
With a hand on his throat
He wants to make up for lost opportunities
He wants to be again
God knows where
And he adjusts his tie.

The two attitudes to life the poem evokes: activity, bravery/passivity, timidity, have their equivalents in great literature. The man who wants to change everything can be seen as Don Quixote, or at least Don Quixote as construed by some of Cervantes's readers, such as Ivan Turgenev (see Schapiro 1980). The one who adjusts his tie can be compared to Hamlet, understood as a man who hesitates, has no faith and is preoccupied mostly with himself (the tie in the poem can be interpreted as a sign of the protagonist's narcissism). Although Don Quixote and Hamlet are normally regarded as contrasting characters, in literature and especially in Polish literature we find personages who are a fusion of their traits. A model example is Kordian in Juliusz Słowacki's romantic poem of the same title (1834). Kordian is a (fictitious) nineteenth century conspirator, who attempted to assassinate Russian Tsar Nicolai I when he came to Warsaw in 1829 to be crowned as Polish king. However, paralysed by fear and distaste for murder, Konrad fails to commit this act. Don Quixote, Hamlet and Kordian are all evoked in Skolimowski's films. One of his etudes, *Little Hamlet*, set among Warsaw's lumpenproletariat, as the title suggests, attempts to connect contemporary Poles with Shakespeare's most famous creation. The characters in Skolimowski's Polish films, especially Leszczyc, compare themselves with romantic characters (see Chapter 2 and 3). One of Skolimowski's later characters, Colonel Gerard, as I will argue in due course, is largely modelled on Don Quixote.

The poem about a man adjusting his tie most obviously concerns Leszczyc, Skolimowski's alter ego. However, this version of Skolimowski is somehow different from the persona he created in his published poems. He is depicted in the film from a distance, as conveyed by a third person narrative and its bitter irony, referring to the gap between his desires or ambitions and their outcome. Although both Skolimowski's poetry and cinema are personal, his poetry strikes one as more intimate, which partly results from the nature of the medium (poetry is regarded as the most intimate of all arts) and partly from the shift which took place in Skolimowski's attitude to art, namely his realisation that, to achieve the desired artistic outcome, pathos and self-pity must be counterbalanced by irony.

Skolimowski and Dygat

Together with drawing on his own poetry, in his early films and in some measure also in his later ones, Skolimowski was inspired by the work of Stanisław Dygat (1914–1978), one of the most popular Polish writers of the 1960s. They met for the first time when Skolimowski was a student at the Łódź Film School. As the director himself reveals, 'Staniław Dygat was at this time the Polish Guy de Maupassant. He wrote short stories, in which one could find virtually everything which one wanted … So I decided to "do a Dygat"' (Skolimowski, quoted in Krubski 1998: 133). The final result was *Money or Life*, based on Dygat's short story, *Pięć tysięcy złotych* (*Five Thousand Zloties*) and with the writer playing the main part. As an actor, Dygat was outstanding; he played his role in *Money or Life* so well that he received an award at the 1962 festival of students' etudes in Warsaw. It should be mentioned that casting well-known people, such as writers and musicians, was a common practice among students of the Łódź Film School at this period (ibid.: 120). For example, the famous absurdist playwright, Sławomir Mrożek, was cast in the main part in Agnieszka Osiecka's etude *Słoń* (*The Elephant*, 1959), based on Mrożek's own story.

Although *Money or Life* only lasts five minutes, it is packed with motifs which can be found in subsequent Skolimowski films and Dygat's novels. Set during the

Second World War, it depicts an encounter of two men: a crook, played by Dygat, and his Jewish victim, played by Bohdan Łazuka, squabbling about money.

The setting of the story is a funfair, a scene rich in connotations. Funfairs, pertaining to carnivals, constitute a separate sphere of reality where rules of normal behaviour are suspended (see Bakhtin 1984). In 1943, the Germans erected merry-go-rounds near the Warsaw ghetto, to draw the attention of Poles away from the uprising. However, the funfair, through disavowing of the cleansing of Jews, also pointed to the hidden reality of the Holocaust. This paradox was later discussed in numerous works, including in Czesław Miłosz's poem *Campo di Fiori* (see Miłosz 1996: 28–29). Although we do not see the ghetto in Skolimowski's film, it can be written into the narrative, precisely thanks to the presence of the funfair. Skolimowski also plays on the dialectic of concealed and revealed, visible and suggested, real and pretended in a scene in which 'Dygat' approaches the shooting gallery in order to shoot a clay bird, and is shouted at, 'Don't shoot!' This cry foretells another war command, 'Hands Up!', that provides the title of Skolimowski's last film made in Poland before his exile. In a wider sense, it anticipates the motif of 'playing at war', which is present in *Hands Up!* as well as in *Identification Marks: None* and *Walkover*, where we find scenes of children pretending to take part in fake executions.

The 'real war', as represented by Skolimowski, is rendered unrealistic, as if staged by somebody who does not have any memory of this event, having only learnt about it from films on the subject, such as Wajda's *A Generation*. This impression is conveyed by the mannered acting of the men playing German policemen and the setting, which comes across as staged, with no 'accidental' characters, only those used in the action. The effect of artificial war was intended. Skolimowski did not try to shoot a war film, only its simulacra, and in this way show the war as it was imagined almost twenty years after it ended. Such an interpretation is encouraged by the repeated pronouncement by 'Dygat': 'If it was a real war, I would behave like a hero'. Dygat as a crook is a formidable character, but he is more similar to gangsters from American films than any Polish models of criminals, which might be explained by the writer's fascination with American cinema (see Kurz 2005: 158). Thus his role adds to the feeling that *Money or Life* is a film about war films, rather than the reality of the war.

The men's arguing over money also conveys the idea, which most likely came from Dygat, that the Second World War did not fundamentally change human morality, and especially did not make heroes of the majority of Poles. Crooks remained crooks, eager to better themselves at the expense of others. However, it affected everyday situations and conflicts, as depicted by the ultimately decent behaviour of 'Dygat'. Dygat also proposes such an attitude to the war in his later novel, *Disneyland* (1965), as shown in an episode of a quarrel between the parents of the protagonist over some broken porcelain. Their argument ends when a German policeman visits them, angry that they do not obey the curfew. In this way he draws the couple's attention away from the reason for their quarrel and effects their temporary reconciliation.

After *Money or Life*, Skolimowski and Dygat stopped working together, but they constructed matching realities, so to speak. For Aleksander Jackiewicz, the thematic, ideological and stylistic similarities between their works were so striking, that he began his essay on the early films of Skolimowski with the description of Marek Arens, the main character of *Disneyland*: 'Marek is a long distance runner. He achieved serious international successes. But he is fragile and his sporting career is uneven. "Przegląd Sportowy" [a popular sports journal] calls him a chameleon of the track. Previously he was a boxer' (Jackiewicz 1983: 381). Jackiewicz finishes with the sentence: 'This is not *Walkover* by Skolimowski. This is *Disneyland* by Dygat' (ibid.). Indeed, the description of Marek Arens perfectly fits Andrzej Leszczyc. For this reason I propose to look in more detail into Arens's life and persona, as well as other aspects of *Disneyland*. Not only should they reveal similarities between Dygat and Skolimowski, but also help to guess Leszczyc's past and future (about which we learn very little from the films) and to fill some of the gaps the director left in his films.

Apart from sport, Arens is interested in women; women and sport practically fill his life, which can also be said about Leszczyc in *Walkover*. Arens sleeps or at least flirts with many women, but his relationships lack passion and commitment. He believes that his true and only love is Jowita, whom he saw only once at a costume ball, when she was in the guise of a Muslim woman. After this incident he meets Agnieszka, who appears very similar to the pretty stranger from the ball, but claims to be Jowita's best friend. Although Arens is attracted to Agnieszka, he is unable to commit to her, being obsessed by Jowita. Jowita is really Arens's mental construction, although built from some 'tangible' elements. The novel finishes when Agnieszka reveals to Arens that she was, in fact, Jowita. For him, however, this information comes too late, as Agnieszka is about to marry another man.

Arens's erotic trials and tribulations are similar to those of Leszczyc in the sense that for both characters women appear not individually but in a sequence. No girl is truly unique for them because the value of none of them is intrinsic, but results from her relationship to another girl, real or, more likely, imaginary and her ability to fulfil his desire (which is both sexual and non-sexual). The non-uniqueness of women, as Iwona Kurz observes, is reflected in *Disneyland* in the use of the plural when discussing women, as in the sentence 'Women cry when they do what they decided not to do' (Kurz 2005: 170). Men, by contrast, are not met with such sweeping generalisations. Arens's main dilemma, whether to choose between the familiar Agnieszka or the mysterious Jowita, excellently illustrates Freudian, and even more so Lacanian, ideas about sexuality and love: love as a sustained relationship or feeling is impossible. This is because, as Elizabeth Grosz puts it in her feminist reading of Lacan

> The woman can be man's object of desire in so far as she 'veils' the 'mysteries' for which he searches, only, that is, in so far as her 'lack' is veiled or hidden. He desires conquest of these mysteries initiating a cycle of desire and frustration: if his conquest is successful, its mystery vanishes and the object loses its fascination. This may lead to frustration or disappointment and a sense of betrayal for not living up to his image of her. The nearer satisfaction comes, the more impossible is its attainment … His 'exploration', 'contest' and 'appropriation' of her enigma forces him to confront the question of

castration. This is why, even if the man distinguishes two types of women, one, an alter-ego he respects but who holds no mystery for him; the other, a phallus, object of fascination and desire, the latter collapses into the former after a period of close familiarity. His sexual partner becomes more an object of affection than of desire after sustained intimacy. Then his desire diverges to another woman, and the cycle starts again. (Grosz 1990: 136–37)

However, Arens reaches the point where he cannot accept that the 'two sexes love a phase apart', which he expresses by such words: 'I cannot stand any more that in my life women first mean everything for me and then mean nothing, that first I say the most saintly words to them and then lies. I cannot stand this lack of loyalty to everybody and everything because this is lack of loyalty to myself' (Dygat 1975: 85). The last sentence is crucial because it links a stable identity with a stable relationship with a woman. Accordingly, Arens promises Agnieszka that she will be the last woman in his life, and when she leaves him, revealing to him Jowita's identity, he is devastated; his identity shattered. Leszczyc never reaches this painful stage. Like a butterfly, he moves freely from one female 'flower' to another. Women are transient to him, therefore their disappearance does not shatter his identity.

From the fact that Arens's life revolves around women, we should not derive that he is 'female friendly'. His fascination with Jowita and his attraction to Agnieszka is accompanied by hatred and contempt for most women. He regards them as whores and is especially contemptuous of older women, who seduce and control men, such as the woman who drove his previous coach to suicide. Again, we find a similar attitude to older women in Skolimowski's films (see Chapter 2). However, while the director limits himself to presenting the status quo, Dygat suggests that his young character's sexist attitude to women is a consequence of his childhood. Arens's self-description begins with the sentence: 'My father was a complete bungler' (ibid.: 9). Dygat's protagonist has even less good to say about his mother. He describes her as a jealous, tyrannical and egocentric person, and suggests that she never loved him, only performed on him the rituals of motherly love. Moreover, she betrayed Arens's father with another man. Arens thus loathes women because they remind him of his mother and the more they remind him of her (the older and more promiscuous they are), the more he loathes them. At the same time, his resentment of his mother and the lack of any memories of maternal comfort are the cause of his obsessive search for the ideal woman.

Does Leszczyc and other Skolimowski characters hate older women and desperately search for the female ideal because of their inadequate relationship with their mothers? Although such an interpretation amounts to reading into the film what was not written, it can be supported by some episodes, such as the telephone conversation Leszczyc has with his mother in *Identification Marks: None*, in which she comes across as somebody whom he fears rather than loves, or his admission in *Walkover* that he never had a house. We can also support it by the director's accounts of his life, in which his mother features mostly as an absent figure.

Although Arens prefers his father(s) than his mother, his description of them is by no means flattering. Father figures are present in his life more than his mother, but they are negative models, making the son aware of what he does not want to become. Arens's natural father did not even want to mould him in his own image, but tried to make his son as different from him as possible, therefore he forced him to do sport, especially disciplines which allowed the boy to defend himself, such as boxing. Yet because sport was imposed on him, Arens lacks passion for sport and does it for trivial reasons, such as being popular with girls or out of loyalty to his coaches. On the whole, Arens feels that his fathers' weakness is partly his own, therefore his derision of them is accompanied by self-mockery. Not only does he mock his father and stepfather, but practically all men he encounters. For him all of them grow old before growing up, which he fears will be his fate too. As for him, he claims that he would like to live differently, to sacrifice his life for some noble goal. But it is not easy to find such a goal in peace time and even if it were possible, Dygat leaves some doubt as to whether his protagonist would be able to take advantage of this opportunity. Again, these opinions and concerns are similar to those experienced by Leszczyc. He also disrespects older men and would like to be a hero, do something extraordinary, but lacks the passion.

Apart from the characters, the works of Dygat and Skolimowski are linked by the way they are narrated and their emotional tone. *Disneyland* is told in the first person; it is Arens's story, just as *Identification Marks: None* and *Walkover* come across as Leszczyc's stories, not only in the sense of being concerned with his life, but also presenting his point of view. Moreover, there is a certain nostalgia or melancholia in all of them. In *Disneyland*, it is a consequence of the novel's form: a retrospective in which the male protagonist muses on his life, especially his lost opportunity of loving and living with Agnieszka.

Identification Marks: None and *Walkover* are set in the present, but this present feels as if it is already past. This is because Leszczyc is aware that soon he will be somewhere else and little will remain of what he is currently experiencing. There is also a certain irony in the works of both authors. As Aleksander Jackiewicz observes, *Disneyland* is simultaneously lyrical and ironic (see Jackiewicz 1983: 320). Irony, which is mainly self-irony, results from Arens telling us not only how he sees himself, but also how other people perceive him. Their opinions appear more important to him than his own self-image, therefore he wants to be faithful to a woman as she can offer him a mirror in which he can see a coherent reflection of himself. Secondly, he looks at himself through the prism of popular culture, chiefly American cinema, as a minor or grotesque version of his heroes, for example, as a caricature of Gregory Peck.[2] The importance of other people in Arens's self-perception is also transmitted by the motif of putting on a mask, of pretending to be somebody else. On the one hand, the mask hides features of which its owner is ashamed, on the other, it helps avoid being imprisoned in stereotypes. Putting on a mask is ultimately a sign of Arens's weaknesses. The mask is his armour; without it he would be naked or perhaps not exist at all.

There is also irony in *Identification Marks: None* and *Walkover*, although it is used more sparingly. Leszczyc is critical of himself, for example when he explains to the military draft board why he chose to study ichthyology, but his words can be taken at face value. The previously quoted verse, which accompanies Leszczyc's peregrinations, is ironical, because it points to a gap between the protagonist's intentions and results. We can also talk about visual irony (see Chapter 3). Interestingly, in *Identification Marks: None* and *Walkover*, Leszczyc does not compare himself to cinematic characters and certainly not to any popular American heroes. On the whole, there is more irony in Dygat's novel, more lyricism in Skolimowski's films.

Both Marek and Leszczyc can be construed as post-romantic and Hamletian characters. They are post-romantic because they gaze nostalgically at the times when 'men were men': fought in wars and conquered women. Moreover, sport, as I argued previously (see Chapter 2) might be seen as their attempt to live romantically in un-romantic, thwarted times. Narcissism, relentless introspection and, connected with them, an inability to act decisively, on the other hand, link them to Hamlet. Like Hamlet, Arens and Leszczyc are also fatherless men, who try to come to terms with this condition.

Disneyland was screened in 1967 by Janusz Morgenstern under the title *Jowita*. Although I regard this film as successful in many ways, I agree with the critics who consider it as an unfaithful representation of Dygat's work (see, for example, Jackiewicz 1983: 319–21). The main difference between these two texts concerns the construction of the main character and the mode of narration. In Morgenstern's film, Arens is played by Daniel Olbrychski, at the time already a major star of Polish cinema and a decade later its greatest male star. Unlike the 'opaque' Leszczyc, Olbrychski's Arens lacks any of the self-doubt or fragility with which Dygat imbued his character. Instead he gives the impression of being a strong man who knows very well what he wants from life and how to get it. Secondly, Morgenstern's narration, despite preserving the form of a retrospective, comes across as objective. We look at Arens from outside, never being privy to his musing on women, family and himself. Actually, such a mode of narration suits the actor; as an introspective Arens, Olbrychski would be ridiculous or at least unbelievable.

The connection between *Disneyland* and early Skolimowski films is probably more visible now than at the time these works were created. This results from the fact that the type of characters we find in them practically disappeared from the Polish screen and literature in the next decade. They were replaced by rougher men and women, who did not greet their college colleagues with 'Sir' or 'Miss', and did not search for the intangible goal of identity, but used coarse language and strove for career, high social position and money. Roughness and greed dominate the behaviour of the protagonists of the stories of such popular writers and scriptwriters of the 1970s as Janusz Głowacki and Ireneusz Iredyński, and of the Cinema of Moral Concern that followed the Third Cinema of Skolimowski, Majewski and Kluba. This change was also reflected in visual style: the poeticism and surrealism of the Third Cinema gave way to the 'coarse' realism of *Wodzirej* (*Dance Leader*, 1977) by Feliks Falk, *Aktorzy prowincjonalni* (*Provincial Actors*, 1978) by Agnieszka Holland or Wajda's *Bez znieczulenia* (*Rough Treatment*, 1978).

I shall finish this section by mentioning that the last time Dygat is evoked in Skolimowski's films is in *Ferdydurke*. His wife, Kalina Jędrusik, plays the wife of Professor Filidor. Although her role is very small, it is symbolic for the continuous attachment of Skolimowski to Dygat and his world.

Skid, or the Missing Link

In the 1970s, Skolimowski made no films in Poland, but one of his scripts, *Skid,* was adapted by Jan Łomnicki, a respected director with a background as a documentarist, yet without any distinctive style as a feature film maker. *Skid* is one of Łomnicki's better films, as testified by the main award at Karlovy Vary, although in Poland the director was accused of creating it out of clichés and conveying his messages too bluntly (see Oleksiewicz 1972; Jackiewicz 1983: 359). Probably the most distinctive feature of the film and the main reason for its relative success is the camerawork of Zygmunt Samosiuk, the most talented Polish cinematographer of the 1970s and one of the best Polish cinema ever had, who died in 1983, at the age of only forty-three years. Among Samosiuk's other works are Andrzej Wajda's *Krajobraz po bitwie* (*Landscape after the Battle,* 1970), Walerian Borowczyk's *Dzieje grzechu* (*Story of a Sin,* 1975) and, most importantly, Janusz Morgenstern's *Trzeba zabić tę miłość* (*To Kill This Love,* 1972), which was shot the same year as *Skid* and bears many similarities with Łomnicki's film. Samosiuk's very mobile camera gives the impression of catching the stream of reality, with all its ugly sides, such as streets full of worn-out, unglamorous people, dingy bars and restaurants, run-down houses and small garages on the outskirts, operating in the grey economy. At the same time, it captures the new, consumerist Poland of department stores where one can buy such luxuries as foreign cosmetics (the advert of Old Spice aftershave accompanies the protagonist's search for one of his ex-girlfriends) and an affluent driver has a miniature television set installed in his car. This Poland, unlike the Poland in Skolimowski's films made in the 1960s, is shot in colour, although Samosiuk uses a limited palette, in which shades of green and grey dominate, to underscore the harshness and monotony of 'real socialism'.

Marek, the main character in *Skid,* has much in common with his 'ancestors' in *Identification Marks, Walkover* and *Barrier,* because he is also a drifter (see Skwara 1972: 4; Jackiewicz 1983: 359). We learn that he is a student, but on the verge of being expelled from the university. He earns some money by taking photographs and selling them to newspapers, but his income is not sufficient. He lives in a dingy room rented from an old woman, in a ruined tenement block. We can derive from conversations with his landlady that she does not like him to invite female friends to his room, but he ignores her disapproval. Erotic conquests are, in fact, his main achievements; women fall easily to his boyish charm but his relationships do not last.

However, unlike Leszczyc, who has the courage to own up to his failures, as demonstrated by his talks with the draftee board, Marek is unable to admit to himself or anybody else that he did not succeed. When people point out to him his shortcomings, he reacts aggressively, blaming others for his own mistakes. He is also prepared to use others, including women, to support his freewheeling style. What in Leszczyc could be seen as romanticism, in Marek is only irresponsibility. Another reason why Marek cannot be classified as a romantic is his utter materialism, epitomised by his desire to acquire a car, which he pursues ruthlessly. His only redeeming feature is his sincere love for a married nurse, but it is difficult to say whether it is a lasting feeling or only a temporary infatuation, because his attempt to gain her heart by acquiring a car and driving it like a rally driver leads to her death.

The features which distinguish Marek from Leszczyc can be regarded as pertaining to the times when *Skid* is set, namely the 1970s, the period when Edward Gierek was the leader of the Party. It was 'the decade of the propaganda of success', when Poland for the first time in its postwar history opened itself up to Western influences that, paradoxically, helped lay bare the inadequacies of the country's economy, politics and culture. In the 1970s, the ideals of socialism, such as social equality and collective effort, if not altogether forgotten, played a smaller role in official discourses. Similarly, the memory of the war, which haunted the characters of Skolimowski's films in the 1960s, faded. War became a 'boring' subject and even war films were shunned by the younger viewers. On the whole, the 1970s was the most un-ideological decade in postwar Poland and, understandably, this period is remembered primarily for its focus on private life and materialism. Partly because of the propaganda and partly because of the real successes of some sections of the population, young people believed that it was possible to achieve success relatively easily. Marek's attempt to get a car perfectly illustrates this belief, which in his case proves not only naïve but disastrous. Similarly, his attempt to gain identity and a place in society through a woman can be regarded as symbolic for the times in which *Skid* is set.

Even if we make allowances for the fact that *Skid* is set in 'Gierek's Poland' rather than 'Gomułka's Poland', it strikes one as very different from Skolimowski's own films, both those he made in Poland and abroad. To begin with, Jan Englert, the actor playing Marek, although full of energy and frantic, does not come across as youthful. Moreover, he lacks the enigma or opaqueness which Skolimowski's Leszczyc displayed (see Chapter 1) or even Nowicki's charisma, which furnished the protagonist of *Barrier* with a darkish charm. Consequently, Marek is a less interesting and sympathetic character than Leszczyc. Englert's later career, including in Łomnicki's films, such as *Wielka wsypa* (*Botched Job*, 1992) and *Szczur* (*Rat*, 1994) or the popular comedy *Kiler* (1997) by Juliusz Machulski, reinforced and developed his image as a selfish and shallow man, who would sacrifice everything and everybody to enrich himself materially. As Janusz Skwara testifies, Łomnicki also expanded and changed the role of Halina, the nurse with whom Marek falls in love. Like many women in Skolimowski's films, she is a 'working woman', having an affair with a young drifter. Yet, unlike previous Skolimowski women, she does not encapsulate materialism or conformity to the dominant ideology, but reveals decency, even idealism, which the male character is missing. She does not care about Marek's car or any consumer goods he can offer her and becomes a victim of his materialist ambitions. *Skid* is also Łomnicki's rather than Skolimowski's film, because of its smooth narration and lack of ambiguity – it is a realistic film through and through. The only trace of double meaning is created by Skolimowski himself, who plays the owner of a garage, watching on television as Polish ski jumper, Wojciech Fortuna, wins the Olympic gold medal, which can be read as an allusion to his interests in sport and his ambition to be a winner on the international arena. *Skid* demonstrates that Leszczyc, as we know him, would, in 1970s cinema, come across as an anachronism and be more of an outsider than he ever was. All in all, *Skid* can be regarded as a film that somehow prolongs the Polish chapter of Skolimowski's career, linking this director with Polish cinema of the 1970s. At the same time, it points to the fact that in this period he was, literally and metaphorically, elsewhere and knew Poland mostly from television.

Between Arthur Conan Doyle and Joseph Conrad

The Adventures of Gerard, based on the book by Arthur Conan Doyle, is Skolimowski's first 'proper' adaptation and the first film made after the banning of *Hands Up!* It was a strange choice for this director, who by then did not have any costume or historical films in his portfolio, or even films based on scripts not written by himself. It also has the reputation of his lesser work. This opinion is reinforced by the director, who claims that he embarked on this project completely unprepared, having no training in making 'ordinary' films and being spoilt by the film's high budget (see Uszyński 1990a: 21–23; Smader and Demidowicz 2004: 107). The problems were apparently so huge that the film was on the verge of being taken away from Skolimowski by its producer. It was rescued by Claudia Cardinale, who played the main female part. Cardinale announced that if Skolimowski was fired, she would leave the film as well (see Uszyński 1990a: 22–23; Lichocka 1994: 8). The actress had reasons to defend the director, because her role of Teresa, Countess de Morales, not only perfectly suited her type of feisty southern woman, but also allowed her to surpass it by exhibiting qualities normally ascribed to men, such as bravery, lack of sentimentality and an absurd sense of humour.

I do not intend to argue that *The Adventures of Gerard* is a masterpiece, but find it accomplished according to the criteria of a specific film genre, in this case a parody of an adventure film. It sustains its fast rhythm from beginning to end and comes across as coherent, therefore easy to follow, in spite of being packed with characters and events. This is a remarkable achievement, as Conan Doyle's *The Adventures of Gerard* is fragmented, with each chapter taking place in a different corner of Europe, devoted to a different story and different characters, and united only by the protagonist, Colonel Etienne Gerard. Moreover, contrary to the director's claim that the film was spoilt by its large budget, it looks as if the money was spent rather well. The costumes shine, the scenes of battles and pursuits are handled professionally and the setting is rich in decorative detail. Again, it should be complimented, as the setting had to be invented: Conan Doyle's book is poor in picturesque description, as a consequence of its mode of narration. Gerard, who is the book's narrator, is so preoccupied with depicting his own adventures that he pays little attention to the wider world. In addition, the film is well played, especially by Peter McEnery as Gerard and the previously mentioned Cardinale. In Tom Milne's opinion:

> The fatuous Gerard, constantly confiding his self-esteem in asides to the camera, could all too easily become a stock comic caricature, *Carry On* style, but in Peter McEnery's characterisation he emerges, enchantingly, as the

perfect embodiment of Conan Doyle's Hussar of Conflans, gay-riding, plume-tossing, debonair, the darling of the ladies and of the six brigades of light cavalry. Entering every hazardous engagement with an insouciant twitch of his moustachios, and exiting on horseback with right hand on hip in a gesture of supremely nonchalant insolence, McEvery gives a perfectly calculated performance. (Milne 1971: 3)

Indeed, although we laugh at Gerard, it is not a contemptuous sneer, but rather a sympathetic giggle, in which amusement with the grenadier's cockiness is mixed with admiration for his bravery, commitment to serve his leader and his country, optimism and good luck. We find many of these features in Don Quixote and this association is strengthened by the setting of the film in the vast deserts of Spain. Gerard also recollects Cervantes's hero because, as Carlos Fuentes writes in regards to Don Quixote, 'he leaves his village, goes out into the world, and discovers that the world does not resemble what he has read about it' (Fuentes 1988: 49).

Skolimowski's attitude to the lucky Colonel, although inherited from Conan Doyle, can also be regarded as the director's own. He subtly conveyed this attitude in his films about Leszczyc, as well as off-screen. Gerard possesses what Leszczyc admires in Polish war heroes: their heroism and readiness to die and, at the same time, he lacks what he despises in them: their tendency to suffer and lose. Comparison with previous Skolimowski films is invited, especially in the episode

Figure 4.1 Skolimowski and his actors during shooting of *The Adventures of Gerard*

when the brave Colonel asks a fellow hussar to wound him, so that he can show off his scars, as so far he has remained uninjured, having emerged unscathed from every battle. 'False scars' also appear in Skolimowski's films, but they result from the old men's attempt to ascribe to themselves experiences which were not their own and in this way be seen as more heroic than they really were.

Gerard's limited intelligence can be seen as his asset, because it prevents him from excessive introspection and forces him to find practical solutions to problems encountered. Besides, both in Conan Doyle's rendering and Skolimowski's re-working, Gerard turns out to have more wit than people are prepared to grant him. One of the chapters of the book, 'How the Brigadier Captured Saragossa', is devoted to the Colonel's triumph over his new army companions, who at first laugh at his boastful stories, only to find out that he is indeed braver and luckier than they (see Conan Doyle 2004: 40–69). At the end of this chapter the mocking tone gives way to a true pathos. In the film, Gerard also proves to be more perceptive and imaginative than his peers and superiors grant him. For instance, he notices that the handsome young man whom he encounters is in fact a woman but sustains the game of disguise. He is also able to overcome the dilemma 'motherland or woman', which poisoned the lives of Polish romantic heroes, by using the simple formula 'motherland first but, when possible, women too', and on his way to fulfilling his military duties he takes advantage of any available women. It can even be suggested that his profession as a soldier allows him to enjoy the pleasures of the female body more than if he were a civilian. This is because brothels await soldiers in every village they pass, young women are used as tools to extract military information from them and men are forgiven for raping the daughters and sisters of their enemies. Besides, wars do not last forever, therefore women can wait for their sweethearts. This truth is revealed at the end of the film, when Gerard receives a medal from Napoleon and Teresa agrees to wait for him while he goes in search of further adventures and glory.

Skolimowski's focus on an indestructible hero of the kind we find in comic books does not exclude his recognition of the cruelty of war. However, he acknowledges it by using his trademark black humour, which in this case brings associations with Monty Python productions. For example, in one scene Gerard is told that the hostile army buried his companion and when he thanks them for what looks like a humanitarian act, he is informed that the man was buried alive. In another scene Gerard's beloved Teresa uses a huge axe to torture a man from the enemy's side. Although the victim appears to be more interested in kissing his tortureress than alleviating his suffering, we learn that in the end he died. War is not only cruel, but also absurd; its victors and victims are chosen at random. A perfect example of its absurdity is the destruction of a castle not due to military attack or conspiracy, but thanks to pure chance – Teresa's blind uncle throwing a cigar butt on the ammunition dump.

Despite such images, *The Adventures of Gerard*, as Tom Milne notes, 'is not saddled with self-conscious contemporary messages as it was in, say, *Waterloo* or *The Charge of the Light Brigade*' (Milne 1971:3). It is even difficult to situate the director's attitude to war on the scale militarism–pacifism. The only clear idea we get is that war, as presented by Skolimowski, is a fact of life, from which nobody can remain aloof. And when it takes place, the only victor is the one who kills his enemies, saves his life and wins the girl.

Captain Miller, the main character in *The Lightship*, based on a novella by the German author Siegfried Lenz, can be regarded as the character most contrasting to Colonel Gerard that Skolimowski ever created, because he opposes using arms, even when it appears to be the best solution to a problem, which in this case is defeating a band of criminals invading his ship. In Lenz's book, where Miller's prototype is called Freytag, his motives are clearly articulated. They derive from his desire to preserve his own life and those he is responsible for, distaste of violence, a wish to fulfil his everyday duties and contempt for heroism, which in Freytag's view results from egotism (as was largely the case of Gerard). These motives are conveyed in the answer, given by Freytag to his son, when he accuses him of cowardice:

> You know nothing. So long as you imagine that the only course open to an unarmed man is to argue with gun muzzles I don't give a damn for what you know. I'll tell you something, lad. I have never been a hero and I don't want to become a martyr; both of those types have always seemed very suspect to me: they died too easily and even in death they were still certain of their cause – too certain, I think, and that is no solution. I have known men who died in order to settle something. They settled nothing, they left everything behind. Their death helped them but nobody else. A man with no weapons and no power still has more chance than a dead man, and I often think that behind this desire to offer oneself at any price to the muzzle of a gun lies the worst egotism. (Lenz 1986: 65)

Freytag's utterance resonates especially in the original, German context of the novel, set only ten years after the end of the Second World War. By opposing the use of arms, Freytag, with whom the author sympathises, implicitly criticises German militarism, which originated in the worst type of egotism, revealed by Hitler and his followers, led to the Second World War and was disastrous for everybody concerned, including Germany. Yet by moving the action of *The Lightship* from the Baltic coast to the coast of Virginia and changing all the characters into Americans, Skolimowski obliterated any pacifist message transmitted by the original setting. Moreover, as Peter Christensen observes, in the film these crucial words are never said, therefore Miller's motives are more difficult to fathom (see Christensen 1990: 89). As I argued in Chapter 2, on the whole, Miller emerges from the events as a stronger and more victorious character than his chief adversary, Calvin Caspary. Yet his heroism can be appreciated only at the end of the film and even then it is more subdued than in the novel. For example, unlike Lenz, Skolimowski does not make clear in the film that Miller's procrastinating amounts to a coherent strategy of getting the intruders into a position from which they will not be able to escape, but he creates an impression that Miller has no strategy at all and his crew's enforced cohabitation with Caspary and his henchmen might be permanent.

The 'clouding' of Miller's psychology and morality might result from external factors, especially Skolimowski's dislike of the actor cast in this role, Klaus Maria Brandauer (see Chapter 2). His attempt to strip Miller of some of the glory with which his equivalent was furnished by Lenz might also derive from the director's ambiguous attitude to the general situation represented in the book. This ambiguity used to be explained by critics and the director himself by reference to the work of Joseph Conrad, whom Skolimowski lists as an important source of inspiration for a number of his films. As he puts it, 'There [in *Lightship*] are similarities to Joseph Conrad's *Victory*, which is something I've always wanted to do. Maybe the geographical situation of Poland makes people specialists in those kinds of issues. *Victory* has been a project of mine for fifteen, twenty years now, so in a way I could make use of the Conradian philosophy which I'd been accumulating on *The Lightship*. Robert Duvall is almost like Mr Jones in *Victory*, although Lenz had already described that character pretty well', and adds 'Conrad should be counted too [as one of the writers of his film], so we have seven writers involved in the whole thing' (Combs 1986: 133).

If *Victory* is the main perspective from which to look at *The Lightship*, then we should ask what links these two literary works, or Skolimowski's interpretation of them. One, as Christensen observes, is the choice of characters. Conrad's Alex Heyst, like Freytag and Miller, lives on the periphery of 'real life', in this case in Samburan in the East Indies, in near solitude and inactivity as the manager of a collapsed enterprise with a grandiose name, the 'Tropical Belt Coal Company'.

The second similarity between Conrad and Lenz's novels, and Skolimowski's film, is the motif, very common in Conrad's other works, of some past deed, regarded as infamous, that tarnishes the current reputation of the character. He is wrongly accused or blames himself for crimes which he did not commit or could not prevent. In *Victory*, Heyst's adversary, the owner of a dingy hotel named Schomberg, spreads the rumour that Heyst is responsible for the death of Morrison, his business partner and a man whom in reality Heyst helped in a moment of crisis, when Morrison was about to lose his brig. The horrible accusation that 'Heyst turned hermit from shame' (Conrad 1973: 39) comes to obsess Heyst, making him believe that he did indeed play a part in Morrison's demise. In Lenz's novel, Freytag also lives under the shadow of an apparently shameful act committed during the war, of not saving the life of his comrade Natzmer, who was taken prisoner by the Greeks. Unlike in the case of Heyst, who did not commit the act attributed to him (Morrison died a natural death when he was visiting his native England), Freytag indeed did not save Natzmer nor even try to save him. However, he claims that he did not try because he had no chance of succeeding. Although his own son does not accept this explanation, it is presented by Lenz as entirely convincing. Finally, Miller is accused of abandoning the crew of an American military ship attacked by an enemy submarine. It is true that he did not rescue his comrades, but not because he could not do it, but because he decided to follow the enemy ship and then there was no time to rescue the attacked crew. Unlike Freytag, who drew the only reasonable conclusion under the circumstances, Miller faced a profound dilemma (see

Christensen 1990: 90–91). Not surprisingly, after the war Miller was put on trial and, although he was cleared, his career did not progress. His position as captain of the lightship might be taken as a legacy of this unfortunate war episode. Although the moral position of each of the three men is quite different, they are similar in the sense that rumours of their dishonourable behaviour keep them on the defensive and affect their future choices. They have to prove themselves, which they do, and ultimately they achieve a moral victory. But again, Miller's victory is most blurred; he pays the heaviest price, not only with his own life but also with that of one of his people, for what can be regarded as the smallest triumph.

Conrad's novel finishes with Heyst's lover perishing and his own suicide, which renders its title, *Victory*, problematic. It can be regarded as ironic, matching the mocking tone with which the author treats Heyst's 'nirvana' (see Cox 1974: 130). More often, however, the title is regarded as serious, relating to the alleged victory of the characters who, in their death, proved that for them love matters more than life. This exaltation of lofty values over more tangible goods, including the gift of life, can be explained by Conrad's Polish background, the tragic history of his country and even of his family. His father, the impoverished poet Apollo Korzeniowski, who can be described as a typical Polish romantic, was arrested in 1861 and exiled to Vologda in the north of Russia for belonging to an anti-Czarist revolutionary organisation. The punishment led to the premature death of both of Joseph Conrad's parents (see Miłosz 1982: 44). For people such as Apollo Korzeniowski and all Poles living under partition, there were no other victories than moral. As Conrad himself wrote in a letter to an English friend, Edward Garnett: 'You seem to forget that I am a Pole. You forget that we have been used to go to battle without illusions. It's you British that "go in to win" only. We have been "going in" these last hundred years repeatedly, to be knocked on the head' (Conrad, in Karl and Davies 1988: 492). However, Maria Janion maintains that Conrad transformed Polish (collective) experience into an existential (individual) experience (see Janion 1998: 264–65). Czesław Miłosz, on the other hand, claims that 'The Poles sought support in Conrad for a desperate and gratuitous heroism, and they tried to imitate those of his characters who embodied a fateful loyalty to a lost cause' (Miłosz 1982: 44).[3] Drawing on these opinions, I suggest that Conrad's *Victory* is a product of such a metamorphosis of Polish, collective experience into universal and individual experience which, in due course, becomes perceived by Poles, including Skolimowski, as 'theirs'. The issue of moral victory features prominently in many other Skolimowski's films, but the director's attitude towards it changed over the years. In *Walkover*, Leszczyc loses to a man whom he previously beat through a walkover, but it is depicted as his moral victory. By standing up to a stronger opponent he proves his courage and willingness to act. As he says in the film, he does not want to give away his life in a walkover. Marc in *Le Départ* also achieves some kind of moral victory by giving up his childish dream about racing cars. Of course, in each of these cases moral victory is at the expense of real victory. Gerard, as was previously established, does not know what moral victory is and all the characters in *The Adventures of Gerard* are neatly divided into real winners and losers. A different situation altogether is depicted in *Success Is the Best*

Revenge, where moral victory matters a lot to the Rodaks. Adam Rodak, in particular, wants to fight and sacrifice himself for Poland (see Chapter 2). However, this romantic concept is mocked by Skolimowski within the diegesis and off-screen. In an interview with Richard Combs he says, 'The title is a pure irony, of course. I don't think the characters involved in that film have any chance of success. So the bitterness of the title is that they will never have their revenge. They are all losers' (Combs 1986: 134).

In other words, due to making the most romantic and, in a sense, the most unsuccessful film of his career, Skolimowski became much more negative about 'moral victories' than when he made *Walkover*. He learnt that only an actual victory, measured in money and external recognition, matters. 'Moral victory' is no more than a polite description of defeat. Armed with this opinion Skolimowski was less willing than ever to appreciate characters such as Miller, for whom it is enough to enjoy the conviction that he is right and who does not bother to convince anyone else about his rightness.

In his perceptive essay on Skolimowski's *The Lightship*, Peter Christensen draws attention to an additional feature which links Skolimowski's with Conrad's work, simultaneously differentiating it from Lenz's novel, namely the presence of homosexual motives. Caspary is a homosexual dandy, as is Mr Jones in Conrad's *Victory*. Homosexual attraction is negatively depicted in these works, as castrating and degrading (see Christensen 1990: 92). I entirely agree with this interpretation but, again, would like to offer a 'Polish key' to explaining Conrad and Skolimowski's homophobia. I believe that it derives from Polish culture, marked by extreme militarism, nationalism and, connected with them, the extolling of masculine environments and activities, such as fighting wars and partaking in uprisings. As I argued elsewhere, extreme homosocial pressure is usually accompanied by homophobia, to compensate for the danger of the emergence of homosexuality (see Mazierska 2008).

The final link between Skolimowski and Conrad, not only his *Victory*, but practically all his work, is the aura of foreboding, which in Conrad's work is conveyed by using as the narrator somebody who views the events from a distance of many years, when nothing can be changed and the main dramatis personae are dead. In *The Lightship*, an ominous effect is created by using as the narrator Alex's son, who recounts his father's story when the father is already dead. By contrast, narration in Lenz's book is objective. Again, the aura of foreboding and the utter pessimism permeating Conrad's work can be linked to his Polish, romantic heritage with its 'culture of disaster'. Yet, as the previously quoted Janion observes, 'Historical evil in the novels of Conrad takes the shape of existential evil' (Janion 1998: 264). If this is the case, the metaphorical ancestors of the intruders in *Victory* and Skolimowski's *The Lightship* are the countries which invaded and destroyed Poland.

Although Colonel Gerard and Captain Miller mark two poles of Skolimowski's characters (passivity–activity, real victory–moral victory, life–death), they have something important in common – they are both nonconformists. Each of them single-mindedly follows his own goal, paying no attention to circumstances and others' opinions. Gerard's enthusiasm and urge to act, combined with his foolhardiness, makes him similar to Don Quixote. Miller's reflexivity and apparent passivity links him to Hamlet. The way the director treats these characters suggests that he would like to synthesise their virtues and surpass their shortcomings. However, so far it has not happened either in his original work or his adaptations.

Skolimowski and Nabokov

In the foreword to *King, Queen, Knave*, Vladimir Nabokov includes this passage: 'One might readily conjecture that a Russian writer in choosing a set of exclusively German characters was creating for himself insurmountable difficulties. I spoke no German, had no German friends, had not read a single German novel either in original, or in translation. But in art, as in nature, a glaring disadvantage may turn out to be a subtle protective device' (Nabokov 1970: 7). Further in the foreword, Nabokov explains that the 'disadvantageous advantage' of setting his work in an unknown territory was a 'fairytale freedom' in creating characters and milieu, and allowing the author emotional detachment from the characters (ibid.). Yet some critics argue that *King, Queen, Knave* 'is, in a way, a realistic portrayal of the Russian émigré's way of *not* seeing the natives of the countries into which he had happened to fall except as celluloid or cardboard figures' (Field 1967: 158). If this is the case, it can serve as a model for all artists finding themselves in a position similar to Nabokov's, namely émigrés unfamiliar with their new environment.

I do not know whether Skolimowski read Nabokov's introduction but it seems to me that he adhered to the same recipe Nabokov used in his novel, by giving in to

Figure 4.2 Gina Lollobrigida and Jerzy Skolimowski during shooting of *King, Queen, Knave*

the writer's desire for pure invention, exhibiting utter detachment from the characters and avoiding the temptation to insert into the story any obvious moral lesson. Paraphrasing Nabokov, of all Skolimowski's films 'this bright brute' is the gayest and at the same time the coldest, if not cruellest film in his portfolio. Consequently, of all his adaptations, I will regard *King, Queen, Knave* as simultaneously the most faithful to the literary original and the most 'his own'. Skolimowski achieved what can be regarded as the Holy Grail of adaptation, largely by conveying the book's sense of absurd and irony, but through different means.

Nabokov's absurdism derives mainly from the disparity between characters' self-perceptions and the way others see them. In his book practically everybody lives a solipsistic life because his/her self-image does not match that of others. Martha regards Dreyer as utterly dull and therefore repulsive. Dreyer, on the other hand, regards himself as the opposite of Martha's image of him, as a kind of artist, whose main pleasure in life is manipulating other people. His willingness to invest in the production of automatons is a sign of this desire for invention and manipulation. Moreover, he likes financial risk and does not care much about money. At the same time, he believes Martha to be frigid, which he treats as an insurance policy against her possible unfaithfulness. Yet Martha is not frigid at all, as proved by her passionate affair with Franz, which she initiates and in which she is the active side. Both Dreyer and Martha are also mistaken in their judgement of Franz. Dreyer takes him for a completely unimaginative, provincial boy and does not for a moment consider the possibility of him seducing Martha. Martha, on the other hand, not unlike Anna Karenina or Madame Bovary (see Clancy 1984: 27), construes Franz as the owner of all the positive qualities Dreyer is lacking and, blinded by her own passions, cannot conceive of Franz ever stopping loving her. Finally, for most of the narrative, Franz acts as a kind of screen, reflecting other people's opinions of him. He is clumsy in Dreyer's presence and passionate when visited by Martha. Only gradually does he begin to formulate opinions of his own and distance himself from both Martha (whom he starts to see as an ugly toad) and Dreyer.

Skolimowski, who lacked the novelist's means to convey characters' thoughts and decided not to use the first-person narration, nevertheless manages to transmit this sense of mistaken perceptions. This effect is largely achieved by accumulating chance encounters and various situations that reveal that the characters are clueless about each other's opinions. As a result, 'at first glance *King, Queen, Knave* seems to be no more than frivolous farce' (Milne 1973: 250), in which everybody is always in the wrong place at the wrong time. Another way to convey the inability to see correctly is through the motif of myopia. It exists in Nabokov's hypotext, but Skolimowski amplifies it by making Frank (who replaced Nabokov's Franz) more blind and clumsy than his literary 'ancestor'. However, it is not only Frank who is blind, but Dreyer too, for not seeing the obvious, missing what is in front of his eyes.

The director also enhances the absurd content of the novel by furnishing it with objects which have lives of their own or even conspire against people. I largely described their appearance and functions in the previous chapter. Here I only want to add that they signify the characters' detachment from each other and from themselves, their ultimate solipsism, despite living superficially social lives. The automatons, created by Professor Ritter, fit this description well, but we can also list here the boat which brings death to Martha. Skolimowski also manages to convey what can be described as the rhythm of the novel, which Nora Buhks compares to a waltz, claiming that Nabokov transposed it into the literary work at the level of the schema of the composition and the semantic structure. As Buhks observes,

> In daily life, and in comparison to it, dance appears linked to diversion, to play, and to artifice. It is a movement which is effected by means of a series of figures chosen in advance, appearing in a repetitive order ... In *King, Queen, Knave* the playful process becomes one of the dominant processes for the construction of the novel's structure, of the novel's universe, which is ostensibly offered to the reader as playing at life, at a certain level, and as playing at a novel, at another level ... Thus it is constantly emphasised that Dreyer plays at life, which basically for him is only a pleasant diversion; another example: the invention of the moving mannequins, playful imitation of creative nature; or the multiple variations of Dreyer's murder in the imaginations or conversations of the lovers and, finally, the novel's entire subject itself, presented to the reader; characters included; like the play of a mad old man who takes himself for the wizard Menetekelfares. (Buhks 1987)

Skolimowski mimics the novel's waltz-like rhythm by presenting the characters as if they were dancing, swirling and simultaneously both enjoying and suffering dizziness. Their movements are circular, presented from unusual angles and often unrealistically speeded up, as if they played in silent cinema. Moreover, his narrative develops through presenting us couples changing partners, as in a ball. First Martha dances with Dreyer, then with Frank, then Dreyer plays with his young female companions. The director even 'waltzes' further than Nabokov, by showing that the last couple in the game is constituted by Dreyer and Frank, who is about to inherit his uncle's fortune. Such a suggestion is not included in the novel, where Dreyer keeps his nephew in contempt till the end, and there is no chance that the youngster would inherit anything from his rich relative. This difference, however, does not result from Skolimowski's search for cinematic equivalents of the literary original, but rather from his different approach to certain issues and themes present in the novel. In particular, in this book Nabokov gives little thought to the issue of the relationship between younger and older generations. For Skolimowski, on the other hand, this topic, especially the relationship between younger and older men, is very important, therefore he twists the plot of *King, Queen, Knave* to elaborate it. For example, unlike Nabokov's Martha, who dies of pneumonia, the Martha in Skolimowski's film drowns in circumstances rendered ambiguous. Apart from making for a more 'cinematic' death, it is plausible to interpret the change as pointing to the possibility of the two men subconsciously contributing to her demise. Her 'disappearance from the picture' allows male friendship to blossom, as Frank and Dreyer demonstrate on their return from Martha's funeral, when they behave as if they were the best of friends. This scene, which has no equivalent in Nabokov's novel, harks back to the earlier films of this director, such as *Identification Marks: None* and *Walkover*, in which a young heterosexual man scorns the pleasures offered to him by women and chooses male company and masculine pursuits. To put it crudely, the director uses the material offered by Nabokov's novel to create an Oedipal story *à la* Skolimowski. In this story, Frank adopts the position of an Oedipus by sleeping with his uncle's wife, but rather than this leading to a mortal conflict between 'father' and 'son', it brings them closer. It could be suggested that Martha is a vehicle of Frank's maturation, which his uncle needs to ensure the successful future of his business. Her erotic (and economic) tutelage completes the young man's transition to his position as Dreyer's successor. She plays this role well and at the end of her education, Frank is indeed transformed, coming across as a self-confident young man, ready to free his uncle from the clutches of responsibility.

One striking feature of Nabokov's novel is the abundance of various literary and 'cinematic' moments, such as the characters' visits to the cinema or the building of a cinema theatre in close proximity to Franz's lodging. The new cinema is to show a filmed version of a successful play by Goldemar entitled *King, Queen, Knave*. These references can be seen as a way to underscore the parodic, artificial nature of Nabokov's characters (see Clancy 1984: 28). Denis Donoghue suggests that 'Perhaps the novel should be read as a form of literary criticism, since the incidents assume the presence of similar incidents in other books, standing between this new fiction and the begging world' (Donoghue 1982: 204). Conversely, the literary and cinematic references can be seen as increasing the novel's realism by choosing as its protagonists people who model themselves on popular culture. Skolimowski, however, chose to ignore them. In particular, he did not transfer to the film a scene in which Franz discovers that his landlord's wife in reality is 'only a grey wig stuck on a stick and a knitted shawl' (Nabokov 1970: 175). To include this scene would probably make his film look like a parody of or a homage to Hitchcock's *Psycho* (1960). It should be added that such avoidance is in tune with Skolimowski's overall approach to cinema, his unwillingness to be compared with other film makers.

In an interview given in 1990, Skolimowski described *King, Queen, Knave* as the worst film of his career and an artistic disaster from which he could not rise for a long time. He regards the main reason for his apparent downfall as his inability to translate Nabokov's text into film (see Uszyński 1990a: 27–28). In my opinion, the opposite is true; his *King, Queen, Knave* belongs to his best films and is perhaps the most accomplished adaptation of Nabokov's work.

The Shout, or Filling the Gaps

The Shout, based on a short story by Robert Graves, is listed not only as the most accomplished of Skolimowski's adaptations, but also one of the most successful movies of his career. It is also a film with which the director is particularly content, both with the way it was made and the overall result. Its success is not a surprise, as the literary original lends itself perfectly to the treatment of a director such as Skolimowski, who is happiest when working with a short story, so to speak, which allows him to fill the gaps with his own imagination and improvisation. Indeed, *The Shout* (not unlike *Barrier*), was conceived by Skolimowski practically as he went along (see Strick 1978: 147). The second attraction of Graves's prose Skolimowski describes as 'the ambiguity and the sense of absurd' (ibid.: 146). The director not only transmitted these features to his film but heightened them. His *The Shout* is also more thought-provoking than Graves's, thanks to elaborating certain themes which the writer only outlined. On the whole, his adaptation can be compared to endowing a skeleton with a well-developed body.

The story of Charles Crossley, a man who spent twenty years among Australian aborigines and his intrusion upon the lives of a bourgeois English couple, Anthony and Rachel Fielding, both in the literary version and in the film, is set against a cricket match. As William Johnson notes, this setting works better in the film, 'where even the briefest cutback presents the viewer with the full ironic contrast between the game code that more or less unites the players and the urgent private codes that compel some of them to run amuck' (Johnson 1979: 54). Cricket, being regarded as the ultimate English pastime, a game for gentlemen with unlimited time at their disposal, also underscores cultural differences. Anthony, as depicted by Skolimowski, is a model Englishman: polite and friendly, but indecisive and lacking in strong emotions. Crossley's emotions, on the other hand, are so strong and immediate that he can use them as a tool of physical destruction, even of murder. Moreover, he attaches no importance to comfort, money or technology, and gives the impression of utter composure and moral strength. However, there are flaws in the Anthony Fielding – Charles Crossley dichotomy, because their differences are conceived not by an objective, detached observer, but by Crossley himself, who 'is trying to project his own weaknesses onto Anthony while reserving all possible strengths for himself' (ibid.: 55). Nevertheless, even only as imaginary, their conflict points to weaknesses of both models of behaviour: civilised and uncivilised. On the one hand, there is an emptiness and sterility at the heart of bourgeois culture, as epitomised by the Fieldings' childlessness and Anthony's affair with the cobbler's wife from a nearby village. On the other hand, the uncivilised, aboriginal culture, represented by Crossley, comes across as cruel, as conveyed by his admitting to killing his own children after they were born, so that nothing would remain of him after his departure from Australia. Ultimately, these two cultures in their 'mature' forms prove infertile, being unable to produce either children or valuable cultural goods. Only through their synthesis can something of value be created. This possibility, however, is not tested in the film.

Both Graves's short story and Skolimowski's film lend themselves to psychoanalytical interpretation. Crossley's murder of his own children (which is not mentioned in the literary original) can be explained by his fear of his son(s) sleeping with their mother (Crossley's wife) and of children killing their father. Oedipal anxiety also permeates Crossley's relationship with his English hosts. As Johnson maintains, Charles's desire for Rachel and his antipathy to Anthony suggests that 'they stand for him for his parents, and if he shouted Father to death (an apt revenge

Figure 4.3 Alan Bates as Charles Crossley and Susannah York as Rachel Fielding in *The Shout*

for the common paternal sin of shouting at one's son) he could enjoy Mother all by himself ... At the same time, guilt at wishing Father dead drives Charles to accuse himself of murder' (ibid.: 55).

Johnson also persuasively suggests that the story of Crossley's intrusion can be interpreted as a parable about Marxist revolution.

If Crossley's story is taken at face value, Anthony embodies the evils of the bourgeoisie: he toys with art, lives at a remove from society (the cottage is isolated on the moors) except when supporting repressive institutions (playing the organ for the church), is self-indulgent and individualistic. Charles, by contrast, has broken with his bourgeois background (having spent years among victims of colonialist repression) and spurns its blandishments; he is a revolutionary prepared to use violence (the shout – an imaginative symbol on the lines of Dovzhenko's talking horse or unkillable Red soldier). Although Charles is the stronger, Anthony tricks him and breaks his soul-stone (divides and conquers the proletariat). Charles is placed behind bars. But the shout remains… (ibid.: 55)

I find both interpretations, psychoanalytical and 'Marxist', plausible, and coherent within the larger body of Skolimowski's work. As an Oedipal story, *The Shout* can be treated as a variation on the theme introduced in *King, Queen, Knave*. As a parable of the proletariat cheated by the weak but clever bourgeoisie, it can be regarded as a forerunner to *Success Is the Best Revenge*, where the chief capitalist, sick and emasculated but ultra-successful Montecurva, is played by John Hurt, Anthony in *The Shout*.

The strong physical opposition between slim and frail John Hurt and muscular and broad Alan Bates, playing Crossley (a contrast, of course, absent in Graves's version) excellently visualises the ideological dichotomies suggested by Skolimowski. They are further accentuated by the use of Francis Bacon's paintings in the film. Bacon's twisted, suffering figures convey the suffering and weakness of Anthony. They can also be viewed as signs of invisible forces making the bodies and souls of both men suffer, of the absurdity which is not so much present in the external world as permeating the human psyche. Skolimowski also heightens the surrealist content of Graves's story by multiplying objects which, rather than serving humans, acquire lives of their own and conspire against people, such as pieces of wood that break the window when Anthony tries to chop them. The whole of nature is shown as unfriendly to humans: the beach is cold, the wind sounds like moaning souls and, finally, lightning kills Crossley and the doctor.

Although, at first sight, Graves's short story offered Skolimowski little opportunity to 'write himself' into it, the final product is very self-reflexive. This is because what Crossley tells in his monologue about his own story sounds very similar to what the director has said off-screen about making this film. Crossley admits to changing the sequence of events and mixing the temporal order to make the story 'alive' and thus enticing for the viewer; Skolimowski lists editing as the crucial means of furnishing the film with meaning (see Strick 1978). Crossley thus becomes a kind of deputy to the director, who on his behalf tells us what the director is doing. Moreover, his place in a little hut, from where he observes the cricket match and asks his companion or assistant to write down his observations, is similar to that of any film director, as well as to the position Skolimowski himself often took in his later films: that of an observer. Some visual motifs, such as mirrors and other reflective surfaces, add to the impression that we do not see any true 'reality' here, only its distorted reflection.

Torrents of Spring and the Nature of Love

Skolimowski adapted *Torrents of Spring* in 1989, but he came under the spell of Turgenev's novel when he was a teenager, in 1952, which was the depth of Polish Stalinism (see Combs 1990: 36). He admits that he identified with the situation of Turgenev's protagonist, who has to choose between two women, cannot decide, and loses both, which makes his life meaningless forever after. 'Dimitri Sanin is the kind of person I might have been at 20 or 22. I think this is the typical vulnerability of a young man who is not yet sure what the traps are in life. And love is the most dangerous one. One can say he is my type of hero, a man in between – like me living in the West while my heart is still over there in Poland' (Skolimowski, quoted in Combs 1990: 36).

For me this confession not only states the significance of Turgenev's novel for the director, but also provides a key to his interpretation. For Skolimowski, *Torrents of Spring* essentially concerns the difficulty of choice and the perilous results of male indecisiveness in matters of the heart. However, the novel can be interpreted somewhat differently, as the story of a man who makes a firm decision after meeting the second of his loves, Maria, and bears the consequences of his choice, which is his virtual abasement and enslavement by her. This interpretation is invited by such passages in the novel as Sanin's address to Maria, 'I am going wherever you are, and I will be with you until you drive me away' (Turgenev 1980: 168). It is also encouraged by Leonard Schapiro, the author of the English translation of Turgenev's novel, who in the essay accompanying it, regards *Torrents of Spring* as a largely autobiographical novel due to the similarity between Sanin's love for Maria and Turgenev's love for his married lover, the singer Pauline Viardot. Unconditional love enslaved and degraded both men, but also constituted the most important chapter of their lives (see Schapiro 1980: 202–3). Schapiro also notes that 'Fear, almost hatred, of the enslavement to love or desire runs like a thread of scarlet throughout Turgenev's life work, from the earliest to the latest' (ibid: 205). With that is connected the writer's exaltation of will above all other human attributes (ibid.: 207). It is strong will, rather than any other feature, physical or mental, which attracts Sanin to Maria in the first place and sustains his obsessive interest in her till the very end.

The difference between the film and the book results on this occasion from the opposing attitudes to women and female–male relationships of these two artists. Turgenev's 'erotic philosophy' is informed by Schopenhauer, while Skolimowski's, as I argued in Chapter 2, by Freud. Skolimowski's reading of *Torrents of Spring* is thus in tune with the way he portrays male–female relationships in his other works, namely as man's neverending search for an ideal and the numerous displacements of one woman by another in his life. Such a reading and re-writing of *Torrents of Spring* is suggested by the director ignoring these fragments of the book in which Dimitri endures humiliation in order to be with Maria, as when he dutifully peels an orange for her husband. Instead, he includes in the film two scenes which do not have their equivalents in Turgenev's novel and which point to Dimitri's indecisiveness about which woman he loves. In one of them Maria makes Sanin confront both his

Figure 4.4 Valeria Golino as Gemma and Timothy Hutton as Dimitri in *Torrents of Spring*

women: herself and his fiancée Gemma. Unlike Turgenev's Sanin, who since meeting Maria practically forgot Gemma and followed Maria slavishly, Skolimowski's Sanin during this encounter cannot make up his mind and at one point literally hides from both women behind a curtain. Dimitri's inability to choose and Maria's exposure of his indecisiveness and dishonesty towards both women, rather than his slavish devotion to Maria, is the ultimate source of his shame. We can assume that if he had the option, Skolimowski's protagonist would keep both lovers till he got bored with them, while Turgenev's Sanin rejects this possibility. The second scene added by Skolimowski presents Sanin searching for Maria in Venice. Maria in this episode is a very elusive, perhaps an absent figure, a ghost, which gives the impression that what Sanin is really looking for is not her as a concrete person but his mental image of an ideal woman.

Although substituting the writer's message with the director's message during the process of adaptation is not a sin as such, it becomes unfortunate when such substitution leads to a film which is unsatisfactory due to the change, as is, in my opinion, the case of Skolimowski's *Torrents of Spring*. By making a film about a wavering man, rather than a man madly and unhappily in love, Skolimowski missed the opportunity of telling a great male love story. Consequently, his film comes across as elegant but lukewarm.

In most other aspects, however, Skolimowski is faithful to the vision of the Russian writer. The setting, the pace of action, the subjective style of narration, thanks to the extensive use of subjective shots, close-ups and introducing the figure of Maria's friend who appears to know the fate of the characters, testify to Skolimowski's desire to create a truthful rendition of Turgenev's work. Even Skolimowski's Sanin is in some ways similar to his literary antecedent by looking remarkably 'Russian'. Timothy Hutton was chosen for the role of Sanin because of his similarity to Pushkin (see Combs 1990). More importantly, as a weak man (although for different reasons than those presented in the book), he is also similar to Turgenev's other men. He can be seen as a relative of Turgenev's Bazarov from *Fathers and Sons* and Litvinov of *Smoke* (as well as a cousin of Skolimowski's own Andrzej Leszczyc from *Identification Marks: None* and Marc from *Le Départ*). The gap between his dream of greatness and his ability to achieve it is excellently portrayed by his duel with Baron von Doenhof, the man who offended Gemma. Rather than being a serious fight, leading to one of the men losing his life, it is a fake duel, in which the men only pretend to kill each other. It is worth adding here that Skolimowski probably holds a world record among directors for representing duels in which both adversaries survive. The first we find in *The Adventures of Gerard*, the second in *Torrents of Spring*, the third in *Ferdydurke*. Taken together these pseudo-duels signify his men's inability to live up to a romantic ideal of masculinity. They desire to be Don Quixotes, while in reality they are only Hamlets.

Skolimowski and Gombrowicz

In the final section of this chapter I consider Skolimowski's relationship with the Polish émigré author, Witold Gombrowicz, regarded by many critics as the greatest Polish writer of the twentieth century. There are several important similarities between Skolimowski and Gombrowicz that pertain both to their work and artistic personas. Maria Janion describes Gombrowicz as an artist who 'consciously excludes himself: from society, dominant artistic trends and accepted modes of speaking and writing' (Janion 1991: 178). Skolimowski also, as I mentioned in the Introduction, was construed by critics as an outsider and in due course accepted this label. In one interview he even compared himself to Gombrowicz by saying, 'Like my favourite Polish author, Witold Gombrowicz, I was a cultural outsider' (Yakir 1982: 28).

This self-perception is reflected in their work, which frequently poses the question of the individual's right and ability to live a truly independent life. Gombrowicz does this in *Ferdydurke*, *Ślub* (*The Marriage*), *Pornografia* and *Trans-Atlantyk*. Connected with this issue is the problem of the relationship between generations, the right of the son to disobey his father and the Law of the Father: institutions and cultural forms created by his elders. In *Trans-Atlantyk*, Gombrowicz even coins the term 'synczyzna' (son-land), in opposition to 'ojczyzna' (fatherland), to describe the model of the relationship in which the Law of the Son dominates over the Law of the Father. They are also united in their fascination with youth.[4] However, Gombrowicz appears to me a more critical adulator of youth than Skolimowski. In Gombrowicz's work, for example, we find such an opinion, 'For me youth is inferior and inadequate in everything except for one thing: in that it is young, it is youth "in itself". So there is nothing surprising about the fact the action of the young, in as far as it constitutes a political, social or ideological programme, should be of such poor quality' (Gombrowicz 1973: 130). Skolimowski, on the other hand, not only gives in to youthful charm, but treats the views and ideas of the young very seriously. Although undoubtedly Gombrowicz revealed astonishing insight by predicting that youth will be the main 'fashion of tomorrow', he only drew conclusions from what he experienced in his time, because this elation of youth began after the First World War, when he matured as a person and writer (see Jarzębski and Zawadzki 2006: 286).

Another link between Skolimowski and Gombrowicz is their interest in revolutions and other drastic political changes, riddled with upper-class fear of the uneducated masses. Their styles are not dissimilar either, thanks to their leaning towards absurdism, grotesquerie, but not as an aim in itself, but as a means to represent reality more accurately. Both authors also show a predilection for certain narrative motifs such as the mask; masks serve their characters as a means to counteract forms imposed on them by culture. Finally, Gombrowicz's work, like Skolimowski's, is largely autobiographical, as conveyed by the fact that his protagonists often share the author's name.

From Skolimowski's original projects, I will regard *Success Is the Best Revenge* as closest to Gombrowicz's oeuvre. Its plot bears resemblance to one of Gombrowicz's early stories, *Stefan Czarniecki's Memoir*. Gombrowicz's character, a half-Polish, half-Jewish youth, attempts to overcome his lack of any distinct identity and alienation from his surroundings by joining the Polish Army, becoming an *uhlan*, an emblem of Polish bravery and patriotism. However, his attempt to gain a wholesome identity ends in failure when he sees how his fellow uhlan is mortally wounded. Adam Rodak, in *Success Is the Best Revenge*, can be regarded as Stefan Czarniecki's modern analogue because, although he is not of mixed race, the years spent in London changed him into the kind of 'colourless being' Gombrowicz's Czarniecki is: neither a proper Pole, nor a Brit. The physical assaults and verbal abuse Adam suffers at school from his fellow pupils is also similar to the alienation experienced by Gombrowicz's character. Equally, his decision to assert his Polishness by returning to Poland under martial law is not dissimilar to Stefan's joining the *uhlans*. Unlike Czarniecki, we do not know how Alex's attempt to find a wholesome identity will finish, but we can guess it will also be unsuccessful.

Screening *Ferdydurke*, which is the story of a thirty-year-old man's return to the times when he was a schoolboy, offered Skolimowski an opportunity to explore the common interests and attitudes between himself and Gombrowicz and assert his place as Gombrowicz's successor, albeit working in a different medium. Another potential charm of Gombrowicz's masterpiece for the director, who dreamt of revenging his Polish-British flop, *Success Is the Best Revenge*, was the fact that *Ferdydurke* was conceived as an act of revenge on ignorant and unsympathetic critics who had scorned Gombrowicz's previous novel, *Pamiętnik z okresu dojrzewania* (*Memoirs of a Time of Immaturity*, 1933). Perhaps this was one of the reasons why Skolimowski decided to shoot his film in English, with the British actor, Iain Glen, in the main role of Józio, who was chosen largely because he looked like a young

Gombrowicz (not unlike Michael York, who shared some similarity with Skolimowski). The script was written by Skolimowski with the help of two authors, whom he described in interviews as 'American students of literature', John Yorick and Joseph Kay, and who in reality are Skolimowski's own sons. Again, this involvement of his sons is reminiscent of *Success Is the Best Revenge*, which was largely based on the diary of Skolimowski's elder son, this time using the penname Michael Lyndon. A careful reader will also note that *Ferdydurke* includes the word 'Skolimów', which could be regarded as a secret sign for Skolimowski.

Yet, *Ferdydurke* also poses a great challenge to the film maker. Firstly, it is not only rich in ideas, but is also structurally very complex. The adventures of the novel's protagonist, Józio, are intersected with interludes containing characters and situations not connected with the main course of action: *Filidor dzieckiem podszyty* (*Philifor Honeycombed with Childishness*) and *Filibert dzieckiem podszyty* (*Philimor Honeycombed with Childishness*), and their introductions. The interludes refer to a duel between Filidor (Philifor) and Filibert (Philimor), adherents of different philosophical and practical positions, which Gombrowicz describes as synthesis and analysis. Leaving the interludes out would help the film's coherence; including them would give a chance to explore Gombrowicz's iconoclastic attitude to the inherited modes of writing. The price of the second option, however, is the risk of making a movie which, even at its basic level, as a story, becomes obscure for viewers unfamiliar with Gombrowicz's work. Skolimowski's approach to this problem was to try 'to have his cake and eat it' or, more precisely, to eat half of the cake and leave the other half. Filidor and Filibert are present, but their narrative role is very small and there is no attempt within the narrative to explain the ideas which they embody. For sympathetic viewers who know the book, their presence can be interpreted as a kind of shorthand, allowing the director to communicate maximum meaning with the minimum of words. For those who do not know the original, the inserts are simply confusing.

Another, perhaps greater, challenge of screening Gombrowicz derives from the fact that the situations described in his works lend themselves to metaphorical rather than literal interpretation, and the metaphorical meaning is far from obvious, not least because Gombrowicz's ambition was to create his own system of metaphors.[5] This conundrum is partly solved by narration, in which metaphorical meanings are often explained. For example, the duel of grimaces between Miętus and Syfon in *Ferdydurke* figuratively refers to the problem of various identities (forms) with which culture tries to furnish young men, their attempts to resist these forms and their failure to do so. Skolimowski also included in his film the duel of grimaces, giving it even more prominence than in Gombrowicz's work, but this scene does not convey its metaphorical meaning convincingly and looks like a boyish game, only more extreme (see Werner 1992: 8–9).

A frequent method of Gombrowicz, used in *Ferdydurke* as well as in *Pornografia* and *Kosmos*, is to show how a small shift in a situation, caused by using a particular word or introducing a discordant object into a pattern, leads to total chaos. It can be the word 'mamusia' (mummy), which Józio utters when his ostentatiously modern landlords, the Młodziaks, boast about their liberal approach to erotic behaviour, which includes accepting their daughter's (hypothetical) child out of wedlock. This word, taken from a different discourse (not liberal, but the traditional language of 'old aunties'), causes the disintegration of the Młodziaks' talk, as demonstrated by their hysterical laughter and, in due course, the collapse of their 'modern' world. Similarly, the single act of spanking Miętus, the upper-class friend of Józio, by a simple farm hand, overturns the traditional world of the gentry and leads to a revolution. The purpose of such scenes is to demonstrate that language does not passively mirror the world, but transforms it. This idea, nowadays associated largely with the classics of postmodern theory, such as Derrida or Foucault (which can also be found in the works of their 'intellectual ancestors', such as Antonio Gramsci and Ludwig Wittgenstein), although widely accepted, is difficult to grasp when represented visually without additional commentary. This is because, although language indeed changes the world, it does not do so rapidly. The new word or phrase has to circulate and be repeated many times, before it affects human behaviour.[6]

By seeing the situations I just described in their concrete forms, devoid of the author's commentary, the viewer might overlook their metaphorical content. Of course, the less familiar one is with Gombrowicz's work, the more likely it is that his ideas would elude one. In order to preserve the intellectual content of the scene, the film maker might attempt to replace it with one which will convey the same idea, but in a way easier to understand by the viewer – be unfaithful to the book's letter, in order to achieve faithfulness to its spirit. Yet Skolimowski decided to transfer the scenes 'of linguistic chaos' from the book to the film almost verbatim, hoping that they would be understandable. In my opinion this does not happen at all in the first scene. The hysterical laughter of the Młodziaks as a reaction to the word 'mummy', despite enriching it by Józio's gesture of hugging a baby, comes across as simply bizarre. For viewers unable to grasp the metaphorical meanings of Gombrowicz's prose, a scene like this confirms the hostile stereotype of this writer as an author of unintelligible prose. Easier to understand is the metaphorical content of the second situation, that of spanking a member of the gentry that leads to revolution, not least because on this occasion metaphorical meaning is closer to its literal meaning, so to speak. Historical books are full of descriptions of wars and revolutions that began by a single act of subversion of the political or cultural order.

Skolimowski is not faithful to the literal content of the book on all occasions, but his divergences from the hypotext appear to derive not from the need to transfer to the film the intellectual content of the book, but to make it more accessible to an English audience. *Ferdydurke*, in common with practically the whole of Gombrowicz's oeuvre, is little known among English-speaking readers (although he enjoys cult following in France and, of course, in his native Poland) and is even less known among English-speaking cinema-goers. Hence the double risk of shooting it in English. As a means to cater for different capacities of understanding we should list the change of the original title of the film to *Thirty Door Key*. This is because 'Ferdydurke' does not mean anything or, more precisely, did not mean anything when Gombrowicz invented the word, although phonetically it resembles Freddy Durkee, the protagonist of Sinclair Lewis's novel, *Babbitt* (see Jarzębski and

Zawadzki 2006: 265). Susan Sontag suggests that Gombrowicz 'opted for jabberwocky' to provoke his critics who rejected his first book, *Memoirs of a Time of Immaturity* (Sontag 2002: 97). However, in due course the word 'Ferdydurke' gained a life of its own. It is possible, for example, to identify Gombrowicz as Ferdydurke or treat it as a metaphor of the systematic destruction of existing cultural forms, examples of which I provided. By contrast to 'Ferdydurke', 'Thirty Door Key' has a more specific meaning. It bears associations with the age of the protagonist, who had just turned thirty years, and suggests that it will take issue with the 'key' to this age. Other adjustments to the foreign audience include giving up on certain scenes pertaining specifically to Polish culture, such as the episode of a Polish lesson, in which one of the pupils claims that everybody at school hates the Polish romantic poet Juliusz Słowacki, contrary to the canon that heralds him as great. In passing, it should be mentioned that this scene could easily be adapted to a foreign audience by changing Słowacki into Shakespeare or Byron. Gombrowicz himself within the text suggests that this episode has a universal meaning, by including the sentence: 'It may be that Słowacki doesn't move you, my dear Kotecki, but don't tell me, don't tell me that you're not profoundly moved by Mickiewicz, Byron, Pushkin, Shelley, Goethe...' (Gombrowicz 2005: 46).

Polish film critics also noted that the school, which is one of the main settings of the book and the film, looks more like an English public school than its humble Polish equivalent (see Janicka 1992: 6; Werner 1992: 9). By such transformation, Skolimowski misrepresented Gombrowicz, who in his book mocked Polish schools and, being himself openly and provocatively snobbish, probably would be impressed

Figure 4.5 Schoolboys in *Ferdydurke*

by a place such as Eton. Skolimowski himself in due course admitted that he regards as unfortunate his decision to shoot *Ferdydurke* in English (see Lichocka 1994: 9), as the English version alienated a large section of Polish viewers, eager to listen to Gombrowicz's idiosyncratic, quasi-archaic language, while doing little to attract an international audience.

Although in the reviews of *Ferdydurke* one could encounter the word 'baroque', which was also used in relation to Skolimowski's earlier films, principally *Barrier*, in this case it refers to overcrowding the film with characters, plots and subplots in order to preserve the literal content of the original, rather than packing it with meanings or inventing new means of artistic expression. Nevertheless, in this chaotic criss-crossing of characters and plots we can identify several distinctive ideological strands. One concerns the dichotomy of maturity–immaturity. In Gombrowicz's version, Józio presents himself as a man who is, despite his age of thirty years, immature or hanging perilously between maturity and immaturity. For this reason his peers and elders treat him with distrust and derision. Skolimowski's Józio, on the other hand, as I already mentioned (see Chapter 2), finds himself in a school full of men looking as if they were a similar age to him. He thus comes across not as an exception to the rule, but as a typical exemplar of a generation of people who would do anything to cheat time and remain young. This disparity pertains to the different epochs in which these two *Ferdydurkes* were conceived. In the 1930s, when Gombrowicz wrote this novel, thirty-year-old men were expected to be mature; near the end of the twentieth century this is no longer the case.

Another distinct motif present in both the hypotext and the hypertext is that of revolution. The motif of a drastic change of political and social order gets central stage in a later work of Gombrowicz, *Operetka* (*Operetta*, 1966). In *Ferdydurke*, it is only sketched near the end of the novel. Gombrowicz, as Maria Janion observes, sees revolution as a revenge of the servants over their masters, who take their positions, eat their food, sleep in their beds, without changing any deeper structure of social relations (Janion 1991: 184–85). Such revolution only destroys what existed without constructing anything positive.[7] Similarly, revolution, as represented in the film, is a revolt of servants against their masters that brings only chaos and mayhem.

Skolimowski's critical attitude to revolution should not surprise a viewer who knows his earlier films representing the class of 'servants': *Moonlighting* and *Success Is the Best Revenge*. In particular, the image of peasants copulating in a dog kennel, which we find in *Ferdydurke*, brings to mind the scene of looking for Mr Edzio in *Success Is the Best Revenge*. It can also be mentioned in passing that Skolimowski planned to screen *Nie-boska Komedia* (*The Un-divine Comedy*) by Zygmunt Krasiński, which Janion considers, together with Gombrowicz's *Operetta* and *Szewcy* (*The Shoemakers*) by Stanisław Ignacy Witkiewicz, as a work exhibiting an utterly negative attitude to revolution (ibid.: 175–88).

The contrast between the two main male characters in Skolimowski's film, the self-reflexive, shy Józio and the extravert, action hungry Miętus is typical for Gombrowicz's works.[8] It also reflects the way Skolimowski structures his world, namely into passive, withdrawn Hamlets and active and foolhardy Don Quixotes.

However, in the majority of his earlier films, these two types were kept separate. Placing Józio and Miętus in one story lays bare the shortcomings of both of them, perhaps even the impossibility to find a compromise between the types they represent.

While Gombrowicz's ambition was to furnish his work with universal, rather than historical meaning (the writer was contemptuous of the bulk of Polish literature, which he regarded as provincial due to its preoccupation with entirely Polish affairs), Skolimowski's film is born out of an opposite impulse. He invites one to see the meaning of the represented events in a distinct historical context, that of the last moments before the outbreak of the Second World War. The approaching war is suggested by radio announcements, Józio's cousin's Zosia's engagement to a German officer, and images of people and horses wearing gas masks. Moreover, the film finishes with archive footage of bombs dropping on Warsaw. What Gombrowicz mocked in his book, the director treats with nostalgia. This nostalgia can be interpreted as autobiographical; the mourning for prewar Poland standing for Skolimowski's yearning for Poland after his self-exile, following the problems with *Hands Up!* It can also be seen in the context of the time when Skolimowski shot his film, namely the early 1990s, when Poland finally rejected communism and discussions on its future were dominated by the question of whether it should model itself on prewar Poland.

The strategy of changing universal into historical is not uncommon in the work of literary adaptation. As examples we can list François Truffaut's *La Chambre verte* (*The Green Room*, 1978) and Raoul Ruiz's *Le Temps retrouvé* (*Time Regained*, 1999), based respectively on the works by Henry James and Marcel Proust. In the first film the protagonist's obsessive desire to commemorate all dead is explained by his partaking in the First World War – the greatest experience of mass death prior to the Second World War. In Ruiz's film the subject of the First World War is also underscored, to accent the importance of remembering and immortalising in literature a world which will soon perish. In all these cases, Skolimowski's *Ferdydurke* included, the result is to create a film which, intellectually, fails to live up to the reputation of its main hypotext and even distorts the original message.

Ferdydurke did not achieve international success, but in Poland received predominantly good reviews, although it failed to awaken enthusiasm comparable to Skolimowski's early Polish films. The reviewers praised Skolimowski's faithfulness to the original and, somehow conversely, his ability to update Gombrowicz and make him accessible to foreign viewers (see Janicka 1992; Płażewski 1992; Wojciechowski 1992). He was also complimented for his visual flair (see Wojciechowski 1992). I do not share these compliments and instead, agree with Mateusz Werner that Skolimowski's take on Gombrowicz was pedestrian (see Werner 1992). Judging from the long silence which followed *Ferdydurke* and the character of his subsequent film, *Four Nights with Anna*, for Skolimowski it was a lesson that he should avoid revenging his unsuccessful Polish-English films by producing new variants of *Success Is the Best Revenge* and, following Gombrowicz's diagnosis about the artistic and political potential of young people, trust his own artistic intuition instead of that of his sons.

Conclusions

Despite the heterogeneity of literary sources on which Skolimowski drew throughout the later part of his career, his films reveal a high degree of consistency in terms of construction of characters, choice of problems and visual style. Irrespective of whether he bases his films on original scripts or works of literature, the final products are films packed with surrealist imagery and depicting 'boys' entangled in Oedipal conflicts of some sort. These boys can be construed as versions of Hamlet and Don Quixote, therefore we can regard the masterpieces of Shakespeare and Cervantes as the ultimate hypotexts of Skolimowski's films. They are always incomplete, internally divided and facing a dilemma: be decisive or let others decide for them; act or think, focus on the external world or live one's life in one's head. This dilemma is never successfully resolved, perpetuating their adventures and giving their creator an impulse to make new works, according to the idea advocated by Gombrowicz that the incomplete and imperfect is superior to the perfect because it is more constructive.

Notes

1. Judging by the director's interviews, Skolimowski wanted to screen many more literary works than he succeeded in doing. Among his unfulfilled projects are novels by Joseph Conrad, such as *Victory* and *Secret Agent*, Knut Hamsun's *Hunger*, *The Un-divine Comedy* by Zygmunt Krasiński and *In America* by Susan Sontag.
2. Poland in the 1960s was so different from the West, that it was assumed that Poles cannot seriously compare themselves with Hollywood heroes.
3. Czesław Miłosz draws attention to the romantic symbolism embedded in the name 'Conrad', being also the name of Konrad Wallenrod, the protagonist of Adam Mickiewicz's poem, *Konrad Wallenrod*. Miłosz writes, 'When he signed his first book "Conrad", dropping his family name of Korzeniowski as being too difficult for an Anglo-Saxon public, he was well aware of its double meaning' (Miłosz 1982: 36).
4. In Gombrowicz's case this fascination is often linked by critics with his homosexuality (see Płonowska Ziarek 1998)
5. For this reason Gombrowicz's dramas are also very difficult to stage and are used predominantly as texts for reading.
6. Gombrowicz seems to be well aware of the effectiveness of repetition in creating reality. In *Ferdydurke*, for example, we find such a sentence, 'It is by repetition that myths are created' (Gombrowicz 2005: 72).
7. Gombrowicz's moral and political views are riddled with ambiguities and paradoxes. Crucially, however, he shows distrust of people who try to detach their moral views from their social position and material situation. In his work we find, for example, provocative praise of the aristocracy (see, for example, Gombrowicz 1997: 76–83) and such a criticism of Marxist morality, 'As far as Marxism is concerned I cannot see the point of that self-violation practised by men who are bourgeois by birth and education and who try to identify themselves with the proletariat by invoking a doctrine. That's all hot air!' (Gombrowicz 1973: 79).
8. Again, such a way of structuring his work can be linked to the writer's homosexuality and, connected with that, lack of interest in female characters.

CHAPTER 5

'I Don't Like Obvious Film Scores': Music and Other Sounds in Skolimowski's Films

Contrary to the widely held opinion that film music is 'unheard' (see Gorbman 1987; Prendergast 1992), we hear Skolimowski's films as much as we see them, and their scores often remain in our heads long after the memory of the plot fades. This is not an accident, as this director always attached great importance to music, and not only in his films, but also, as I will argue in due course, in his life. Its significance results largely from his conviction (typical for those who identified with youth culture), that music is a perfect way to characterise people. By accompanying a character's actions with some kind of music or by making him listen to a particular piece, the author can describe his tastes and feelings more effectively than by making him engage in lengthy dialogue or monologue. Moreover, Skolimowski always strove to furnish his films with 'polyphonic' meaning, to be cinema's poet rather than a professional story teller. Again, music is a perfect tool to achieve this goal as it can convey a film's deeper or hidden meaning, saying what the author does not want to or cannot say by other means.

The director's interest in scores also derives from his overriding concern for the film's aesthetic form, his belief that an inventive soundtrack adds to the film's artistic value. I regard the words Skolimowski himself once uttered and which I am using as the title of this chapter: 'I don't like obvious film scores', as the key to capturing the specificity of soundtracks in his films. In a large proportion of them the scores are anything but obvious, therefore we pay attention to them. This does not imply that they follow the same pattern. If this was the case, they would probably become obvious after some time. On the contrary, the scores in Skolimowski's films evolved, in step with changes in music fashions and the evolution of his musical and cinematic interests. For this reason, I am dividing this essay into three sections, corresponding to different approaches to music he revealed in different chapters of his career.

The 1960s: Boxing and Jazz

Probably the most quoted sentence ever uttered by Skolimowski is the advice he gave to Jerzy Andrzejewski and Andrzej Wajda in the early 1960s, about how to make a contemporary film, which later became *Innocent Sorcerers*: 'There must be boxing, there must be jazz, there must be a cool guy who has a scooter and meets pretty girls, and from time to time has some reflections' (Skolimowski, quoted in Krubski 1998: 102). These words attest to the importance the young Skolimowski attached to jazz in film of this period and the context in which he wanted it to appear – it had to be the music of the young, even of youth itself.

In regard to jazz, Skolimowski perceives himself as an early innovator – somebody who discovered this music before others. Talking to Jerzy Uszyński, he admitted that in Poland the explosion of jazz took place after 1956, the year which started a political and cultural 'thaw' in Poland, but he fell in love with this music two years earlier. He mixed with Polish jazzmen and was particularly close to Krzysztof Komeda.[1] Komeda (1931–1968), real name Krzysztof Trzciński, was not only a first-class author of film scores, but also a principal force in developing modern jazz in Poland as composer, pianist and leader of the Komeda Sextet. He achieved this position despite dying at the young age of thirty-seven, following an accident. His individual style resulted from an ability to intertwine various sources of inspiration, such as Polish classical music and folklore, and the sound of the popular jazz combos of that time: The Modern Jazz Quartet and the Gerry Mulligan Quartet (see Kowal 1995).

Skolimowski was labelled the first fan of the Komeda Sextet. The band even offered him collaborative work – making lighting effects at their concerts. He agreed, and in the middle of the 1950s travelled for a year with the musicians all over Poland. Skolimowski also tried to write lyrics to a piece written by Komeda, entitled *Kotek w chmurach* (*A Kitten in the Clouds*). Although, as he later admitted, the text was rather naïve and was met with laughter by Komeda, he did not give up writing (see Uszyński 1990a: 6). The subsequent films in which Skolimowski used jazz can be seen as a continuation of this early attempt to write poetry to music.

As Roman Kowal argues, the specificity of Komeda's style as a composer of film music was a clash between the lyricism of the leading musical motif and the aggressive sound of jazz (see Kowal 1995: 120). The lyricism, which assured him the title of the greatest 'poet' of Polish jazz, is conveyed in the titles of his compositions, containing words such as 'ballad' or 'lullaby'. As an author of film scores he was also not afraid to venture beyond jazz, into pop, dance and religious music (see Sowińska 2006: 235). Critics also draw attention to the elusive and mysterious quality of Komeda's scores and his innovative use of individual instruments that often mimic natural sounds, including the human voice (see Kowal 1995: 120). Komeda himself, in an interview given in 1961, identified two types of film music. The first type consists of a leitmotif that reappears in various episodes of the film, although possibly in different instrumentations. The second type is more varied, with different musical motifs used in different parts of the film. Although the composer did not state clearly which approach he favoured, he suggested that the first type is more effective. The viewer remembers such scores better, while the nuances of the second type are typically overlooked (see Komeda-Trzciński 1961: 37). In films with a leitmotif there is a stronger link between the music and the individual character – a feature that proved very important for Skolimowski. Of course, jazz music, which consists of improvisations on a theme, is particularly appropriate for film music of the first type. In the same interview, Komeda also emphasised the link between music and other sounds used in film, such as city noises (ibid.: 35). Furthermore, he declared himself an adherent of film music that is functional, even subservient to the narrative.

Although jazz was important to Skolimowski even before he started making films, in his student etudes Skolimowski did not use jazz scores, unlike Polański, who 'packed' his early films with this type of music. In *Little Hamlet* and *Money or Life*, the music can be described as a pastiche of Polish urban folk music. In the first film, it is a song resembling an 'urban ballad', sung by bands performing on the streets of Polish towns before the Second World War, which typically presented the story of some tragic character. In this case the song summarises and comments on the story of Little Hamlet, a humble Polish version of one of the most famous of Shakespeare's creations. The source of the sound is diegetic: an old, barely functioning record player, around which the characters of the film gather. The start-stop and dishevelled sounds of the music correspond to the mechanical movements of the film's personages, recollecting characters of silent cinema. In *Money or Life*, which is set at a funfair, we hear tunes typical for this environment, such as simple, very rhythmical tunes and fragments of popular songs, including *Sto lat, sto lat*, which is a Polish version of *Happy Birthday to You*. Although we do not see the source of the sounds, we can assume they are diegetic, because the sound is mechanical and butchered, as if coming from some poorly working equipment. Moreover, the sounds of *Sto lat, sto lat* are activated by a well-aimed shot. The score includes a short fragment of one of the most popular funeral marches, Chopin's Piano Sonata No. 2 in B Minor, op. 35, played on a mouth organ; this being used as a sign by some conspirators. This fragment deserves special attention, as it provides a model of using classical music in the early part of Skolimowski's career, by presenting it in a degrading context. *Erotyk* is practically devoid of any music, except at the beginning and the end when the heroine sings in a childish voice *Spotykamy się tylko w lustrze* (*We Only Meet in a Mirror*). The songs in *Little Hamlet* and *Erotyk* not so much strengthen the meanings conveyed visually, which is the typical function of songs in films, as explain what we see on screen. Without the song it would be next to impossible to identify the connection between Skolimowski's film and Shakespeare's *Hamlet*. Similarly, the song in *Erotyk* makes it clear that the reality depicted in this film is *surreality*: the stuff of dreams and daydreams.

After completing his school etudes, Skolimowski turned to jazz, making six films with jazz scores. This does not mean that their scores are similar. On the contrary, they are very diverse. Skolimowski began with films where the sound of jazz serves to characterise the protagonist, rather than convey the perspective of the film author. This is the case in *Identification Marks: None* and *Walkover*, the scores for which were written respectively by Krzysztof Sadowski and Andrzej Trzaskowski, both popular Polish jazzmen, but not of the same stature as Komeda. The jazz music, accompanying Leszczyc's peregrinations, accentuates his edginess, the richness of his inner life which he is unwilling or unable to transmit. It also underscores the fast and chaotic life of the city in which the protagonist finds himself, and his desire to escape. In these films jazz competes with other sounds emitted by the radio, such as fragments from Piotr Tchaikovsky and Johann Sebastian Bach in an educational programme for children. Using Bach in such a programme is a subtle commentary on the communist approach to culture – whilst it had a mainly negative attitude to Western culture, especially popular music, regarding it as decadent, it looked more benevolently on old and high culture. In short, Bach was good, even for small children, while the Rolling Stones was bad, even for teenagers. At the same time, by offering many different versions of one motif, badly played and incorrectly introduced by the speakers, Skolimowski lays bare the disrespectful approach to classical music in socialism: the music, in common with culture at large, was no more than an instrument to educate society. Leszczyc typically ignores the classical music filling the rooms which he enters. Some sounds from the radio, however, startle him, as if they captured his deepest emotions, conveyed what he was unable to express. Mariusz Dzięglewski suggests that the sounds of the radio reveal the conscience of the character (see Dzięglewski 2002: 168).

As in his etudes, in *Identifications Marks: None*, Skolimowski uses a song as a way to characterise the protagonist. On two occasions we hear the song *Eurydyko, nie czekaj na mnie* (*Eurydice, Do Not Wait For Me*). First a group of soldiers sing it outside the building where Leszczyc, together with other young men, wait to be examined by a draftee board. Secondly, we hear it when the protagonist is already on a train, going to the army. The song, written by Andrzej Jarecki and presented in the satirical STS theatre in 1962, roots the film, as Iwona Kurz observes, in a particular period of Polish cultural history – the early 1960s, when Poles were largely preoccupied with (small) consumption, although the earlier, romantic ideas were not entirely dead (see Kurz 2005: 253–54). Secondly, it betrays Leszczyc's unconscious: his simultaneous rejection of and yearning for love. Up to this point all the songs in Skolimowski's films emphasised the importance of love and its impossibility, especially for male subjects. Ophelia, evoked in a song heard in *Little Hamlet*, and Eurydice, in *Identifications Marks: None*, are figures of death, therefore love in the respective films cannot be happy.

In *Walkover*, even more than in *Identifications Marks: None*, music merges with other sounds. On many occasions we are not sure whether the sounds we hear belong to music or not, and whether they are diegetic or extraneous. For example, the sounds accompanying a scene when Leszczyc is on a train with Teresa might result from the wheels on the rails or could be extradiegetic. Certainly, the main source of jazz in this film is diegetic: the transistor radio carried by Leszczyc. Both the fact of possessing a radio and the sounds of jazz emitted by this machine point to the protagonist's belonging to a young generation. This link between youth, radio and jazz music is especially illuminated in an episode when Leszczyc tries to pawn his radio to an older man. The man says that he does not know about such gadgets – he is simply too old for them. However, Leszczyc does not really listen to music from the radio, in contrast to poems which he approaches as if they were directed to him. He uses it only to build a wall between himself and the external world (see Sowińska 2006: 206).

Jazz also fulfills the role of an enclave, in which youngsters could hide themselves, in earlier Polish films, especially *Innocent Sorcerers*, but in these films music served the whole community while in *Walkover* it is used by an individual (ibid.). The fact that Leszczyc eventually pawns his radio can be interpreted as a sign of him abandoning his solipsistic pursuits and preparing himself for a communal life. On the other hand, the transistor radio also can be used jointly, as Leszczyc is reminded by a young fellow who would like to share a room with him in the workers' hostel, largely because of this fashionable and costly gadget.

The only distinctive piece of nondiegetic music in *Walkover* is used in the scene when Leszczyc fights with a fellow boxer. It is simple and rhythmical, as if mimicking the blows the boxers inflict on each other. This music continues to the end of the film and beyond the narrative, accompanying the film's final credits. This gives the impression that, despite the end of the match, the fight goes on. Perhaps it continues in Leszczyc's mind as he cannot liberate himself from his boxing experiences.

Sowińska claims that, in *Walkover*, jazz is represented as music which has lost its power. The director hardly uses it and the character pays little attention to it (ibid.: 207). I find this assessment plausible. However, it can also be suggested that it did not so much lose its significance as become dislocated – from culture and individual consciousness to the unconscious. In particular, the rhythmical, syncopated sounds finishing the film signify its continuous presence which has engraved itself on Leszczyc's unconscious. It is worth adding here that the music finishing a film is regarded as especially important as it summarises and concludes the score.

Komeda was the composer of the scores for the three following films by Skolimowski, *Barrier*, *Le Départ* and *Hands Up!* From a musical point of view, these are the most accomplished films in Skolimowski's career, albeit for different reasons. In *Barrier*, the soundtrack is most versatile and surprising; *Le Départ*, as the director himself puts it, 'is a test case as to how much music a film can take' (Thomsen 1968: 142); in *Hands Up!*, Komeda succeeded in creating the most 'catchy' piece of music ever heard in a Skolimowski's film.

Barrier belongs to the 'late Komeda'. With the passage of years Komeda learnt to utilise various musical traditions and venture outside jazz (see Sowińska 2006: 235). He also became more interested in the soundtrack as a whole rather than in its purely musical component. *Barrier* is an excellent example of the freedom with which Komeda draws on various strands of music, creating a versatile, but simultaneously a coherent and original, musical whole. The music in *Barrier* appears constantly to clash with the image. These clashes point to a layer of reality which initially the images do not reveal, forcing the viewer to move beyond the façade of a thin plot. Sowińska in her perceptive analysis of *Barrier* goes as far as claiming that sounds 'prolong reality' (ibid.: 236). This opinion links with Komeda's conviction that jazz is not equally suitable to all film genres, but best serves films with a mystery or a hidden meaning which the music helps to unleash (see Kowal 1995: 120).

The first such clash between sound and image opens the film, when the singing of *Hallelujah* accompanies four men who one by one are trying to catch a matchbox in their mouthes, while their wrists are bound with electric cable. Christians use the word *Hallelujah* to express their joyful praise of God, therefore *Hallelujah* psalms are popular at Easter, as a way to celebrate Christ's resurrection. The most famous work of classical music using this word is George Frideric Handel's *Messiah* (1741). However, rather than imitate Handel's work, Komeda uses it as an anti-model. Instead of using the major key, he wrote his *Hallelujah* in a minor key; instead of using a large variety of instruments to accentuate the triumphant character of the event celebrated, he used human voices, treated like instruments (see Sowińska 2006: 238). The vocal parts of the score were performed by the NOVI (New Original Vocal Instruments) SINGERS. This jazz group, which did not use any instruments, could be compared to the band Manhattan Transfer or even to a gospel choir. However, it was a highly unique phenomenon on the Polish music scene at the time. NOVI made its debut in 1965, only a year before *Barrier* was shot, which was, as Sowińska observes, a very fortunate coincidence (ibid.: 268). Indeed, it is difficult to fathom this film without the distinctive sounds of NOVI's voices.

The deviation of *Barrier*'s score from the musical and religious tradition suggests that the focus of the film is not masses of people performing a certain ceremonial, but an individual who must establish his attitude towards it. Equally, Komeda suggests that the story Skolimowski is to tell us will be far from euphoric. During the film, *Hallelujah* is presented in four variations, typically announcing the character's downfall or crisis. The music thus conveys the discord between the mood of the country, preparing itself for Easter celebrations, and the mood of the protagonist, who is focused on his private, unsuccessful life. Yet we cannot describe it as ironic because gradually the protagonist gives in to the festive mood. Krzysztof Kornacki even suggests that like Christ, who returns from the dead, the character is reborn thanks to the power of love (see Kornacki 2004). If there were no music, the link between the Boy's peregrinations and the special time they take place would be more difficult to capture, as it was difficult to notice the link between Leszczyc's peregrinations in *Identification Marks: None* and the anniversary of the outbreak of the Second World War. Music thus provides a context for the narrative and works as a commentary on the behaviour of the character, endowing him with lyricism or melancholy which he tries to suppress or does not want to show in 'external' life. The very use of jazz, rather than classical music, in a film set during Easter time, is meaningful. It betrays the director's disapproval, conveyed also by other means, of Polish rituals as ceremonies frozen in time, and his proposition to update them. The whole film can be regarded as an attempt to look at Easter afresh, from a more individualistic and contemporary perspective.

Although, unlike in previous films by this director, nondiegetic music dominates over diegetic, the former by no means disappeared in *Barrier*. We hear it when the Boy visits a restaurant where a large party is about to start, to celebrate the end of Lent. Here people perform songs, for example, *Eurydice, Do Not Wait For Me*, which summarise the tragic condition of themselves, their countrymen and perhaps the whole of mankind. One of them is a cleaning lady who, encouraged by the dance leader, sings a modified version of Skolimowski's poem which appeared in his previous films:

Now he,
After bad days
Or after something
Like youth
Or love

With a hand on his throat
He wants to make up for lost opportunities
He wants to be again
God knows whom.
With a hand on his throat
He wants to make up for lost opportunities
He wants to be again
God knows where
And he adjusts his tie.

The poem, as I argued in the previous chapter, concerns the gap between great ambitions and their meagre outcomes, elevation and triviality. On this occasion the gap is conveyed by the contrast between the humble performer (washing floors and public toilets can be regarded as an epitome of trivial, unfulfilled life) and her elevated performance. The current from the ceiling fan blows the kerchief from the old woman's head and blows her hair, making her look like a hero from a socialist realistic sculpture or painting, shown marching against adversity. Moreover, we see the cleaner from a very low angle, monumentalising perspective which, again, adds to the heroic impression (see Sowińska 2006: 239). The song is not sung by the actress playing the cleaner, Maria Malicka, but by Ewa Demarczyk, arguably the greatest Polish singer of the postwar period, famous for dramatic interpretations of Polish poems. It appears as if the director did not bother to create the illusion that Malicka was the true performer of his poem, but attempted to draw attention to the gap between the dignity of her performance and the normal status of the performer. Together, the cleaner's show is disharmonious in the extreme, pointing to the absurdity of her own existence and everybody who identifies with her song.

Another pathetic and disharmonious song is uttered by the war veterans at the same event. This piece in the rhythm of a march is not any real Polish war song, but a kind of composite song consisting of fragments of familiar texts and melodies. We hear such pathetic expressions as 'Our blood and our anger' or 'Hope, faith, love, pride, death'. As in the case of the cleaner, their singing is dissynchronous: every man sings his own song and many only move their lips, as if trying to fake an experience in which they did not really partake. The very accumulation of emotive terms might arouse suspicion that the film's author mocks the performers. This suspicion is corroborated by the ridiculous appearance of the veterans, wearing hats made of copies of a popular women's magazine. Yet their worn faces look sad rather than funny, suggesting that what Skolimowski really questions is the condition of the war veteran, not any concrete bearers of this condition. At the same party, we also hear lively, simple, rhythmical music, which sends the guests into a trance; they make mechanical movements, as if oblivious to anything else but the music. Both the music and the very situation resemble the dancing scenes from *Lásky jedné plavovlásky* (*A Blonde in Love*, 1965) by Miloš Forman, the director to whom Skolimowski was close throughout this period of his career.

In *Barrier*, to a much larger extent than in *Walkover*, natural sounds collapse with unnatural, diegetic sounds with extradiegetic, noise with music. The goose's cackle is magnified and repeated by the echo, the tram scraping the track is unrealistically prolonged, almost hurting the ears, cigarette lighters emit sounds like explosions, a bottle of champagne opens with an enormous crash. On other occasions sounds bear metaphorical meanings. For example, frequently used are bells, keys and glasses rubbed with hands, emitting sounds that bear resemblance to sounds produced by instruments used in the Catholic ceremonies, especially the Easter liturgy. At another moment the music imitates the movement of the character climbing a high building to rescue a goose waiting to be killed for the Easter feast. The use of music on this occasion (known in the jargon of film composers as mickey-mousing), brings to mind the scene from *Knife in the Water* in which the student climbs the yacht's mast. All these devices, apart from having specific narrative and symbolic functions, draw the viewer's attention to the aural aspect of the film, which becomes a true partner of the image. However, this extraordinary aurality of *Barrier* is largely a result of the very sparse use of dialogue. The role of the soundtrack is thus to somehow make up for the lack of words and smooth over the gaps in the narrative.

Krin Gabbard notes that 'since the 1980s, perhaps even since the 1950s, jazz has been about art. The carefully cultivated atmosphere in nightclubs, the photographs on album covers, the insider patter of jazz disc jockeys, the coloured lights that play on musicians in concert halls, the studied aloofness of the performers – what Walter Benjamin would call the "aura" of jazz – are difficult if not impossible to separate from the music' (Gabbard 2003: 120). These words ring especially true in relation to *Barrier*, as this is a very 'arty' film, and jazz contributes in large measure to its sophistication. Moreover, Skolimowski created his own, one can say East European, way of conveying the relationship between art and jazz. There are no Western-style nightclubs in this film, but the restaurant where the Easter ball takes place has a coolness of its own (see Chapter 3). Similarly, his jazz performers are aloof, but again, not in a studied, Western way, but more because they are bored and indifferent to their surroundings. In a similar vein, Skolimowski's dance leader does not attempt to imitate Western disc jockeys but rather accommodates this role to the Polish milieu through inserting irony into his performance. Finally, in *Barrier* there is no reference to the photographs on jazz album covers (there were hardly any jazz records available at the time in Poland), but there is a successful attempt to use jazz to add sophistication to the typically social realistic mise-en-scène, as conveyed in a scene of painting political slogans. Even over forty years after its production, *Barrier* still looks and sounds cool, and its elegance is the cumulative effect of musical and visual elements.

Yet despite the richness and sophistication of the soundtrack of *Barrier*, I find *Le Départ* the most 'musical' film of all those Skolimowski directed. One feels that without music, *Le Départ* would not survive as a coherent artefact, but instead break into a series of disjointed episodes. Unlike other films by this director, music not only illustrates events represented or counterpoints them, but practically replaces them, filling long passages without words and endowing the whole film with amazing energy. As previously mentioned, the soundtrack also plays the role of a 'narrative glue' in *Barrier*, but in *Le Départ* it fulfils it to a larger extent. Take the scene at the motor exhibition or of Marc driving his car through the deserted streets and tunnels of Brussels; they practically cannot exist without music. In the second case the music is very loud and aggressive, conveying Marc's approach to driving as if it was his private war against other people and the forces of nature. However, the sharp tones of Komeda's score are alternated with a lyrical song performed by Christiane Legrand, obviously exhibiting the more delicate and vulnerable side of a young car fanatic. We always hear one of these two leitmotifs when Marc is alone; no other music accompanies him in such situations, which suggests that Marc's 'emotional register' consists of two extremities: frantic energy and melancholia. This impression is also conveyed by the acting of Jean-Pierre Léaud, who is either hyperactive or pensive. The distinctive tone of Christiane Legrand's voice, sister of the famous film composer, Michel, inevitably recollects her most famous performance in Jacques Demy's film, for which Michel wrote the score, *Les Parapluies de Cherbourg* (*The Umbrellas of Cherbourg*, 1964). Even for those unfamiliar with French, the voice of Christiane signifies yearning for wasted or impossible love.

In common with *Barrier*, the music in *Le Départ* is frequently onomatopoeic. For example, in a scene when Marc quarrels with the driver of a motorcycle who caused an accident, the music amplifies the characters' quarrel, making it look more comical. The replacement of words by music suggests that it does not matter what the characters argue about or who is right; the very fact of the quarrel is important. Similarly, in the episode where Marc lies on the tram track, in order to force his girlfriend to step from the tram and join him on his scooter, the music resembles screaming. Such a replacement of words by music and other nonverbal sounds can be construed as an excellent strategy to cover the director's lack of knowledge of the language spoken in his film. In a wider sense, the score in *Le Départ* can be seen as a bridge between his Polish inheritance and the foreign world which the director would soon embrace for good.

While in *Barrier* and *Le Départ* the soundtracks are very rich and versatile, in the main part of *Hands Up!* it is somehow limited. However, the aggressive sounds of jazz at the party of medical school alumni enter the film like a storm, announcing a discord that will prevail in the rest of the film. Subsequently, the music serves as an underscore to the letter read by one of the participants at the ball. It comes across as a way to silence the reader, but at the same time it accentuates the combative nature of the letter. The main characters soon leave the party, but they take the music with them, singing the tune when entering an unused rail carriage, where the remainder of the film is set. The motif stays in their heads and thanks to its simplicity (it feels like it consists of only several notes) and numerous repetitions, it has the same effect on the film's viewers.[2]

As was previously mentioned, after *Hands Up!* was taken off the censors' shelf, the director added the Prologue to it. However, the style of this part of the score is very much in tune with what Skolimowski was doing 'musically' in the 1980s, therefore I shall discuss it in the later part of this chapter.

In this section I will also consider the soundtrack of Skolimowski's segment, *The Twenty-Year-Olds,* in *Dialóg 20–40–60*. Although the music for the entire film was written by a Slovak jazzman, Brano Hronec, in its style and function it is not dissimilar to the scores written by Komeda. Stylistically the music is eclectic, encompassing jazz, folk music, as well as pop and rock, which, by the time the film was shot, had replaced jazz as the principal music of the young. Moreover, diegetic cues tend to continue as nondiegetic, which can be interpreted as a sign that music dominates both the character's external life and his unconscious. Skolimowski casts in the main role a young musician, the leader of a pop/rock band, which can be described as a Slovak version of the Beatles. Their catchy song, performed probably in Vienna, excites the audience, consisting largely of teenage girls. Both the exaggerated performance of these 'Slovak Beatles', adorned in extremely shiny, glam rock clothes, and the hysterical reaction of the audience, underscored by rapid camera movements, invites ridicule. It is not difficult to guess that the whole spectacle is seen throughout the detached and contemptuous eyes of a jazzman, regarding pop and rock taste as a bad taste. We can associate this perspective with that of both Hronec and Skolimowski.

The instrumental version of the song presented at a gig accompanies the protagonist on his way to Bratislava, where he is to meet a woman, whom he used to love, in a dingy flat. When the young man reaches the flat, the music changes into a different type of music, first a jazzy score, then to a Christmas carol (the film is set around Christmas time, as suggested by a meagre Christmas tree, decorating the apartment). These changing melodies are pierced with startling noises such as of an oven exploding when the character puts a match into it. Although, as this description suggests, musically *Dialóg* comes across as a 'mini-*Barrier*', the soundtrack is much less satisfactory, partly because the film itself is not a masterpiece and partly because, unlike in *Barrier*, music does not reveal any hidden meanings, only confirms what we see.

Skolimowski's films from the 1960s are not only full of jazz, but also bear association to jazz compositions. In Michel Ciment's assessment, the director was at the time like a jazz musician: 'all rhythm and improvisation' (see Ciment 1984). Indeed, *Barrier* and *Hands Up!* were improvised. In *Le Départ*, rhythm appears to be the main principle of editing. *Barrier* and *Le Départ* almost feel like films in which the aesthetic form was laid out first, while content (plot and characters) was added later. However, with the passage of time, this freewheeling approach would disappear from Skolimowski's style.

The 1970s: Searching For One's Melody

Skolimowski's emigration coincided with death of Komeda and a decline in jazz's popularity in Poland and abroad. Jazz stopped being the sound of youth and became the music of the elite. Its use in film also declined. Not surprisingly, in his films made as an émigré, Skolimowski does not use jazz scores. Stylistically, from the 1970s, his scores became very eclectic. Not only do films made in a similar period have very different scores, but the film maker tends to incorporate different types of music in one film. Skolimowski's early films made in the West also testify to his search for his 'own' composer.

The music for *The Adventures of Gerard*, Skolimowski's first film as an émigré, was written by Riz Ortolani, one of the most prolific film composers, with over two hundred scores to his credit. About the time he wrote the music for Skolimowski's film, he was mostly known for spaghetti westerns, some of which were very popular in Poland, such as *Old Shatterhand* (1964), produced in Germany and directed by Hugo Fregonese. The fact that *The Adventures of Gerard*, in common with many other spaghetti westerns, was shot in Spain, was the main reason that Ortolani was employed. The composer treated *The Adventures of Gerard* as if it were a spaghetti western. Obviously, this kind of music, by putting the content of the film in brackets, adds to the unrealistic character of the film,[3] drawing attention to the fact that it is not about the Napoleonic wars, but about the twentieth century's rendition of this event. The music works best in the humorous parts of the film. When the events on screen get more serious, the score is less satisfactory, even confusing, giving the impression that the composer did not understand the film. Unlike Skolimowski's 'Polish' jazz films, there is no leitmotif linked to the main or any other character in the film. Ortolani's score acts as an external commentary on the plot, rather than an expression of Colonel Gerard's secret thoughts.

The music plays a somewhat similar role in *King, Queen, Knave*, although it is stylistically a different score to that written by Ortolani. The composer is Stanley Myers (1930–1993), a prolific British film composer, with whom Skolimowski worked on three films in the 1980s. However, Myers's approach to music in *King, Queen, Knave* is very different to that in *Moonlighting* and *Success Is the Best Revenge*. In *King, Queen, Knave*, the score, in common with *The Adventures of Gerard*, serves chiefly to portray the characters from an external perspective. It accentuates the idea that they are superficial, kitschy or even fake in their tastes, emotions and behaviour. One way of conveying this falsity is by using well known musical motifs, but badly played. The film opens with probably the best known funeral march, Chopin's Piano Sonata No. 2 in B Minor, op. 35 (used previously in *Money or Life*), played against the image of Martha and Dreyer returning from a funeral. Not only is the march played too slowly, on an organ which is out of tune, but it is also interrupted by strange noises, resembling sounds emitted by trains, owls hooting and dogs barking. Moreover, the organ music is gradually swept over by the orchestra. The exaggerated and eccentric instrumentation points to the fact that Martha and Dreyer do not really mourn the person whose funeral they attended, only give a typically 'funeral' impression. Such a 'reading' of the music is confirmed by the dialogue, when Martha asks her husband how she looks. The next motif is played when Frank meets Martha for the first time. She sits in the garden and we hear a banal, 'romantic' tune. The music on this occasion underscores her superficial elegance and her desire to live a romance. Later, in a scene when the Dreyers throw a garden party, the music sounds like a pastiche of Bavarian folk music. Bavarian folk is associated with bad taste as displayed at the party, where a piglet, adorned with a ribbon, serves as the main present, and guests amuse themselves in egg-throwing competitions. Here music strengthens the impression of the Dreyers' indulgence in bad taste, which is not even their indigenous taste (as he is an Englishman while she is Italian), but one they adopted, most likely for commercial reasons: to show their business partners, employees and customers that they are true Germans.

When Martha visits Frank for the first time with the intention of seducing him, we hear three distinctive cues, following each other. First some speeded up, tuneless sounds produced by string instruments mimic their growing appetite for sex. This motif is followed by a pastiche of fiery Spanish folk music, with the distinctive sound of castanets, announcing that the affair was consummated. Finally, when Martha and Frank make love for the second time, less hastily, paying more attention to proper facial expressions and body language (which, however, looks caricatured), we hear one of the best known pieces of Baroque music: Adagio in G minor by Tomaso Albinoni. This is, however, a butchered version of the Adagio, played on instruments that are completely out of tune by some hopelessly incompetent player. The use of this sequence of themes is ironic, emphasising that the love affair between Martha and Frank is sordid and clichéd.

Skolimowski also furnished *King, Queen, Knave* with a fair amount of diegetic music. For example, when Frank visits Martha, she puts on a record with some nondescript music recollecting 1960s pop, followed by a record with an aria from an opera. The second tune is played when Charles returns home. The contrast between the two types of music signifies the disparity in taste pertaining to the differing ages of Martha's two lovers or, perhaps, her assumption that if they represent different generations, they cannot like the same type of music. In reality, neither Frank nor Charles pay any attention to any of these tunes; each of them is preoccupied with their own thoughts. Music in this episode acts as a background or smoke screen, behind which the characters play out their dreams and desires. Music is used even more as a camouflage in an episode when the secret lovers go to a guitar concert in some smoky pub. Martha and Frank pay no attention to the performance, which allows them to discuss their lethal scheme in relative security. Martha and Frank's sordid affair is also conveyed by the noises they produce when making love, as well as when they are preparing for or dreaming about sex, such as the sounds of a mattress squeaking on the bed frame, beds groaning against the neighbouring pieces of furniture, apples falling from the wardrobe of an apartment downstairs and a rocking chair crashing against the window. Although the lovers attempt to hide their affair, they are unable to do so, being too carnal.

Although the score of *King, Queen, Knave* is very rich, there are no leitmotifs or indeed any cues that might be identified with the character. Consequently, we see the titular king, queen and knave as shallow people lacking any true interests or memories.

The melange of tunes, representing different periods, genres and styles, not only establishes the main trio as styleless, but prevents us from situating *King, Queen, Knave* in any distinctive place or time, which helps the film to stay 'faithful' to its literary source, Vladimir Nabokov's novel, which also has a timeless feel, despite being ostensibly set in Berlin during the 1930s. As a result of this stylistic eclecticism the music in *King, Queen, Knave* appears low-key, almost 'invisible'. From this respect *King, Queen, Knave* comes across as very different from Skolimowski's films from the 1960s, giving the impression that not only his characters, but also he was looking for his own 'tune'.

A different approach to music is offered in *Deep End* where, for the first time in his career, Skolimowski used a theme song – *But I Might Die Tonight* from the album *Tea for the Tillerman* by Cat Stevens, released in 1970. Although, as Richard Davis observes, in every period of movies there has been the issue of the theme song, pop song or end-title song, in the 1960s and 1970s, following the success of the Beatles films and *Easy Rider* (1969), scores utilising rock 'n' roll and other types of music appealing to young viewers were in vogue. Davis even asks rhetorically, 'How else to express the tone of these times but through the music of popular songs' (Davis 1999: 53–54). As if confirming this assessment, the score in *Deep End* plays two interconnected functions. One consists of rooting the story in British youth culture of the 1970s; the second to act as the voice of the soul of the main character, Mike.

Both roles are perfectly fulfilled by the song of Stevens, who in the 1970s was one of the biggest stars of British pop music. Stevens sang about romantic love, relationships between children and their parents, searching for one's place in the world and lost innocence. Perhaps more than any other pop music of the time, Stevens's songs were associated with a certain vulnerability and quest for spirituality typical of young people of this generation, to which Mike also belongs. Moreover, the very title of the song foreshadows the deadly ending to the film. It is one of the many signs of approaching death, along with red paint covering the walls and the lamp hanging over the pool which Mike will use in his fatal attack on Susan.

But I Might Die Tonight is already played in the title credits and in the film's first sequence, showing Mike cycling to work. Later we hear short fragments of this song on various occasions when Mike is on his own, for example cleaning dirty baths in the bathhouse. When Mike enters into a relationship with another person, the song fades out, suggesting that the approaching death looms in his subconscious. Other music used in the film is that of Can, a German band close to psychedelic rock, which in the 1970s became the lynchpin of 'krautrock'. In this period, Can diverged from traditional song structures towards a fluid improvisational style, very suitable for film scores. In *Deep End*, the music of Can appears when Mike loses touch with reality and either cannot control his emotions or starts dreaming. An example is the episode of Mike searching for Susan in a night club and on the streets of Soho, accompanied by Can's *Mother Sky*. On this occasion Mike appears to be as frantic and uncontrollable as the song we are hearing. Can's music is also used in the scene of his swimming, after being teased by his friend asking whether he has already slept with Susan. When he goes underwater, he starts imagining that Susan is swimming with him naked, and this is accompanied by the 'mermaid' sounds of Can. The sounds are not only dreamy, but also spooky, again foretelling approaching death. It is true that, as David Thomspon remarks, 'today the soundtrack by Can and Cat Stevens would probably win a high cool rating' (Thompson 2007: 20). However, the use of these two distinguished, but rather different types of music, might also suggest that in this period Skolimowski was hesitating between straightforward pop music and more elusive, electronic scores. Always being attracted to poetry and ambiguity, as opposed to clear-cut, literal messages, Skolimowski chose the latter.

Before *Deep End*, Skolimowski used pop and rock in his scores, for example in *Dialóg 20–40–60*. However, this film constitutes a breakthrough in his approach to these styles as here they are not used as 'foreign' sounds from which the author detaches himself, but ones that he embraces. Most likely this sympathy to the songs of Cat Stevens, as conveyed in *Deep End*, was less enduring than to the music of Komeda, but it is a secondary issue here. What really matters is Skolimowski's ability to present them as if he identified with them and in this way also encourage the viewer's identification.

The subject of searching for one's melody or, more exactly, voice, is literalised in *The Shout*, where the two main characters, Anthony Fielding and Charles Crossley, fight a kind of duel about whose music/sound is superior. Anthony, who is a professional musician, in a way typical of modern, industrial times, uses complex equipment to produce music. His method consists of recording simple, often natural sounds, such as that of marbles rattling together in a moving container or a bee buzzing inside a bottle, trying to get out, and then transforming them by a system of synthesisers. As a musician Anthony thus denaturalises the natural. He produces music in a specially designed studio, separated from sounds that might invade his space, which marks the artificiality of his project. We never hear any finished product of Anthony's work, only his endless experimentation with atonal music, which leads to the production of even less tuneful sounds which have an unsettling, almost painful effect on both Anthony and the film audience. This disturbing feature of Anthony's compositions is echoed by the work of Francis Bacon, which decorates the studio. Anthony does not explain to anyone the goal of his struggle with sound, which comes across as a solipsistic and masochistic pursuit. On the whole, Skolimowski creates the impression that Anthony's music is bare because it does not derive from his soul and does not serve anybody, but is the realisation of a self-contained intellectual project. Anthony also plays the organ in the local church. Of course, this is a very different type of music, because it is traditional, serves the community and even, from the perspective of Christianity, fulfils a moral purpose. However, the performer profanes this music by arriving in the middle of the service, when people are already singing without the organ. His playing is even discordant. Moreover, after the service Anthony commits an act of adultery, acting against the message of the priest's sermon and the spirit of Christianity in the wider sense. Hence, as a musician, he has no anchoring in the world.

Anthony's way of producing music is contrasted with that of Charles, who does not need any equipment to make music, only his own, powerful voice. He claims

Figure 5.1 Alan Bates as Charles Crossley before emitting his deadly shout

that his shout is so strong that it can kill and indeed in due course it kills a shepherd. Unlike Anthony, who most likely studied music at college, Charles learnt his craft during eighteen years spent among Australian aborigines. The shout with which Charles kills those around him can be regarded as a metaphor for any music of high value – if it does not move the listener, if it does not change his or her emotions fundamentally, then it is not worth writing and performing. However, there are also similarities between Anthony's electronic music and Charles's shout – both are unsettling and un-musical. They cannot be repeated and shared; they are therefore a domain of the specialists.

From the perspective of the mode of production and style, the soundtrack of *The Shout* is one of the most interesting made in this period in the West. Its centrepiece is a shout, uttered on the dune by Charles. To strengthen its effect, the director used the Dolby system. As he described it in an interview, 'it had to be applied just at the right moment so that we would be hearing something special. The shock of the sound is not a question of loudness or richness – it is sudden and it is complex, because the human voice is fortified on forty or more tracks by all the things that came into my mind that might be helpful, the Niagara Falls, the launching of a Moon rocket, everything. But over the top is the real human voice of a man shouting like hell' (Skolimowski, quoted in Strick 1978: 147). This description suggests that when creating the crucial part of the score, Skolimowski drew on the competing 'ideologies of music', encapsulated within the diegesis by Anthony and Charles. He used the voice but re-worked it, taking advantage of the most advanced technical equipment. The voice belonged to the director himself. The reason was his inability to find anybody able to shout non stop for twenty-three seconds, as this was the length of the scene already shot with Bates. Even professional criers performing at the markets in Britain were not able to sustain such a long yell. In despair, the director uttered it himself, at night, in a Soho music studio. The sound was so dramatic that the police were called by neighbours thinking that some awful crime was being committed (see Skolimowski, quoted in Uszyński 1990a: 32).

The same rule of synthesising the natural with the artificial applied to the rest of the score, composed by Tony Banks and Mike Rutherford of the popular group Genesis, largely based on themes from Banks's record *A Curious Feeling*. Banks and Rutherford's score is nostalgic and ethereal, as if echoing and amplifying the sounds of the wind 'playing' on the dunes. It can also be taken for the sounds of spirits of those released from their bodies, about which Charles tells his hosts. The same ambiguity and sense of foreboding is conveyed by the peacock's screeches that accompany the cricket match held in the grounds of a lunatic asylum. The peacock's announcement of approaching tragedy is confirmed at the end of the film, when a sudden storm causes the death of two people burnt alive in a cabin struck by lightning.

The 1980s and 1990s: The Sounds of Apocalypse

After the 1970s, which was the most eclectic period in Skolimowski's career in terms of subjects, styles and scores, his films gained more thematic coherence, which was also reflected in the styles of the scores. The majority of films he made in the 1980s use electronic music. Such scores were already popular in the 1970s and Skolimowski was at the forefront of the 'synthesiser revolution', using electronic music in *The Shout*. As Richard Davis suggests, initially 'synthesiser and other electronic sounds like the theremin were used in high intensity dramatic situations and science fiction films. They were usually part of a scary, spooky or otherworldly musical landscape' (Davis 1999: 61). This was also the way Skolimowski used them in *The Shout*. However, electronic music is likewise played in his ostensibly more realistic films, such as *Moonlighting* and *The Lightship*, and largely as a result of 'wrapping' them in electronic sounds, they feel spooky and otherworldly.

Stanley Myers wrote the scores for three films from this period, *Moonlighting* and *Success Is the Best Revenge*, which I will discuss in detail, and *The Lightship*. Myers is best known for the score of Michael Cimino's *The Deer Hunter* (1978) but, from my perspective, of more interest is the music he wrote in the 1980s for Stephen Frears, especially *Prick Up Your Ears* (1987) and *Sammy and Rosie Get Laid* (1987), films that expressed a deep criticism of Thatcherite Britain.

Moonlighting and *Success Is the Best Revenge* situate the stories of Polish emigrants against the utterly consumerist and yet repressive Thatcherite culture of the 1980s. The mixture of repression on the one hand, and consumerism on the other, is also conveyed by the scores of these films. In *Moonlighting*, most of the time we hear electronic underscore, played at a low volume. Its function is transmitting the tensions among a group of workers and foretelling the tragedy awaiting them. It becomes even more ominous when their leader, Nowak, wanders the city alone and sees on television screens, displayed in shop windows, the tanks on Polish streets – an obvious sign of the imposition of martial law. Only infrequently the score transforms into a gentler, more lyrical tune, when Nowak is reminiscing about his girlfriend who remained in Poland.

The background extradiegetic music is constantly pierced by louder and more distinctive, diegetic sounds, as in a scene when Nowak and his comrades for the first time enter the house which they are to renovate and are immediately confronted with the sounds of cracking stairs, noises produced by a broken toilet and pigeons cooing. This juxtaposition of diegetic and nondiegetic sounds produces an effect of two types of unpleasantness awaiting the characters: immediate, and distant but ultimately more ominous. This pattern is repeated throughout the whole film, only with the passage of time the 'domestic' sounds become louder and more aggressive, pointing to the frantic speed of workers racing against time, their noisy equipment, such as sledge hammers used to knock down the walls, and the growing rate of incidents happening during their work such as pipes bursting which leads to the collapse of a ceiling. However, the most startling noise is produced by the telephone in a nearby booth. At the beginning its sounds signify news from families in Poland; later, the lack of any news from them and the workers' disappointment. Loud sounds in the house also reflect the lack of contact between the Poles. Being cut off from their motherland, not knowing each other well, hating their boss and, most importantly, lacking any time for socialising, they have no opportunity to counter the industrial noises by their gentler, human voices. Often it is difficult to say whether the sound is diegetic or not, which adds to the atmosphere of tension and anxiety. This effect appears to be intended by the director, who admits that in one scene he used 'a combination of traffic sounds, electronically distorted, as music … Here, I recorded the sound of trucks – played at a very low volume, so one can't really tell what it is. It comes like an unpleasant wave and disappears, a hum that attacks your subconscious' (Skolimowski, quoted in Yakir 1982: 29).

The most obvious sounds of Thatcherite consumerism are heard in the local supermarket, first visited by the whole group and then frequented only by Nowak. When they go there for the first time, preparations for Christmas are already under way. The air is filled with adverts for various goods, which are meant to make their consumers happy, as well as the loud and discordant sounds of jingles and degraded versions of religious chants. The function of this 'music', in common with the religious symbols displayed in the shop windows, is purely commercial – to encourage customers to come inside and spend money. In the supermarket where Nowak does his regular shopping, apart from the music, we hear noises produced by cashiers and the equipment used for surveillance of the customers. As time passes, his money runs out, and Nowak turns into a thief, frightened that his illegal acts will be detected, the noises in the shop become even more sinister, resembling the sounds in an astronaut's laboratory or alien spaceship. Smaller shops mimic the supermarkets in their use of Christmas carols as a way to lure customers. Especially poignant from this perspective is a pawn shop for electrical goods owned by a man of Indian or

Pakistani origin, because most likely he is not a Christian and thus cannot have any spiritual connection with Christmas music. Yet his commercial methods are effective as Nowak buys from him a second-rate television set. The first night the men have a chance to use the television and watch a football match. Again, the sounds are loud and aggressive, and this impression is strengthened by showing us only the back of the television set. The workers do not enjoy the transmission for long, as the set breaks and, after emitting even more discordant sounds, falls silent. After this incident they immediately take to their axes and energetically attack the walls, either because they have nothing else to do, or to vent their frustration.

The high level of noise and refuse produced by the Poles upsets their English neighbours who keep coming to them with complaints, although they are themselves not blameless. For example, when a skip is set in front of the house, the neighbours dump their rubbish there at night, without any concern for the Poles' peace. As time passes, noise is used as a powerful weapon in an undeclared war between natives and the immigrants. This competition to create the greatest noise is both ridiculous and scary, for example, an episode when Nowak tries to retrieve a newspaper from the neighbour's letterbox and is greeted with the vicious barking of a dog holding the newspaper in his teeth on the other side of the letterbox. When the workers are visited by some English children singing Christmas carols,[4] they react by singing their Polish carol even louder, making the children bewildered and ultimately forcing them to leave empty-handed. Scenes like this bring to mind Roman Polański's *The Tenant* (1976), where the ability to create noise without being punished was also a mark of a person's place in the social hierarchy.

Figure 5.2 Renovating the house in *Moonlighting*

The sounds of London streets, as presented in *Moonlighting*, are as unpleasant as the interior sounds. The cars pass very rapidly, therefore loudly, paying no attention to the passers-by; the drunkards sing disjointedly or curse; the dogs bark. Moreover, often Nowak returns home in stormy weather, with thunder sounding like God's angry cries. The only oasis of aural peace and serenity is the Catholic church, but for the Polish migrants this oasis is practically unreachable. The three workers cannot go there because Nowak does not allow them to waste any time or money on 'spiritual pleasures' and Nowak himself has neither time nor courage to go to the church, feeling like a sinner who lost faith in God. However, he goes there once in order, as he puts it, to recover his self-respect and be human again.

On the whole, the soundtrack of *Moonlighting* comes across as the music of the approaching apocalypse. It broaches and amplifies the hellish life of Polish migrants; life that can only get worse, if the Poles remain in London. The apocalypse itself, however, remains off-screen, most likely because it concerns Poland under martial law, to which characters have only indirect access.

Unlike *Moonlighting*, *Success Is the Best Revenge* begins with the serene and melancholy music of Frédéric Chopin, accompanying the opening credits. Gradually the playing becomes more dramatic and eventually changes into an electronic score of the type used in *Moonlighting*, but louder, more tuneful and therefore distinctive. This change foretells the story, which begins lyrically and nostalgically, but finishes dramatically. The whole score can be regarded as a build-up of the film's momentum, which is the theatrical performance created by the exiled director, Alex Rodak. It is achieved predominantly by nondiegetic music with some help of diegetic sounds, such as the sounds of peacocks living in the garden of Rodak's shadowy friend, Montecurva.

The link between the film's score and the music used in Alex's theatrical 'event' is only revealed at the end of the film. The apocalyptic soundtrack comes across as puzzling, because it does not suit the contemporary subject of the film. On some occasions the music somehow takes us to a world which is an exaggerated or distorted version of what we see on screen. Take the scene of the football match, when Alex plays with a group of Polish workers against an English team and we hear some loud, rhythmical clapping. This sound is not dissimilar to the applause heard at football matches, but the stadium must be packed with people in order to produce sounds of this volume, while on this occasion the whole audience consists of Alex's wife and his younger son. When the film is re-watched, the clapping brings association with the heavy patter of soldiers' boots.

A different motif accompanies Adam Rodak in his peregrinations through London, on what turns out to be his last day in the city. The electronic music resembles the 'cosmic' sounds of *Tubular Bells* (1973) and later works by Mike Oldfield, as well as the scores of science fiction films such as *Blade Runner* (1982) by Ridley Scott. Its function is to transmit Adam's sense of alienation, which is a consequence of his ethnic difference and conflict with his father. Although more lyrical, the music is not very different in its genre and texture from the motif associated with Alex Rodak, which gives the impression that the father and son share the same status of aliens in England and the same fate: both are about to experience something apocalyptic. Their imminent doom is also conveyed by the harsh red light in which both Rodaks are often submerged.

Before the apocalyptic sounds are performed with full force at the theatre, Skolimowski introduces one more interlude of Chopin. It happens at the home of Dino Montecurva. Montecurva entertains his guests, Alex and Adam Rodak and the theatre director Monique des Fontaines, who all visit him to raise money for Alex's event, by playing in a virtuoso style, on a grand piano, Chopin's Etude in C Minor, Op. 10, No. 12, 'Revolutionary'. His performance of Chopin, the most Polish of Polish composers (although he left Poland for France when he was twenty), is imbued with irony. Firstly, we expect that it will be Rodak, the perfect Polish patriot, who will enchant Montecurva, the Pole who does not care about Poland, with Chopin, not the other way round. Montecurva's command of Chopin suggests that he carries enough of Polishness within himself, therefore will not be easily taken by Rodak's patriotic 'chant'. The pornographer's dramatic play also evokes another cosmopolitan Polish 'pornographer', writer and philosopher Stanisław Przybyszewski, who apparently charmed with his piano performances such famous artists as August Strindberg and Edvard Munch. The use of Chopin in this episode is quite different to that of Bach and other classical composers in earlier films by Skolimowski. Previously their music worked as a distraction or a neutral background of the characters' behaviour; on this occasion it constitutes an emotional focus and commentary of their actions. The difference results mainly from the use of live classical music, as opposed to poorly recorded and re-mixed sounds, as in the earlier films.

In the theatrical event itself, in a fashion typical for Skolimowski, diegetical and nondiegetical sounds merge. The heavy patter of policemen's boots, the sounds of tanks, the shouts of football fans, the clash of three gigantic balls (the main elements of the setting), hanging from the ceiling, intermingle with the 'cosmic', electronic score. As the play progresses, the sounds become louder, faster and, consequently, more apocalyptic. We can derive from this mixture of sounds that martial law, to which Rodak's play is dedicated, although it was a human tragedy for Poles, had a cosmic impact. The impact of the score is expanded by the lack of any dialogue in the crucial scene of fighting. Not surprisingly, when the music fades away, we know that this is the end of the performance and practically the end of Skolimowski's story.

The score for *Success Is the Best Revenge* was co-written by Hans Zimmer. This was the first film in the career of this prolific German-born composer, who later wrote music for *Rain Man* (1988), *Driving Miss Daisy* (1989), *Pirates of the Caribbean* (2006) and *The Simpsons Movie* (2007). Zimmer was brought into the film because of his knowledge of MIDI (Musical Instrument Digital Interface),[5] which dominated film music in the 1980s, following the phenomenal success of Vangelis's score to the 1981 film, *Chariots of Fire*, directed by Hugh Hudson. Richard Davis even goes as far as to claim that thanks to MIDI a new kind of composer was born: the specialist in electronic, synthesiser scores. Zimmer was one of the first to establish himself in this field and has been at the cutting edge of developing the new technology (see Davis 1999: 61–62). There is no doubt that it is largely thanks to Zimmer's input that the score for *Success* comes across as very contemporary and distinctive, adding immensely to the out-of-this-world feel of the entire film.

In this section I should also refer to the Prologue to *Hands Up!*, because it was shot in a similar period and fits very well with the mood of *Moonlighting* and *Success Is the Best Revenge*. All these films refer to the situation in Poland of the early 1980s, treating it as a time of approaching apocalypse. In the Prologue the apocalyptic mood is transmitted largely by the music of Józef Skrzek, who at the time was the leader of the electronic group SBB and subsequently the popular author of electronic scores for Polish films. However, when Skrzek embarked on a score for the Prologue, he had only one, although very distinctive, film to his credit, *Golem* (1979) by Piotr Szulkin, which (as its very title suggests), is a horror/science fiction film.[6] Most likely Skolimowski turned to Skrzek inspired both by the content of Szulkin's film and its music. Skrzek's score for the Prologue is not dissimilar to that of *Golem*, being atonal, unsettling, even scary. At times the music sounds like a continuous shout or cry, ascending to some invisible climax. The music of Skrzek fluently gives way to a fragment of *Kosmogonia* (1970) by Krzysztof Penderecki. This work, which combines experimental textures with baroque influences, enriches and balances Skrzek's electronic score by providing it with pathos in the form of human voice. Together, the two works excellently convey the theme of apocalypse.

A different musical element appears when the action of the film moves away from the 'grand narrative' of Polish history to the London house of the director. Here he wakes up when we hear some easy-listening, catchy tunes. It is difficult to imagine a greater musical contrast than the one between the unsettling music of Skrzek and Penderecki on the one hand, and the soft, laid-back tunes heard in Skolimowski's private space on the other. No doubt, such a contrast was intended, as it illuminates the gulf between the director's peaceful life in London and the disturbing character of Polish contemporary reality. Although the score in the Prologue is stylistically very different to music used in the main part of *Hands Up!*, both have a similar, disturbing effect on the viewer.

The last Skolimowski film about apocalypse is *Ferdydurke*. In common with *Barrier* and *Le Départ*, it is his most 'musical' film; we hear music throughout most of the narrative. However, unlike *Barrier* and *Le Départ*, where music makes up for scarce dialogue and plot, in *Ferdydurke* it largely takes the form of an underscore, adding to the impression of the film being heavy, if not overburdened, with meaning. The score was written by Stanisław Syrewicz and Michał Lorenc, credited as the author of additional music. After Wojciech Kilar and Zbigniew Preisner, Syrewicz is probably the most internationally renowned Polish composer, who before *Ferdydurke* wrote scores for, among other films, *L'Amour braque* (1985) by Andrzej Żuławski and *The Lair of the White Worm* (1988) by Ken Russell. Syrewicz's scoring style is eclectic, encompassing pop music and pastiches of classical works, but for whatever kind of film he composes music, he makes sure that it is not pushed into the background. His scores often contain catchy tunes that remain in the viewer's ear long after the film is finished. When discussing the score of *Ferdydurke*, we should also mention Krzesimir Dębski, who was responsible for its rich and varied orchestration.

Ferdydurke, as I argued in the previous chapter, can be construed as a story about a dying world, destroyed by an apocalypse or even by a series of apocalyptic events.

However, nobody within the diegesis, including its narrator, Józio, is aware of the approaching tragedy or at least the characters carry on with their lives and perpetuate their obsessions as if they were oblivious to their future. Both the approaching apocalypse and the lack of characters' awareness is conveyed by music. The soundtrack begins with a simple and repetitive melody played on the piano, as if performed by a carefree player, who only amuses himself by plonking away with one finger. Such music bears association with the leisurely lifestyle of the upper classes, which is confirmed by images of the stylishly furnished house whose inhabitant, Józio, is served by an immaculately clad maid. Soon the music develops into dramatic sounds, performed by the symphonic orchestra, as if the easygoing performer was swept away by forces much larger than himself. This pattern is repeated throughout the whole film: a simple melody is enriched by new instruments and finally transformed into a 'wall of sounds'.

Different moods are created by the use of different sets of instruments: a single piano, strings, a brass band. The first is used most widely, including in the 'circular' leitmotif, marking the circularity of (Polish) history and Józio's entrapment in it. We also hear Józio's cousin, Zosia, dramatically playing Chopin on the piano, with tears in her eyes. Her performance, of Etude in C Minor, Op. 10, No. 12, 'Revolutionary' (played in *Success* by Montecurva), signifies her growing erotic passion towards Józio and her affirmation of her Polish identity following the break with her Nazi fiancé. We hear the sound of strings in the love scene between Józio and Zosia; this time, however, the clichéd music can be construed as ironic, pointing to the lack of authenticity of the relationship between the young protagonists. Syrewicz's score also creates an ironic effect in an episode of the pupils' competition in pulling faces. On this occasion we hear a continuously rising tune, played by a brass band, as if the sounds were to rouse people to a real duel or even a battle. Ironic effect is also produced by a cue, used in the scene of Professor Pimko and Józio's journey to his old school, which sounds like a cross between a military march and a waltz. This motif draws attention to the military drill, taking place on the streets, with people wearing gas masks; this being a preparation for the approaching war. At the same time, it renders this preparation pathetic. Music in the film also serves to caricature certain social environments. For example, the song sung by Józio's aunt in a high-pitched voice, when she and her family are driven by car, points to the absurd lifestyles of the Polish aristocracy and their lack of awareness of their imminent doom. Approaching war is also foretold 'intertextually', so to speak, by using tunes similar to those in other films about the prewar period, such as Bob Fosse's *Cabaret* (1972), evoked in the scene of Józio's visit to the school. The approaching disaster, not unlike in *The Shout* and *Success Is the Best Revenge*, is also foretold by the sounds of peacocks. We hear them in the Łazienki park in Warsaw and on the estate of Józio's aristocratic aunt and uncle.

At the film's climax, two narrative and musical motifs are juxtaposed, which can be described as romantic and revolutionary. One is the motif of love between Józio and Zosia, which culminates on a rowing boat, accompanied by a romantic motif played on strings. As the camera moves away from the young lovers, this motif intermingles with and eventually is taken over by a cacophony of sounds, announcing the peasants' attack on the aristocrats. We hear laughter and the cries of the peasants, as well as of Józio's friend, Miętus, crying a butchered version of the slogan of the French Revolution, *Liberté, égalité, fraternité*, guns firing and windows breaking. All these sounds are played against the background of small groups of instruments, in which drums fulfil a prominent role, producing either dramatic or ominous effects. In this part familiar motifs mix and transform into new melodies, including sounds reminiscent of a popular Polish folk song, in the rhythm of *krakowiak*, *Abośmy to jacy tacy chłopcy krakowiacy* (*We are boys from Cracow*), suggesting that the 'lower classes' are responsible for the destruction of the Polish aristocratic culture and, perhaps, of Polish culture at large. Although the image is apocalyptic, this is still only a 'small apocalypse'; hence the lack of orchestral tutti in this sequence. The scene of the peasant/proletarian revolution gives way to an image of Józio, rowing alone in a boat, accompanied by the sounds of one of the most famous pieces of Polish music, the polonaise *Pożegnanie ojczyzny* (*Farewell to the Fatherland*) by Michał Kleofas Ogiński, written at the beginning of the nineteenth century. This romantic composer was also a famous Polish émigré, who lived in Holland, France and Italy. Largely due to its fame, *Farewell to the Fatherland* is used in varied contexts, to which Skolimowski's use refers. For example, it is a traditional accompaniment to the dance of final year college students in Poland, when they celebrate their maturity at a ball called 'studiówka' (taking place one hundred days before their final exam). In Skolimowski's *Ferdydurke*, Józio also achieves maturity; maturity is even the subject of his final talk with Zosia. Moreover, *Farewell to Fatherland* was used in Andrzej Wajda's *Ashes and Diamonds*, where it announces the end of the prewar Poland of decadent aristocracy. In *Ferdydurke*, the use of Ogiński's polonaise thus echoes Wajda's version. Skolimowski saved the orchestral tutti to the end of the film: documentary footage of Warsaw's bombardment during the Second World War, which constitutes the ultimate apocalypse in this film. In this part the loud orchestral tones are punctured by the sounds of the bombs falling from German aeroplanes.

The score of *Ferdydurke* includes a leitmotif, which opens the film and is played several times throughout the film. Its numerous repetitions and its very circular mode creates a nostalgic mood, as if taking us to the same, yet elusive place: prewar Poland, disappearing in front of our eyes. The fact that this theme also closes the film can be interpreted as alluding to the possibility of such a Poland being reborn after 1989, when it regained democracy.

Although stylistically the score of *Ferdydurke* is very different from that offered in *King, Queen, Knave*, it plays a not dissimilar function: conveying the voice of the film's author, who, from a distance, in this case of knowledge accumulated over the years, assesses the behaviour of his characters, finding it sometimes amusing, sometimes pathetic, moaning their demise but also acknowledging that there was no future for them. Consequently, music, along with other elements of *Ferdydurke's* style, such as mannered acting, creates the impression of it being a 'cold' film, made by a director no longer young.

Conclusion

In conclusion, I want to reiterate my claim that soundtracks play an important role in Skolimowski's films, typically being the partners of their visual side. On many occasions this director was in the forefront of musical/cinematic experimentation, such as when he ventured beyond jazz in *Barrier* and used electronic music and Dolby Stereo in *The Shout*. Music also conveys the tension between Skolimowski the nationalist/patriot and the cosmopolite, as reflected by his collaboration with Krzysztof Komeda and the frequent use of Chopin's music; both composers appealing to an international audience but also regarded as very Polish. Finally, music in Skolimowski's films attests to his long-standing desire to be a spokesman for young people and stay young himself. However, his recent films, which apply more classical scores, suggest that finally the director has aged.

Notes

1. The short account of the history of jazz in Poland and in its uses in film is offered in my book on Roman Polański (see Mazierska 2007). More extensive discussion can be found in Polish sources (see Bukowski 1980: Kowal 1995; Batura 2001; Tomasik 2004; Sowińska 2006).
2. I must admit it is the only musical motif from Skolimowski's films which I am able to repeat.
3. Spaghetti western is an unrealistic genre by being doubly divorced from its natural milieu of nineteenth century literature and American scenery where westerns proper are shot.
4. In reality in this episode Skolimowski used his own sons, Michał and Jerzy.
5. MIDI is a language that allows synthesisers and computers of any manufacturer to talk to each other.
6. Later Skrzek wrote music to another film by Szulkin, *Wojna światów – następne stulecie* (*The War of the World: Next Century* , 1981) and to a number of films by Lech Majewski.

Conclusions

A Successful Independent Director

In 2005, when I embarked on writing this book, it felt like an eccentric task, because Skolimowski was an almost forgotten figure. His name was still recognised in his native Poland and was not entirely alien to hard-core Western cinephiles, but it was difficult to find anyone who actually watched and remembered his films, especially amongst the younger generations. Yet, writing this book coincided with the renaissance of Skolimowski's popularity, inside and outside Poland. Signs of this new interest are presentations of his latest film, *Four Nights with Anna*, at numerous festivals, often in the presence of the director, retrospectives of his films, organised in places so varied as Holland, the Czech Republic, Armenia and South Korea, new interviews with the director, published in prestigious journals, including *Sight and Sound*, as well as the release in Poland of his first four films on DVD. This upsurge of interest can partly be explained by the simple fact that the director had 'woken up' from a long rest from cinema, following the artistic and box-office failure of *Ferdydurke*, released in 1991, and his successes as a painter. An equally important reason are those features of his films, which help them to resist the pressure of time and Skolimowski's entire attitude as a film director, which makes his cinema both a unique phenomenon and therefore still attractive to contemporary viewers. To these features I largely devoted my study.

Throughout the book I argued that Skolimowski, by his natural disposition, is an independent director, an *auteur* through and through. This does not mean that he only made the films he wanted and in the way he planned; in his portfolio we find works which, as he himself admits, were commissioned from him and which due to various unfavourable circumstances, did not live up to his expectations. However, such films are in the minority and, more importantly, they caused in their author such discomfort that he decided to give up on them. Conversely, for the chance to make some of his most original films Skolimowski paid a very heavy price in personal terms. His stubborn refusal to self-censor his anti-Stalinist film *Hands Up!* forced the director to leave Poland and search for opportunities abroad. Fifteen years later, the inner urge to talk about the exiled director trapped in London during martial law in

Poland, which coincided with Thatcher's rule in Britain, led to *Success Is the Best Revenge*, which failed spectacularly in commercial terms. As a result of this flop, Skolimowski lost his house and eventually left Britain. Subsequently, his inability to adjust to the way films are made in Hollywood, precipitated his return to Poland. By and large, making films transformed Skolimowski into a nomad.

Most of all, Skolimowski's artistic independence is reflected in the films themselves: their content and style. It is first demonstrated by their autobiographism. In a large proportion, including the first four made in Poland, the difference between the film's author and its main character is blurred. In them Skolimowski appears to talk about himself or somebody very similar to him, plays the main role and casts his relatives and friends in parts which are similar to roles they played in real life. Moreover, his protagonist situates himself or is relegated to the margins of society, due to his stubborn preoccupation with specific values or ideas, which his milieu scorns or simply due to the fact that he came from somewhere else: is an outsider, a stranger, a nomad, searching for a new home or a person in whom he can invest his feelings. Skolimowski's male characters are getting older, but inside they remain fragile and immature, as if they were children entrapped in male bodies. In particular, Leon in *Four Nights with Anna* appears most childish of all the men the director created. It could be suggested that his fragile, insecure male protagonists, who are always in the process of becoming, rather than acting out and imposing on others their firm opinions, epitomise the predicament of the 'new man': a man who cannot adhere to the old ideals of masculinity but equally is unable to replace them with new patterns; is neither a proper hero nor anti-hero. Autobiographical dimension of Skolimowski's films, especially in *Identifications Marks: None*, *Walkover* and *Success Is the Best Revenge*, is also reflected in the way they are narrated. In these films, the camera closely follows a protagonist during the most momentous day in his life.

Skolimowski's films can be regarded as self-reflexive, but their self-reflexivity is of a subtle kind. In his films we rarely find men talking straight to the camera, which became the most common prop in postmodern films (exceptions are *Success Is the Best Revenge* and Prologue to *Hands Up!*). The director rather prefers to draw our attention to the similarities between life and cinema, for example by accentuating parallels between certain ways of looking at reality and watching films, an example being the huge shadow produced by Leszczyc in *Identifications Marks: None* or the way Leon observes Anna in her window in *Four Nights with Anna*. I argued that an especially important aspect of Skolimowski's style is his interest in language – language as a means of communication and, even more so, in mis-communication. With a talent only comparable to that of Godard, Skolimowski explores private and public languages, language as an instrument of power and language as a private expression, in all their absurdity and beauty.

The next reason why Skolimowski's films feel original and resist the pressure of time is their balance between realism and non-realisms. Like Roman Polański and Wojciech Has, he creates his own type of non-realism, drawing on traditions such as expressionism, surrealism and Polish Romanticism, and mobilising many aspects of cinematic technique, including the soundtrack. He does so to heighten certain aspects of reality which otherwise would be difficult to convey, for example the mental turmoil suffered by the main character or his conflict with the society and culture in which he finds himself. The world depicted in his films comes across as at the same time strange and familiar or, more precisely, the familiar world turns out strange, hostile and frightening. In most cases, it is a dark and ugly world, filled with labyrinthine roads, permeated by dirty water and full of places to which the protagonist is denied access.

Skolimowski's *auteurial* personality is conveyed not only in his most personal projects, but also on those based on books and scripts written by other authors. In particular, in the films such as *King, Queen, Knave, Torrents of Spring* and *Ferdydurke* we find the familiar 'Boy', disorientated and searching for a place where he can 'anchor' himself. Moreover, in each of them the familiar world easily changes into a horrifying universe; the surreal overtakes the real.

Although the director of *Hands Up!* was never a follower of fashions, cinematic fashions caught up with him. In particular, autobiographism, and balancing between realism and non-realism are markers of a large part of contemporary art-house cinema. Skolimowski shows his younger colleagues and us, the audience, how to use traditions without becoming derivative, and how to build an organic whole of elements which appear incongruous,.

The success and tranquillity Skolimowski achieved as a septuagenarian acts as a sign that one can achieve success in the art of cinema despite following such an unusual path. Or, to refer to the title of one of his least successful and most interesting films, I will argue that he got his revenge, if not on the communist authorities, ruthless Thatcherism, then on fate, which conspired to prevent him enjoying the fruits of being one of the most interesting Polish, European and transnational directors of all time.

Biographical Note

Jerzy Skolimowski was born on 5 May 1938 in Łódź. His father was an engineer, his mother a teacher and later a diplomat. He spent the war years in Warsaw. In September 1939, a bomb fell onto the house on Rozbrat Street where he was living with his parents. The little Jerzy was buried under the rubble, to be eventually rescued by his mother. This event, in the director's opinion, affected his health for many years to come, and was the likely cause of his stutter.

During the German occupation, Skolimowski's father was involved in the anti-Nazi conspiracy, hiding a printing machine in their flat. In 1942, he was taken to the concentration camp at Majdanek and died the next year in the camp at Flossenburg. In 1943, Jerzy was placed in an orphanage in Otwock near Warsaw where he spent the last years of the war. In 1946, his mother arranged for the little Jerzy to be sent to Adelbaden in Switzerland, as a means to improve the boy's health. At the same time, his mother was deeply engaged in rebuilding the education system in Poland. Her achievements in this field led to granting her the position of cultural attaché in Prague, in 1947. In 1948, Jerzy followed her to Czechoslovakia. In 1949–50 he attended the only public school for boys in Eastern Europe, the gymnasium in Podebrady, where he met such important future luminaries of Czech culture as Václav Havel, Miloš Forman and Ivan Passer. In 1950, Jerzy was expelled from this school, and the following year he returned to Poland.

In Poland Skolimowski continued his education in the Adam Mickiewicz Grammar School (liceum) on Saska Kępa in Warsaw. He passed the final exams there in 1953, and the same year sat the highly competitive entrance exam to art college. He failed, but was accepted on the ethnography course. Despite passing all exams, he did not write his final thesis. In 1953, Skolimowski also began boxing. Till 1955, when he stopped boxing, he took part in sixteen fights. His boxing career ran in parallel with writing poetry, which led to publishing two volumes of poetry: *Gdzieś blisko siebie*, in 1958 and *Siekiera i niebo*, in 1959. Thanks to his successes in poetry he was admitted to the main writing association in Poland (Związek Literatów) and twice, in 1957 and 1958, was invited to spend periods of time in the house belonging to this organisation. There, in 1959, he met Andrzej Wajda and Jerzy Andrzejewski, who were working on the script for what would become *Innocent Sorcerers*. Skolimowski, who by then had gained a reputation as a specialist in 'youth affairs', was invited to join them and played a major role in shaping the script. Encouraged by Wajda, the same year he sat and passed the exam to enter the Łódź Film School. He studied there till 1964. During his period in Łódź he completed a number of students' etudes, as well as the full-length film *Identification Marks: None*. The critical success of this film led to two more films, completed in a short period of time, *Walkover* and *Barrier*, and to the invitation to work abroad, which resulted in making *Le Départ*, in 1966.

In 1965, Skolimowski married Joanna Szczerbic, an actress who played the main part in *Barrier*, as well as in a number of his subsequent films. The couple have two sons, Michal, aka Michael Lyndon, born in 1968 and Jerzy, aka Jerry, in 1970. In 1966, Skolimowski shot his fourth film in Poland, *Hands Up!*, partly set during Polish Stalinism. The film proved to be contentious with the political authorities. Unwilling to cut out the contentious material, which led to the film's shelving, Skolimowski decided to pursue opportunities abroad. In 1969, during editing *The Adventures of Gerard*, he relocated to London and lived there till 1984, making *The Shout*, *Moonlighting* and *Success Is the Best Revenge*. The same year, following the loss of his house, which served as a credit guarantee for *Success Is the Best Revenge*, Skolimowski relocated with his wife and two sons to Santa Monica in California. In the US, he made *The Lightship* and *The Torrents of Spring*, as well as playing in the films of other directors, including Tim Burton's *Mars Attacks!* The American period also witnessed the development of Skolimowski's career as a painter. He exhibited his works, among other places, in Venice and the Wieliczka salt mine in Poland, and sold to such famous collectors as Jack Nicholson. In 1996 Skolimowski and Szczerbic's marriage was dissolved.

Following the fall of communism in 1989, the director returned to Poland to shoot *Ferdydurke*. His disappointment with this film, as well as the difficulty of finding funds to finance his next project, *In America*, based on the novel by Susan Sontag, put the director off cinema for the following sixteen years. During this period he focused on painting. His last film, *Four Nights with Anna*, was met with critical acclaim. The film was co-scripted and co-produced by Ewa Piaskowska, whom Skolimowski married in 2003. The couple now live in the Warmia region in Poland.

Filmography

Films directed by Jerzy Skolimowski
(with technical details and synopses)

Boks (Boxing)
Poland, 1959
Direction: Jerzy Skolimowski
Screenplay: Jerzy Skolimowski
Cinematography: Roman Wionczek
Production company: Polski Komitet Olimpijski
Runtime: unknown.
Black and white
Cast: Jerzy Skolimowski, Feliks Stamm

The film, which is a hybrid between fiction and an instruction film for the boxing novices, starts with a fight on the street. An aggressive youth is encountered by Feliks Stamm, the 'father of the Polish school of boxing'. Stamm starts to teach the young man how to box and in due course he becomes a real boxer.

Oko wykol (The Menacing Eye)
Poland, 1960
Direction: Jerzy Skolimowski
Screenplay: Jerzy Skolimowski
Cinematography: Jerzy Mrożewski
Production company: PWSTiF
Runtime: 2 min.
Black and white
Cast: Iwona Słoczyńska, Wojciech Solarz.

Somewhere in a funfair a man enters a small caravan wielding a knife. We do not see his face, only the lower part of his body. In the next scene a man is practising throwing knives at a woman from a rocking horse. The last throw pierces her wig. The man leaves the caravan.

Hamleś (Little Hamlet)
Poland, 1960
Direction: Jerzy Skolimowski
Screenplay: Jerzy Skolimowski
Cinematography: Jacek Stachlewski
Production company: PWSTiF
Runtime: 9 min.
Black and white
Cast: Zbigniew Leśniak (Little Hamlet), Elżbieta Czyżewska (Little Ophelia), Wiesław Gołas (Little Laertes), Ryszard Ostałowski (Boss), Hanna Skarżanka (Boss's wife).

A group of Warsaw proletarians meet in a destroyed or unfinished building, consisting largely of stairs, littered with newspapers. A couple named the 'Boss' and the 'Boss's wife' play a song from a record. The song introduces the film characters as dwarfed versions of personas from Shakespeare's *Hamlet*: Hamleś (Little Hamlet), Ofelka (Little Ophelia), Learcio (Little Laertes). Little Hamlet behaves as if suspicious of something, Ofelka bathes and Learcio appears to be discontented with something.

Akt (The Nude)
Poland, 1961
Direction: Jerzy Skolimowski
Screenplay: Jerzy Skolimowski
Cinematography: Jacek Stachlewski
Production company: PWSTiF
Runtime: unknown
Black and white

Mock-documentary about the work of a well known Polish female sculptor of Jewish origin, Alina Szapocznikow. The artist, at her studio in the Old City in Warsaw, makes a sculpture of a naked woman, using a model. In reality, Szapocznikow did not use models.

Erotyk
Poland, 1961
Direction: Jerzy Skolimowski
Screenplay: Jerzy Skolimowski
Cinematography: Jacek Stachlewski
Production company: PWSTiF
Runtime: 3 min.
Black and white
Cast: Elżbieta Czyżewska, Gustaw Holoubek.

A man and a woman meet in a room covered with newspapers, the centrepiece of which is a large, dusty mirror, on which she writes the word 'Erotyk'. The woman seems to be simultaneously attracted and repelled by the visitor who might be an innocuous stranger or a rapist. His ambiguous attitude to her is conveyed by his treatment of the woman's white, fluffy dog whose beauty he admires one moment, only to throw him violently to the ground in the next. After that he approaches her and she moves away from him till reaching a wall. Then the light is switched off and the stranger disappears. The woman sings *We Only Meet in a Mirror*, suggesting that her meeting with the stranger took place in her dream.

Pieniądze albo życie (Money or Life)
Poland, 1961
Direction: Jerzy Skolimowski
Screenplay: Jerzy Skolimowski, based on a short story *Pięć tysięcy złotych* (*Five Thousand Zloties*) by Stanisław Dygat
Cinematography: Jacek Stachlewski
Production company: PWSTiF
Runtime: 5 min.
Black and white
Cast: Stanisław Dygat (Large man), Bohdan Łazuka (Slim man), Krystyna Sienkiewicz (Woman at a shooting gallery).

During the Second World War two men meet at a funfair: one slim and one large. The slim one follows the large one to the shooting gallery and merry-go-round, pleading from him to return five thousand Zloties, claiming that his life depends on this sum. The large man refuses and threatens to denounce him to the nearby German gendarmes, telling them that he is a Jew, although he assumes that he is not. However, the slim man follows the large man and when he is about to be betrayed to the Germans, he reveals that he is indeed a Jew. Upon hearing this, the large man gives him the money and asks him to hit him, which makes the Germans laugh.

Rysopis (Identification Marks: None)
Poland, 1964
Direction: Jerzy Skolimowski
Screenplay: Jerzy Skolimowski
Cinematography: Witold Mickiewicz
Production design: Jerzy Skolimowski
Editing: Halina Gronek
Music: Krzysztof Sadowski
Sound: Jan Czerwiński
Producer: Zbigniew Brejtkopf
Production company: PWSTiF
Runtime: 71 min.
Black and white

Cast: Jerzy Skolimowski (Andrzej Leszczyc), Elżbieta Czyżewska (Teresa, Barbara and the woman living in the apartment of the Janczewskis), Andrzej Żarnecki (Mundek).

The 1960s, 1 September, anniversary of the outbreak of the Second World War. Andrzej Leszczyc wakes up in the morning and wakes his partner, Teresa. He leaves their apartment and goes to a gathering point for men who are about to join the army. In his questioning by the draft commission it transpires that he was a student of ichthyology who gave up studying shortly before graduating from the university. Contrary to the expectations of the commission, he does not look for any excuses to avoid the military service. Leszczyc is meant to catch the afternoon train, which will take him to his army unit. He spends the last hours of his freedom arranging various outstanding errands. He takes his dog to the vet, where the pet, assumed to have rabies, is put down. He goes to the university to collect his documents and meets there an attractive female student, Barbara, with whom he goes to the local wood mill, where he used to work. By chance he meets an old friend, Mundek and goes with him to a café. Mundek gives Leszczyc the address of another woman, whom he pimps. It transpires that Leszczyc was erotically involved with this woman, who now lives in the flat of the Janczewskis, who temporarily moved abroad. Leszczyc tries to find Teresa at work, but she is not there. When they meet at home, he is bad-tempered and accuses her of being unfaithful to him. He leaves home again, gives an interview to a radio reporter and goes to the railway station. Once on the train, he bids farewell to Barbara.

Walkower (Walkover)
Poland, 1965
Direction: Jerzy Skolimowski
Screenplay: Jerzy Skolimowski
Cinematography: Antoni Nurzyński
Production design: Zdzisław Kielanowski
Editing: Alina Fadlik
Music: Andrzej Trzaskowski
Sound: Mikołaj Kompan-Altman
Producer: Jerzy Nitecki
Production company: Syrena Film Unit
Runtime: 70 min.
Black and white
Cast: Jerzy Skolimowski (Andrzej Leszczyc), Aleksandra Zawieruszanka (Teresa), Krzysztof Chamic (the manager of the industrial plant), Elżbieta Czyżewska (the girl at the station), Andrzej Herder (boxer Marian), Tadeusz Kondrat (the owner of the pawn shop), Krzysztof Litwin (Miecio), Stanisław Zaczyk (false priest), Henryk Kluba (trainer Rogala).

Andrzej Leszczyc arrives by train to a nameless, newly built industrial town. The purpose of his visit is to take part in a boxing novices' tournament. Leszczyc, however, does not fit this category. He previously took part in a number of 'first steps' and now earns his living by selling trophies from the competitions. Moreover, he will soon turn thirty. From the window of the train he notices a young woman on the platform, who is also a newcomer to the town. She appears familiar but he does not remember her name, which is Teresa. She also recognises him and they begin crossing the town, together arranging their separate errands, as well as trying to decipher their past and find a new place for themselves. It turns out that Andrzej and Teresa were once students at the same university engineering department. Teresa, being then an ardent communist, played a crucial role in his expulsion from the university. Andrzej forgives Teresa her treacherous behaviour and they make love in her new apartment; the flat being a perk attached to Teresa's new, high post in the industrial plant. Leszczyc takes part in the boxing competition. He beats a weaker opponent but leaves the town with Teresa before an encounter with a much stronger boxer who, like him, previously won many 'first steps'. However, persuaded by the worker whom he befriended during his peregrinations, Leszczyc returns to the town, only seconds before the match is due to start. He wins through a walkover and collects a new set of trophies. Soon, however, his opponent arrives and asks Leszczyc to share his prize with him. When Leszczyc refuses, he beats him up.

Bariera (Barrier)
Poland, 1966
Direction: Jerzy Skolimowski
Screenplay: Jerzy Skolimowski
Cinematography: Jan Laskowski
Editing: Halina Prugar
Music: Krzysztof Komeda
Sound: Wiesława Dembińska
Producer: Stanisław Zylewicz, Ryszard Straszewski
Production company: Kamera Film Unit, Film Polski
Runtime: 83 min.
Black and white
Cast: Jan Nowicki (The Student), Joanna Szczerbic (The Girl), Tadeusz Łomnicki (the doctor), Zbigniew Maklakiewicz (magazine seller), Ryszard Pietruski (head waiter), Maria Malicka (charlady), Małgorzata Lorentowicz (lady of the house).

Easter Eve. In a students' hostel four medical students take part in a game of catching a matchbox in their mouthes. The one who wins takes the prize of a piggy-bank, containing their joint savings, and leaves, announcing to his pals that he gives up on his studies. Carrying his belongings in a suitcase, he encounters a mobile blood-donor station and goes to visit his father in the old people's home. The father gives him a pawn ticket and an address for what looks like a home of some aristocrats. The woman who lives there first mistakes the Student for a cleaner and then gives him his father's sabre. The Student meets a pretty tram driver and takes her to an expensive restaurant, after inviting his friends to meet his fiancée. The restaurant is empty, except for the waiters, the band and a charlady who, asked by the master of ceremonies, gives an elevated performance of a song. The friends arrive and soon the restaurant is full of war veterans. The Student and the tram driver leave and climb to the top of an artificial ski-jump. He jumps on his suitcase and the couple are separated. The Student visits a house with a large car in the garage. The girl searches for the Student and joins a students' party. There she is ridiculed, when it turns out that she knows practically nothing about the man whom she tries to find. The couple meet again when he jumps onto her tram.

Le Départ
Belgium, 1966
Direction: Jerzy Skolimowski
Screenplay: Jerzy Skolimowski, Andrzej Kostenko
Cinematography: Willy Kurant
Editing: Bob Wade
Music: Krzysztof Komeda
Sound: Philip Cape
Producer: Bronka Ricquier
Production company: Elisabeth Films
Runtime: 91 min.
Black and white
Cast: Jean-Pierre Léaud (Marc), Catherine Duport (Michèle), Jacqueline Bir (the customer), Paul Roland (friend), Léon Dony (boss).

Nineteen-year-old Marc, who works as a hairdresser's apprentice in Brussels, dreams about becoming a racing car driver. He enters his name for a car rally due to start in two days, but does not have a car and goes to great lengths to acquire one. When it turns out that his boss will not leave his Porsche for Marc to 'borrow' for the event, he poses as the secretary to a friend disguised as a maharaja, who wants to buy a Porsche and steals the expensive vehicle, while trying it. However, the trick does not work and Marc has to return the car. He also attempts to find money for the deposit to hire it officially. For this purpose he goes to a motor show with Michèle, a girl he has met while delivering a wig to a customer. He plans to steal spare parts and sell them, but this idea fails too. Later Marc and Michèle pawn everything he and his girlfriend have of value, but again the money is not sufficient. Neither is Marc able to successfully steal the car – he returns the car he stole at the petrol station after finding a dog on the back seat. Marc's boss returns unexpectedly and Marc's problem appears to be solved – he 'borrows' his boss's car to use in the rally. However, before the event he and Michèle stop at the hotel to get some sleep and they oversleep the rally.

Ręce do góry (Hands Up!)
Poland, 1966, premiere in 1985
Direction: Jerzy Skolimowski
Screenplay: Jerzy Skolimowski, Andrzej Kostenko
Cinematography: Witold Sobociński, Andrzej Kostenko
Editing: Zenon Piórecki, Grażyna Jasińska, Krystyna Rutkowska
Music: Krzysztof Komeda
Sound: Jan Czerwiński, Norbert Zbigniew Mędlewski
Producers: Tadeusz Karwański, Jerzy Nitecki
Production company: Syrena Film Unit
Runtime: 76 min.
Black and white
Cast: Jerzy Skolimowski (Andrzej Leszczyc – Zastava), Joanna Szczerbic (Alfa), Tadeusz Łomnicki (Opel Record), Adam Hanuszkiewicz (Romeo), Bogumił Kobiela (Wartburg).

The 1960s. At a reunion party of medical school alumni, a man, who gradually uncovers his head from bandages, reads a letter from their colleague, who now lives somewhere in provincial Poland. It transpires that the author of the letter has a grudge against his old companions. A group of party guests, consisting of four men and one woman, leave the building and board a freight train, which is meant to take them to the village where their old friend lives. There they reminisce on their university past and comment on their current lives. In the 1950s, when all of them were students, they took upon themselves the task of assembling a huge portrait of Stalin. The portrait turned out to be faulty, having two pairs of eyes. Consequently, they had to explain their mistake to a commission, consisting of the activists of a youth organisation, which accused them of sabotage. At the trial most members of the team tried to defend themselves, paying little attention to how it would affect their co-defendants. Only the sole female in the group protested against such behaviour, appealing to their sense of solidarity. The consequences for one of the students, Andrzej Leszczyc, were dire: he was expelled from the university and even thought about committing suicide, but was dissuaded by his fellow female colleague, the one who is now on the train with him. In the present time, the ex-students use as pseudonyms the names of the cars they drive: Alfa and Romeo (who are married), Record, Wartburg and Zastava. They admit that they have become materialistic, comfort-oriented, even take bribes at work. The only possible exception is Zastava–Leszczyc, who due to his expulsion from the university started his career later and has remained bitter about the past. It is possible that he is the ex-student with the grudge, who wrote the letter to them read at the party. The passengers cover their clothes and bodies with flour, trying to imagine what it was like to be taken by cattle truck to a concentration camp. They also arrange a fake execution of Wartburg. At the end of their journey they discover that the train did not leave the station. They part and each goes to his/her own car.

Prologue to Hands Up!
Poland, 1981
Direction: Jerzy Skolimowski
Screenplay: Jerzy Skolimowski
Production design: Janusz Sosnowski
Music: Józef Skrzek
Production company: PRF Zespoły Filmowe
Colour
Cast: Jerzy Skolimowski, Alan Bates, Jane Asher, David Essex, Bruno Ganz, Karol Kulik, Mike Sarne, Gerald Scarfie, Volker Schlöndorff, Feliks Topolski, Fred Zinnemann.

Jerzy Skolimowski presents the background to the shelving of *Hands Up!* and the context of the ending of the ban in 1981. He addresses an absent officer of the Secret Service, whose decision almost destroyed his life and career. The director also describes his present life. We see him exhibiting paintings of Polish artists in his London flat and chatting to his guests, such as Feliks Topolski and Alan Bates. In other episodes, Skolimowski appears as an actor in Volker Schlöndorff's *Die Fälschung* (*Circle of Deceit*, 1981), shot in the capital of Lebanon, Beirut, and as a supporter of a pro-Solidarity demonstration in London. Documentary footage is intertwined with the staging of a science fiction film of sorts, presenting the invasion and destruction of some fictitious city or country. These events, which look like a premonition of martial law, are observed by Skolimowski through portholes.

Dvadsatrocni (*Twenty-years-old*)
Segment in *Dialóg 20–40–60*
Czechoslovakia, 1968
Direction: Jerzy Skolimowski
Screenplay: Jerzy Skolimowski
Cinematography: Andrzej Kostenko
Music: Brano Hronec
Runtime: 30 minutes.
Black and white

Cast: Jean-Pierre Léaud, Joanna Szczerbic, Viera Strnisková

After finishing a concert, the leader of a popular youth band travels from Vienna to Bratislava. There he enters a department, where he meets a couple. They leave and he waits for another woman. When she comes, they order food over the telephone, quarrel and eventually part.

The Adventures of Gerard

Great Britain/Italy/Switzerland, 1970
Direction: Jerzy Skolimowski
Screenplay: H.A.L. Craig, in association with Henry Lester, Gene Gutowski and Jerzy Skolimowski. Based on four stories from *The Exploits of Brigadier Gerard* and one from *The Adventures of Brigadier Gerard* by Sir Arthur Conan Doyle
Cinematography: Witold Sobociński
Production design: Bill Hutchinson, Luciano Spadoni
Editing: Alistair McIntyre
Music: Riz Ortolani
Producers: Henry Lester, Gene Gutowski
Production company: Sir Nigel Films (Zurich)
Runtime: 91 min.
Colour
Cast: Peter McEnery (Colonel Etienne Gerard), Claudia Cardinale (Teresa, Countess of Morales), Eli Wallach (Napoleon Bonaparte), Jack Hawkins (Millefleurs), Mark Burns (Colonel Russell), Norman Rossington (Sergeant Papilette), John Neville (Duke of Wellington), Paolo Stoppa (Count of Morales).

Colonel Etienne Gerard, who participates in Napoleon's 1808 attack on Spain, is determined to prove that he is the bravest hussar in the Emperor's army. Gerard is entrusted with an important message for Marshal Massena, whose troops have been pinned down during the siege of the Castle of Morales. Gerard is unaware that he is given this assignment in the hope that, thanks to his famous stupidity, he will fall into English hands. Gerard suffers various setbacks on his way to Massena and several times is on the brink of losing his life. Moreover, he becomes romantically involved with Teresa, Countess of Morales, a Spanish patriot who attempts to capture the message from Napoleon. Yet he manages to deliver the message to Massena intact. At the same time he learns that it was not what the Emperor had in mind. He decides to blow up the Castle of Morales, but is imprisoned by a dashing Englishman, Colonel Russell. He escapes and the castle is blown up by Teresa's blind uncle, the Count of Morales, who throws his cigar-butt into the castle ammunition dump. Gerard receives a medal from Napoleon and embarks on further adventures while Teresa agrees to wait for him.

Deep End
West Germany, Great Britain, 1971
Direction: Jerzy Skolimowski
Screenplay: Jerzy Skolimowski, Jerzy Gruza, Bolesław Sulik
Cinematography: Charly Steinberger
Production design: Tony Pratt, Max Ott Jr.
Editing: Barrie Vince
Music: Can, Cat Stevens
Sound: Karsten Ullrich
Producer: Lutz Hengst, Helmut Jedele
Production company: Bavaria Studios
Runtime: 91 min.
Colour
Cast: John Moulder-Brown (Mike), Jane Asher (Susan), Diana Dors (Mike's customer), Karl Michael Vogler (swimming instructor), Christopher Sandford (Susan's fiance), Erica Beer (baths cashier), Jerzy Skolimowski (passenger on the metro train)

Mike, a boy from a working class family who has just finished school, finds a job in the public baths/swimming pool in Fulham, London. There he becomes interested in Susan, who is slightly older than him and has been working in the baths for several years. Unlike Mike, who is still a virgin, Susan is sexually very experienced. She has a boyfriend, as well as having an affair with her previous PE teacher, who still keeps visiting the swimming pool, each time bringing a new group of schoolgirls to whom he gives swimming lessons. The girl proves to be friendly and helpful, telling Mike how to make extra money by attending to the sexual needs of his female clients. However, Mike wants more than just friendship and he starts to stalk Susan, following her to an adult cinema and night club, which she visits with her boyfriend. He also causes a false fire alarm when Susan makes love to the swimming instructor and he steals a full-sized cardboard cut-out image of an expensive prostitute, standing in front of a Soho brothel, because she looks exactly like Susan. Mike confronts Susan on the underground train, asking her if she posed for the picture and when she says 'yes', he gets very angry, drawing the attention of the other passengers to the couple. Back at the baths, he swims with the 'cardboard Susan'. Some time later Susan accompanies her lover during a running race for the pupils. Mike takes part in the race despite being asked by the teacher not to do so. When the race is finished he punctures the tyres of the teacher's car to prevent Susan leaving with her lover. When the girl finds out about his plot, she hits him, losing a diamond from her engagement ring, which falls into the snow. Mike and Susan collect the snow and go together to the deserted baths, to retrieve the diamond. They succeed and make love. However, when Susan reveals to Mike that she does not regard having sex with him as anything special and attempts to leave, Mike kills her.

King, Queen, Knave
West Germany, USA, 1972
Direction: Jerzy Skolimowski
Screenplay: David Shaw, David Seltzer, based on the novel *Korol', Dama, Valet/King, Queen, Knave* by Vladimir Nabokov
Cinematography: Charly Steinberger
Editing: Melvin Shapiro
Music: Stanley Myers
Sound: Kersten Ullrich, Hans-Joachim Richter
Producer: Lutz Hengst
Production company: Maran-Film (Munich)/Wolper Pictures (Los Angeles)
Runtime: 92 min.
Colour
Cast: Gina Lollobrigida (Martha Dreyer), David Niven (Charles Dreyer), John Moulder-Brown (Frank Dreyer), Mario Adorf (Professor Ritter), Barbara Valentin (optician).

After returning from the funeral of his brother, Charles Dreyer, the wealthy owner of a department store in Munich, persuades his wife Martha that they should take care of his newly orphaned nephew Frank, the likely successor to Charles's business. Martha is hostile towards this idea, but when Frank arrives at their mansion, she warms to the boy, touched by his clumsiness and near blindness, caused by his glasses being broken. Martha takes Frank to an optician and finds him a room. Soon Frank and Martha start to conduct an affair there, to the avid interest of Frank's landlord, Professor Ritter. Ritter uses the connection with Frank to offer Frank's uncle his invention: an artificial skin, which perfectly imitates human flesh and which he names 'voskin'. Dreyer likes voskin and commissions Ritter to use it to build mannequins for his store. The first set of mannequins is unsuccessful, but Dreyer asks Ritter to carry on, using as his new model the woman who visits Frank in his room. Martha decides to get rid of her husband, in order to have both his wealth and Frank. She persuades Frank to murder Charles when they are all on holiday by the sea. They lure Charles, who cannot swim, into a boat. Charles tells Martha that he is about to make a very profitable deal and she decides to postpone the murder. This leads to a confusion – everybody ends up in the water and Martha drowns. Charles invites Frank to live with him in his mansion. Ritter visits their house bringing the new mannequin which looks exactly like the woman who used to visit Frank – Martha.

The Shout
Great Britain, 1978
Direction: Jerzy Skolimowski
Screenplay: Michael Austin, Jerzy Skolimowski, based on the short story *The Shout* by Robert Graves
Cinematography: Mike Molloy
Production design: Tony Woollard
Editing: Simon Holland
Music: Anthony Banks, Michael Rutherford, Rupert Hine
Sound: Alan Bell, Tony Jackson
Producer: Jeremy Thomas
Production company: Recorded Picture Company, for the National Film Finance Corporation and Rank
Runtime: 86 min.
Colour
Cast: Alan Bates (Charles Crossley), Susannah York (Rachel Fielding), John Hurt (Anthony Fielding), Robert Stephens (Chief Medical Officer), Tim Curry (Robert Graves), Julian Hough (Vicar), Carol Drinkwater (Cobbler's Wife), Nick Stringer (Cobbler).

The 1970s. A woman inspects some human corpses in a mental asylum. Then the action moves to a small village in Devon, some years earlier. A childless couple, composer and performer Anthony Fielding and his wife Rachel, are visited by a traveller named Crossley. He claims that for many years he lived among Australian aborigins and has learnt their magic, including a deadly shout. Anthony wants to check Crossley's power and one morning they go to the dunes, where Crossley utters his shout. It kills a shepherd and some sheep, but Anthony survives, only faints during their expedition. At the same time a local cobbler, the husband of a woman with whom Anthony has had an affair, falls seriously ill. The Fieldings' marriage disintegrates due to Rachel's sexual attraction to Crossley. Anthony goes to the dunes and finds some stones, representing the souls of his hosts. He breaks what appears to be Crossley's soul. The police come for Crossley, claiming that he is a madman. Crossley tells this story to Robert Graves, while watching a cricket match, in which Anthony is taking part, in a mental asylum. Lightning strikes the cabin in which Crossley sits, killing him and his companion. The action moves to the present. Rachel recognises the corpse as belonging to Crossley.

Moonlighting
Great Britain, 1982
Direction: Jerzy Skolimowski
Screenplay: Jerzy Skolimowski
Cinematography: Tony Pierce Roberts
Production design: Tony Woollard
Editing: Barrie Vince
Music: Stanley Myers, Hans Zimmer
Sound: Alan Bell, David Stevenson
Producer: Mark Shivas, Jerzy Skolimowski
Production company: Michael White, with the assistance of the National Film Development Fund and Channel 4.
Runtime: 97 min.
Colour
Cast: Jeremy Irons (Nowak), Eugene Lipinski (Banaszak), Jiri Stanislaw (Wolski), Eugeniusz Haczkiewicz (Kudaj), Denis Holmes (neighbour), Judy Gridley (supermarket supervisor), Jerzy Skolimowski (Boss).

At the beginning of December 1981, four Polish men cross the British border at a London airport, armed with one-month tourist visas. They claim that they are coming to buy a second-hand car with their joint savings of twelve hundred pounds, but in reality their aim is to renovate the house of their Boss. Only one man in the group, Nowak, can speak English and he is responsible for persuading the customs officer to let them in, bringing the builders to the place of their work. The task proves very difficult. The house lacks basic amenities, the men are harassed by their neighbours and the money is not sufficient to buy the working material and food. Consequently, Nowak is reduced to stealing food from a local supermarket. He also changes the time on the workers' watches, so that they sleep less and labour many more hours than they intended; this is his strategy to finish the work on time. Moreover, during their stay contact with their families is severed due to the introduction in Poland of martial law. Nowak attempts to hide this information from his companions, anxious that they might refuse to finish their task if they know what awaits them back in Poland. He himself is tormented by the lack of contact with his girlfriend Anna and imagines her betraying him with the Boss. The three men, deprived of almost everything, become rebellious and one night Nowak is forced to sleep outside. The work is eventually completed. Lacking any money, the four Poles set out on a six-hour walk to the airport. During their journey Nowak tells them about the situation in Poland and is attacked by his angry and frustrated companions.

Success Is the Best Revenge
Great Britain/France, 1984
Direction: Jerzy Skolimowski
Screenplay: Jerzy Skolimowski, Michael Lyndon
Cinematography: Mike Fash
Production design: Voytek
Editing: Barrie Vince
Music: Stanley Myers, Hans Zimmer
Sound: Mike Crowley, Jim Roddan
Producer: Jerzy Skolimowski
Production company: De Vere Studio (London)/Gaumont (Paris), for the Emerald Film Partnership.
Runtime: 91 min.
Colour
Cast: Michael York (Alexander Rodak), Joanna Szczerbic (Alicja Rodak), Michael Lyndon (Adam Rodak), Jerry Skol (Tony Rodak), Michel Piccoli (government official), Anouk Aimée (Monique des Fontaines), John Hurt (Dino Montecurva), Jane Asher (bank manager), Eugeniusz Haczkiewicz (Genio).

Famous Polish theatre director, Alex Rodak, receives the Legion d'honneur in Paris, where he meets his wife and sons for the first time in two years. Their separation was caused by martial law in Poland; Rodak could not leave his country, while his family were awaiting him in London. The award allows Rodak to re-unite with his family and embark on a new project: staging a theatrical performance about martial law in Poland with the assistance of the French theatre producer, Monique des Fontaines. For this purpose he has to use a large number of Polish extras – emigrants working in London illegally. However, Rodak suffers financial problems. He has to borrow money from the bank to finance the birthday present for his son Adam and is refused a loan to buy a new car. The extras suspect that Rodak exploits them and threaten not to participate in his project. Monique also grows exasperated by Alex's financial demands. Reluctantly Rodak approaches a fellow expatriate, Dino Montecurva, to raise the money. In addition, Rodak has domestic problems. Inspectors from the council regard Rodak's house extension as illegal and begin to dismantle the roof. His wife, Alicja, grows inpatient with his eccentric project, which might severe them from Poland for good. Adam exchanges his father's costly gift of a movie camera for a walkman and a one-way ticket to Warsaw. He runs away from school, has sex with his girlfriend and boards a plane where he paints his hair and his face red. Rodak and Monique find the leader of the Polish extras and persuade him to encourage the others to take part in Rodak's performance for a fee of twenty pounds each. The show entitled *Success Is the Best Revenge* begins. It depicts Polish history, culminating in the introduction of martial law. The viewers witness various events travelling in specially hired buses. Montecurva brings the money. Alicja gives Alex a letter from Adam which informs him that his son has returned to Poland.

The Lightship
USA, 1985
Direction: Jerzy Skolimowski
Screenplay: William Mai, David Taylor, based on the novel *Das Feuerschiff* by Siegfried Lenz
Cinematography: Charly Steinberger
Editing: Barry Vince, Scott Hancock
Music: Stanley Myers
Sound: Guenther Stadelmann
Producer: Moritz Borman, Bill Benenson
Production company: CBS
Runtime: 88 min.
Colour
Cast: Robert Duvall (Calvin Caspary), Klaus Maria Brandauer (Captain Miller), Michael Lyndon (Alex), Tom Bower (Coop), Robert Costanzo (Stump), Badja Djola (Nate), William Forsythe (Eugene Waxler), Arliss Howard (Eddie Waxler).

The mid 1950s. Captain Miller, commander of the lightship 'Hatteras', floating off the coast of Norfolk, Virginia, takes his rebellious teenage son Alex on board. Alex and Miller are distant from each other and Alex appears to be unhappy to be 'imprisoned' on the lightship. The monotony of their existence is broken when three men, drifting in a disabled boat, approach the ship asking for shelter. Soon it turns out that the men, Calvin Caspary and Eddie and Eugene Waxler, are gangsters on the run. They terrorise the crew. Caspary mocks Miller for being the captain of a ship that does not go anywhere and Eugene kills the cook's pet crow. Although the crew puts pressure on Miller to resist the invaders, suggesting that during the war Miller's passivity led to disaster, Miller refuses to use arms. Yet crewman Stump overpowers Caspary and ties him up, but is killed by Eddie, and the cook Nate kills Eugene. Alex tries to pull his gun on Eddie, but is unable to kill him. Finally, when Caspary attempts to raise the anchor and use 'Hatteras' to escape, Miller confronts his opponent. Miller is shot and mortally wounded. Alex kills Eddie and Caspary is overpowered. Using voice-over, Alex admits that finally he understands his father.

Torrents of Spring
France/Italy, 1989
Direction: Jerzy Skolimowski
Screenplay: Jerzy Skolimowski, Arcangelo Bonaccorso, based on the novel *Torrents of Spring* by Ivan Turgenev
Cinematography: Dante Spinotti, Witold Sobociński
Editing: Cesare D'Amico
Music: Stanley Myers
Sound: André Hervée
Producer: Angelo Rizzoli

Production company: Erre Produzioni/Reteitalia (Rome)/Les Films Ariane/Films A2 (Paris), in association with Curzon Film Distributors (London).
Runtime: 101 min.
Colour
Cast: Timothy Hutton (Dimitri Sanin), Nastassia Kinski (Maria Nikolaevna Polozov), Valeria Golino (Gemma Rosselli), William Forsythe (Ippolite Polozov), Urbano Barberini (Baron von Doenhof), Francesca De Sapio (Signora Rosselli), Jacques Herlin (Pantaleone), Krzysztof Janczar (Herr Kluber), Jerzy Skolimowski (Victor Victorovich).

The 1840s. On his way back to Russia, a young aristocrat, Dimitri Sanin, stops in Germany, where he saves the life of an Italian boy and falls in love with his sister, Gemma, the daughter of an Italian patisserie family. He also takes part in a duel with a German officer, who offended Gemma in the presence of her cowardly and narrow-minded fiancé, Herr Kluber. Sanin decides to marry Gemma, sell his Russian estate and use the money to revive their failing business. He has the opportunity to fulfil his plan thanks to meeting an old acquaintance, Ippolite Polozov. Polozov is married to a rich Russian woman, Maria, with whom he is currently staying in Germany. Maria turns out to be interested in buying Sanin's estate and, in order to discuss the particulars of the future deal, Polozov organises a meeting between Maria and Sanin. Maria turns out to be a very beautiful and seductive woman, and Sanin falls under her spell. They make love on their horse trip to the countryside, with the apparent knowledge and approval of Polozov. Shortly after their return Maria organises a meeting between herself, Sanin and Gemma, during which Sanin turns out to be unable to make up his mind with which of the two women he wants to spend his life. Ashamed of himself, he cries and hides from Gemma. Soon afterwards Maria leaves Sanin in order to chase new men. Sanin follows her to Venice but cannot trace her. Maria suddenly dies and they never meet again. As on old man, standing on a barge, Sanin muses on what happened to him in the past. He learns that Gemma emigrated to America, is happily married and remains grateful to Sanin for saving her from marrying Kluber.

Ferdydurke (Thirty Door Key)
Poland/Great Britain/France, 1991
Direction: Jerzy Skolimowski
Screenplay: Joseph Kay, John Yorick, Jerzy Skolimowski, based on the novel *Ferdydurke* by Witold Gombrowicz
Cinematography: Witold Adamek
Editing: Grażyna Jasińska
Music: Stanisław Syrewicz, Michał Lorenc
Sound: Mariusz Kuczyński, Jerzy Szawłowski
Producer: Jerzy Skolimowski
Production company: Million Frames Ltd, Thirty Door Key Ltd & Cinema,
Runtime: 98 min.
Colour

Cast: Iain Glen (Józio), Robert Stephens (Professor Pimko), Crispin Glover (Miętus), Marek Probosz (Syfon), Artur Żmijewski (Kopyrda), Judith Godreche (Zuta), Dorota Stalińska (Młodziakowa), Jan Peszek (Młodziak), Beata Tyszkiewicz (aunt), Tadeusz Łomnicki (uncle), Fabienne Babe (Zosia), Zbigniew Zamachowski (farmhand Tom), Jerzy Skolimowski (school Headmaster).

Warsaw, the summer of 1939. The country prepares for war with Germany. Józio, a man who has just turned thirty and published his first book, is visited by his old teacher, Professor Pimko. Pimko claims that Józio is still immature and orders him to return to school. The most distinctive pupils there are Miętus, who dreams about a simple and brutal life in the country, among ordinary farmhands, and Syfon, who epitomises youthful innocence. These two men have a duel in pulling faces, which Miętus wins, stripping Syfon of his innocence. Pimko finds accommodation for Józio with the Młodziaks, who pride themselves on being an utterly modern family. Józio is enchanted by the beautiful Zuta Młodziak, but in order to avoid falling in love with her, creates a situation which reveals that the Młodziaks, deep down, are quite conventional people. Józio and Miętus leave Warsaw to visit Józio's aunt and uncle, a traditional Polish noble family. There Józio rekindles his love for his cousin Zosia who, in order to be with Józio, breaks her engagement with a German officer. Miętus, on the other hand, locates his attraction in Tom, a farmhand and servant at Józio's estate. His attempt to fraternise with Tom leads to overturning the traditional social order. The farmers attack and set fire to the estate. Józio and Zosia escape in a small boat, 'Transatlantyk'. Their disappearing into the darkness is accompanied by the sound of sirens. Documentary footage shows German planes flying over Warsaw, dropping bombs. The city is in flames.

Cztery noce z Anną (Four Nights with Anna)
Poland/France, 2008
Direction: Jerzy Skolimowski
Screenplay: Ewa Piaskowska, Jerzy Skolimowski
Cinematography: Adam Sikora
Production design: Marek Zawierucha
Editing: Cezary Grzesiuk
Music: Michał Lorenc
Sound: Frederic De Ravignan
Producer: Paolo Branco, Jerzy Skolimowski
Production company: Skopia Film, Alma Films
Runtime: 101 min.
Colour
Cast: Artur Steranko (Leon), Kinga Preis (Anna), Jerzy Fedorowicz (director of the hospital), Redbad Klijnstra (judge), Barbara Kołodziejska (Leon's grandmother).

North-east Poland. Leon, who was brought up by his grandmother, is a somewhat dreamy, if not slow-witted, middle-aged man, who cannot fight for himself. As a result of this weakness, those around him repeatedly abuse him. One day Leon witnesses the rape of a young woman. He informs the police and in due course is accused of committing this brutal act and is sent to prison. There his fellow inmates torment, rape and humiliate him. After his release Leon finds work in a hospital, with the medical waste incinerator. He also becomes obsessed with a nurse called Anna, who works in the same hospital and lives in the workers' hostel, opposite his house. Leon believes that Anna was the woman whose rape he witnessed. While Anna is sleeping, drugged by sleeping pills, with which he spiked her drinks, he sneaks into her room, washes the dishes, brings her flowers and even tries to put a diamond ring on her finger, bought with his redundancy money. However, during his fourth night with Anna, he is caught and sent back to prison, although at the trial he protests that he did not want to have sex with her or steal anything from her flat. Anna visits him in prison, returning to him the diamond ring he left in her room. She tells him that she believes in his innocence, but wants him to leave her in peace. After being released for the second time, Leon returns to his old house, but this time there is no chance to get into Anna's room, as a wall was erected between the neighbouring buildings.

Other films, in which Skolimowski participated

Niewinni czarodzieje (Innocent Sorcerers)
Poland, 1960
Direction: Andrzej Wajda
Jerzy Skolimowski: co-author, with Jerzy Andrzejewski, of script; actor in the role of a boxer

Nóż w wodzie (Knife in the Water)
Poland, 1961
Direction: Roman Polański
Jerzy Skolimowski: co-author, with Roman Polański and Jakub Goldberg, of script

Przyjaciel (Friend)
Poland, 1965
Direction: Marek Nowicki, Jerzy Stawicki
Jerzy Skolimowski: co-author of dialogues

Sposób bycia (Manner of living)
Poland, 1965
Direction: Jan Rybkowski
Jerzy Skolimowski: actor in the role of a lover of the female protagonist

Poślizg (Skid)
Poland, 1972
Direction: Jan Łomnicki
Jerzy Skolimowski: author of script, actor in the role of a garage's owner

Die Fälschung (Circle of Deceit)
West Germany, France, 1981
Direction: Volker Schlöndorff
Jerzy Skolimowski: actor in the role of journalist Hoffmann

White Nights
USA, 1985
Direction: Taylor Hackford
Jerzy Skolimowski: actor in the role of colonel Chaiko

Big Shots
USA, 1987
Direction: Robert Mandel
Jerzy Skolimowski: actor in the role of Doc

Motyw cienia (The Hollow Men)
Poland, Great Britain, 1993
Direction: Joseph Kay and John Yorick (Michał and Jerzy Skolimowski)
Jerzy Skolimowski: producer

Mars Attacks!
USA, 1996
Direction: Tim Burton
Jerzy Skolimowski: actor in the role of doctor Zeigler

L.A. without a Map
Great Britain, France, Finland, 1998
Direction: Mika Kaurismäki
Jerzy Skolimowski: actor in the role of minister

Operacja Samum (Samum Operation)
Poland, 1999
Direction: Władysław Pasikowski
Jerzy Skolimowski: actor in the role of Hayes, CIA agent

Before Night Falls
USA, 2001
Direction: Julian Schnabel
Jerzy Skolimowski: actor in the role of Professor

Eastern Promises
Great Britain, Canada, USA, 2007
Direction: David Cronenberg
Jerzy Skolimowski: actor in the role of Stepan

Bibliography

Andrew, Dudley (1992). 'Adaptation', in Gerald Mast et al. (eds), *Film Theory and Criticism*, fourth edition (Oxford: Oxford University Press), pp. 420–28.

Bachelard, Gaston (1994). *The Poetics of Space*, trans. Maria Jolas (Boston: Beacon Press).

Bakhtin, Mikhail (1984). *Rabelais and his World*, trans. Helene Iswolsky (Bloomington and Indianapolis: Indiana University Press).

Batura, Emilia (2001). *Księżycowy chłopiec: O Krzysztofie Komedzie-Trzcińskim* (Warsaw: Alfa-Wero).

Bauman, Zygmunt (2005). 'Między nami, pokoleniami...', in Piotr Nowak (ed.), *Wojna pokoleń* (Warsaw: Prószyński i S-ka), pp. 173–87.

Bly, Robert (1991). *Iron John: A Book About Men* (Shaftesbury: Element).

Błoński, Jan (1961). *Zmiana warty* (Warsaw: Czytelnik).

Boniecka, Ewa (1983). 'Skolimowski na filmowym ringu', *Życie Warszawy*, 27 July, p. 8.

Bonitzer, Pascal (1981). 'Partial Vision: Film and the Labyrinth', trans. Fabrice Ziolkowski, *Wide Angle*, 4, pp. 56–64.

Buckley, Jerome Hamilton (1984). *The Turning Key: Autobiography and the Subjective Impulse since 1800* (Camridge: Harvard University Press).

Buhks, Nora (1987). 'The Novel-Waltz (On the Structure of *King, Queen, Knave*)', *Zembla*, http://www.libraries.psu.edu/nabokov/buhks1., retrieved February 2007.

Bukowski, Krzysztof (1980). 'Muzyka Komedy', *Magazyn Muzyczny Jazz*, 7–8, pp. 8–11.

Christensen, Peter G. (1990). 'Skolimowski's *The Lightship* and Conrad', in Graham Petrie and Ruth Dwyer (eds), *Before the Wall Came Down: Soviet and East European Filmmakers Working in the West* (Lanham, MD: University Press of America), pp. 85–101.

Chyła, Wojciech (1992). 'Jerzy Skolimowski: Europeizacja polskości', *Literatura*, 6, pp. 13–17.

Ciment, Michel (1984). 'Skolimowski', in Christopher Lyon (ed.), *International Dictionary of Films and Filmmakers*, vol. 2 (London: St James Press).

Clancy, Laurie (1984). *The Novels of Vladimir Nabokov* (London: Macmillan).

Combs, Richard (1984). '*Success is the Best Revenge*', *Monthly Film Bulletin*, 12, pp. 389–90.

———— (1986a). '*The Lightship*', *Monthly Film Bulletin*, 5, pp. 131–32.

———— (1986b). 'Under Western Eyes: Skolimowski's Conradian Progress', *Monthly Film Bulletin*, 5, pp. 133–34.

———— (1990). 'Heart Like a Wheel', *The Listener*, 24 May, p. 36.

Conan Doyle, Sir Arthur (2004). *The Adventures of Gerard* (Fairfield: 1st World Library).

Conrad, Joseph (1973). *Victory: An Island Tale* (Harmondsworth: Penguin).

Cowie, Elizabeth (2000). '"Woman as Sign"', in E. Ann Kaplan (ed.), *Feminism and Film* (Oxford: Oxford University Press), pp. 48–65.

Cox, C.B. (1974). *Joseph Conrad: The Modern Imagination* (London: J.M. Dent and Sons).

Czerwiński, Marcin (1965). 'Skolimowskiego tragikomedia optymistyczna', *Film*, 23, p. 7.

Davis, Richard (1999). *Complete Guide to Film Scoring* (Boston: Berklee Press).

Donoghue, Denis (1982). 'Denis Donoghue in *Listener*', in Norman Page (ed.), *Nabokov: The Critical Heritage* (London: Routledge and Kegan Paul), p. 204.

Dygat, Stanisław (1975). *Disneyland* (Warsaw: Państwowy Instytut Wydawniczy).

Dzięglewski, Mariusz (2002). 'W poszukiwaniu własnej tożsamości: Fenomen debiutanckich filmów Jerzego Skolimowskiego', *Kwartalnik Filmowy*, 37–8, pp. 166–76.

Eberhardt, Konrad (1967). 'Skolimowski', *Kino*, 9, pp. 14–20.

——— (1982). *Konrad Eberhardt o polskich filmach* (Warsaw: Wydawnictwa Artystyczne i Filmowe).

Eagleton, Terry (1997). *Literary Theory: An Introduction*, second edition (Oxford: Blackwell).

Ezra, Elizabeth and Terry Rowden (2006). 'General Introduction: What is Transnational Cinema', in Elizabeth Ezra and Terry Rowden (eds), *Transnational Cinema: The Film Reader* (London: Routledge), pp. 1–14.

Field, Andrew (1967). *Nabokov: His Life in Art* (London: Hodder and Stoughton).

Foster, Hal (1993). *Compulsive Beauty* (Cambridge: MIT Press).

Fuentes, Carlos (1988). *Myself with Others* (London: Picador).

Gabbard, Krin (2003). 'Whose Jazz, Whose Cinema?', in Kay Dickinson (ed.), *Movie Music: The Film Reader* (London: Routledge), pp. 121–32.

Gazda, Janusz (1966). 'Bunt i zazdrość', *Ekran*, 48, p. 7.

——— (1967a). 'Trzecie kino polskie – kino poetyckie', *Ekran*, 16, p. 3.

——— (1967b). 'Trzecie kino polskie – kino ironiczne', *Ekran*, 17, p. 3.

——— (1968). 'Nadzieja na trzecie kino polskie', *Kultura Filmowa*, 4, p. 4.

Gombrowicz, Witold (1973). *A Kind of Testament*, trans. by Alastair Hamilton (Philadephia: Temple University Press).

——— (1997). *Dziennik 1953–1956* (Kraków: Wydawnictwo Literackie).

——— (2005). *Ferdydurke*, trans. Eric Mosbacher (London: Marion Boyars).

——— (2006). *Ferdydurke* (Kraków: Wydawnictwo Literackie).

Gorbman, Claudia (1987). *Unheard Melodies: Narrative Film Music* (London: BFI).

Grosz, Elizabeth (1990). *Jacques Lacan: A Feminist Introduction* (London: Routledge).

Hall, Stuart (1992). 'The Question of Cultural Identity', in Stuart Hall et al. (eds) *Modernity and its Futures* (Cambridge: Polity Press).

Hanáková, Petra (2005). 'The Construction of Normality: The Lineage of Male Figures in Contemporary Czech Cinema', in Uta Röhrborn (ed.) *Mediale Welten in Tschechien nach 1898: Genderkonstructionen und Codes des Plebejismus* (Munich: Kubon and Sagner), pp. 149–59.

Hauschild, Marta (2007). 'Trzecia fala polskiego kina', *Kwartalnik Filmowy*, 57–58, pp. 103–17.

Havel, Václav (1985). 'The Power of the Powerless', in John Keane (ed.), *The Power of the Powerless* (London: Hutchinson), pp. 23–96.

Hayes, Kevin J. (2002). '*JLG/JLG – Autoportrait de Décembre*: Reinscribing the Book', *Quarterly Review of Film and Video*, 19, pp. 155–64.

Heller, Margot (ed.) (1999). *Diary* (Manchester: Cornerhouse).

Helman, Alicja (1974). 'U źródeł trzeciego kina', *Film*, 20, p. 12–13.

―――― (ed.) (2002). *Bolesław Michałek: Ambasador polskiego kina* (Kraków: Rabid).

Hodsdon, Bruce (2003). 'Jerzy Skolimowski', *Senses of Cinema*, http://www.sensesofcinema.com/contents/directors/03/skolimowski.html., retrieved January 2007.

Hughson, John (2005) 'The Loneliness of the Angry Young Sportsman', *Film & History*, 2, pp. 41–48.

Jackiewicz, Aleksander (1964). 'Nasza "nowa fala"', *Film*, 19, p. 7.

―――― (1977). 'Skolimowski', in *Mistrzowie kina współczesnego* (Warsaw: Wydawnictwa Artystyczne i Filmowe), pp. 169–74.

―――― (1983). *Moja filmoteka: Kino polskie* (Warsaw: Wydawnictwa Artystyczne i Filmowe).

Janicka, Bożena (1966). 'Nie jestem wcale taki modny – mówi Jerzy Skolimowski', *Film*, 51–2, p. 8–9.

―――― (1985). 'Nocna rozmowa sprzed lat', *Film*, 8, p. 9.

―――― (1992). 'Szyderca jako prorok', *Film*, 2, p. 6.

Janicki, Stanisław (1966). '*Bariera*: Notatki z planu', *Kino*, pp. 37–50.

Janion, Maria (1989). *Wobec zła* (Chotomów: Verba).

―――― (1991). *Projekt krytyki fantazmatycznej* (Warsaw: PEN).

―――― (1998). *Płacz generała: Eseje o wojnie* (Warsaw: Sic!).

Jankun-Dopartowa, Mariola (1997). '*Rysopis* jako duchowa biografia pokolenia', *Kwartalnik Filmowy*, 17, pp. 98–104.

Jarzębski, Jerzy and Zawadzki, Andrzej (2006). 'Zachwyca – nie zachwyca', in Witold Gombrowicz, *Ferdydurke* (Kraków: Wydawnictwo Literackie), pp. 265–89.

Jocher, Witold (1967). 'Jerzy Skolimowski', *Litery*, 7, pp. 24–25.

Johnson, William (1979). '*The Shout*', *Film Quarterly*, Fall, pp. 53–59.

Kałużyński, Zygmunt (1965). 'Czy Polska ma nową falę?', *Polityka*, 51, p. 8–9.

Karl, Frederick R. and Laurence Davies (eds) (1988). *The Collected Letters of Joseph Conrad*, vol. 3, 1903–1907 (Cambridge: Cambridge University Press).

Kilian, Jarosław (1992). 'Feliks Topolski – kronikarz XX wieku', in Marta Fik (ed.), *Między Polską a światem: Kultura emigracyjna po 1939 roku* (Warsaw: Krąg), pp. 177–84.

Klejsa, Konrad (2004). 'Jerzy Skolimowski – gry, maski, tęsknoty, ucieczki… (cztery spojrzenia na wczesną twórczość)', in Grażyna Stachówna and Joanna Wojnicka (eds) *Mistrzowie kina polskiego* (Kraków: Rabid), pp. 91–107.

―――― (2006). 'Obcy we mnie, obcy wśród nas: Doświadczenie emigracyjne w brytyjskich filmach Jerzego Skolimowskiego (*Fucha* i *Najlepszą zemstą jest sukces*)', *Kwartalnik Filmowy*, 53, pp. 142–57.

Komeda-Trzciński, Krzysztof (1961). 'Z ankiety "Rola muzyki w dziele filmowym"', *Kwartalnik Filmowy*, 2, pp. 35–38.

Kornacki, Krzysztof (2004). 'Baśń Wielkanocna, czyli *Bariera* Jerzego Skolimowskiego obejrzana na nowo', *Kino*, 4, pp. 59–61.

Kowal, Roman (1995). *Polski jazz: Wczesna historia i trzy biografie zamknięte: Komeda, Kosz, Seifert* (Kraków: Akademia Muzyczna w Krakowie).

Kreutzinger, Krzysztof (1984). '*Bariera*', *Film*, 34, p. 9.

Krubski, Krzysztof et al. (1998). *Filmówka: Powieść o Łódzkiej Szkole Filmowej* (Warsaw: Tenten).

Krzemiński, Adam (1991). 'Zmiana kodu: Rozmowa z Marią Janion', *Polityka*, 48, pp. 17–18.

Kurz, Iwona (2005). *Twarze w tłumie: Wizerunki bohaterów wyobraźni zbiorowej w kulturze polskiej lat 1955–1969* (Izabelin: Świat Literacki).

Lacan, Jacques (1977). *Écrits: A Selection*, trans. Alan Sheridan (London: Tavistock).

Lachnit-Lubelska, Ewa (1983). 'Konstrukcja *Rysopisu* Jerzego Skolimowskiego', *Powiększenie*, 2, pp. 52–62.

Laderman, David (2002). *Driving Visions: Exploring the Road Movie* (Austin: University of Texas Press).

Lejeune, Philippe (1989). *On Autobiography*, trans. Katherine Leary (Minneapolis: University of Minnesota Press).

Lenz, Siegfried (1986). *The Lightship*, trans. Michael Bullock (London: Methuen).

Lenarciński, Michał (1994). 'Potrzebuję trzech pór roku', *Wiadomości dnia*, 21, 3 January, p. 5.

Levy, Silvano (1997). 'Introduction', in Silvano Levy (ed.), *Surrealism: Surrealist Visuality* (Edinburgh: Keele University Press), pp. 7–10.

Lichocka, Joanna (1994). 'Z dołu do góry, z góry na dół...', *Uroda*, 2, pp. 6–9.

Liehm, Antonín (1983). 'Miloš Forman: the Style and the Man', in David W. Paul (ed.) *Politics, Art and Commitment in the East European Cinema* (London: Macmillan), pp. 211–24.

Lubelski, Tadeusz (1989). '*Rysopis*, czyli wprowadzenie outsidera', *Kino*, 11, pp. 1–3 and 24–26.

Maddox, Conroy (1997). 'Only Chaos within One Gives Birth to a Dancing Star', in Silvano Levy (ed.), *Surrealism: Surrealist Visuality* (Edinburgh: Keele University Press), pp. 11–14.

Malt, Johanna (2004). *Obscure Objects of Desire: Surrealism: Fetishism, and Politics* (Oxford: Oxford University Press).

Marszałek, Rafał (1971). '*Na samym dnie*: próba opisu', *Kino*, 6, pp. 41–45.

Mazierska, Ewa (2007). *Roman Polanski: The Cinema of a Cultural Traveller* (London: I.B. Tauris).

——— (2008). *Masculinities in Polish, Czech and Slovak Cinema: Blue Peters and Men of Marble* (Cambridge: Berghahn).

Mazierska, Ewa and Laura Rascaroli (2004). *The Cinema of Nanni Moretti: Dreams and Diaries* (London: Wallflower Press).

Michałek, Bolesław (1966). 'Film i literatura, filmowcy i pisarze', *Kino*, 3, reprinted in Alicja Helman (ed.) (2002). *Bolesław Michałek: Ambasador polskiego kina* (Kraków: Rabid), pp. 137–50.

Michałek, Bolesław and Frank Turaj (1988). *The Modern Cinema of Poland* (Bloomington: Indiana University Press).

Milne, Tom (1971). '*The Adventures of Gerard*', *Monthly Film Bulletin*, 1, p. 3.

——— (1973). '*King, Queen, Knave*', *Monthly Film Bulletin*, 12, p. 250.

Miłosz, Czesław (1982). 'Joseph Conrad in Polish Eyes (1957)', in R.W. Stallman, *The Art of Joseph Conrad: A Critical Symposium* (Athens: Ohio University Press), pp. 35–45.

——— (1996). *Selected Poems*, trans. Louis Iribarne and David Brooks (Kraków: Wydawnictwo Literackie).

Mirska, Dorota (1994). 'Ręce do góry!', *Twój Styl*, 7, pp. 52–56.

Morrey, Douglas (2005). *Jean-Luc Godard* (Manchester: Manchester University Press).

Moullet, Luc (1986). 'Jean-Luc Godard (April 1960)' in Jim Hillier (ed.) *Cahiers du Cinéma*, vol. 2 (London: Routledge and Kegan Paul), pp. 35–48.

Mulvey, Laura (1996). 'Visual Pleasure and Narrative Cinema', in E. Ann Kaplan (ed.), *Feminism and Film* (Oxford: Oxford University Press), pp. 34–47.

Nabokov, Vladimir (1970). *King Queen Knave* (London: Panther).

Naficy, Hamid (2001). *An Accented Cinema: Exilic and Diasporic Filmmaking* (Princeton: Princeton University Press).

———— (ed.) (1999). *Home, Exile, Homeland* (London: Routledge).

Newman, Kim (2007). 'The Sound of Fear: The Influences and Production of *The Shout*' (Essay accompanying the DVD version of Jerzy Skolimowski's film) (Network).

Oleksiewicz, Maria (1965). 'Dwadzieścia dziewięć ujęć', *Film*, 32, p. 11.

———— (1969). 'Podarunek dla aktora', *Film*, 10, p. 5.

———— (1972). 'Kalki', *Film*, 43, p. 4.

Orr, John (1993). 'Commodified Demons II: The Automobile', in *Cinema and Modernity* (Cambridge: Polity Press).

Ostrowska, Elżbieta (1998). 'Filmic Representations of the "Polish Mother" in Post-Second World War Polish Cinema', *The European Journal of Women's Studies*, 5, pp. 419–35.

Owen, Jonathan (2008). *The Avant-Garde Tradition in Czech New Wave Cinema*, Ph.D thesis, University of Manchester.

Pascal, Roy (1960). *Design and Truth in Autobiography* (London: Routledge and Kegan Paul).

Paul, David (1986). '*The Lightship*', *Film Quarterly*, Fall, pp. 14–17.

Piątek, Waldemar (1983). 'Gdzieś blisko siebie', *Powiększenie*, 2, pp. 28–36.

Płażewski, Jerzy (1965). 'Trzecie kino polskie? Uwagi o produkcji 1965', *Ekran*, 51–2, p. 3.

———— (1992). 'Zastrzeżenia szacunkiem podszyte', *Kino*, 7, pp. 9–10.

Płonowska Ziarek, Ewa (ed.) (1998). *Gombrowicz's Grimaces: Modernism, Gender, Nationality* (Albany: State University of New York Press).

Pogorzelska, Joanna (2001). 'Sukces jest najlepszą zemstą', *Magazyn Gazety* (supplement to *Gazeta Wyborcza*), 8 February, pp. 20–24.

Polanski, Roman (1984). *Roman by Polanski* (London: Heinemann).

Popiel, Michał (2006). 'Skolimowski: jestem leniem', *Dziennik*, 31 May, p. 36.

Prendergast, Roy M. (1992). *Film Music: A Neglected Art* (New York: W.W. Norton and Company).

Richardson, Michael (2006). *Surrealism and Cinema* (Oxford: Berg).

Ronduda, Łukasz (2007). 'Skolimowski, Królikiewicz, Żuławski, Uklański, czyli wypisy z historii polskiej nowej fali', *Obieg*, 1 November, http://www.obieg.pl/text/07110101.php., retrieved January 2008.

Ronduda, Łukasz and Barbara Piwowarska (eds) (2008). *Nowa Fala: Historia zjawiska, którego nie było* (Warsaw: Instytut Adama Mickiewicza, CSW Zamek Ujazdowski).

Roszak, Theodore (1995). *The Making of a Counter-Culture* (Berkeley: University of California Press).

Rutkowska, Teresa (2002). 'Zaczarowany Opel Rekord', *Pamiętnik Literacki*, 3–4, pp. 286–302.

Salecki, Jerzy Andrzej (1970). 'Klęski i zwycięstwa scenarzysty', *Sportowiec*, 17, pp. 14 and 21.

Schapiro, Leonard (1980). 'Critical Essay – *Spring Torrents*: Its Place and Significance in the Life and Work of Ivan Sergeyevich Turgenev', in Ivan Turgenev, *Spring Torrents*, trans. Leonard Schapiro (London: Penguin), pp. 183–239.

Schopenhauer, Arthur (1923). *The Wisdom of Life* (London: George Allen and Unwin).

Seed, Patricia (1999). 'The Key to the House', in Hamid Naficy (ed.), *Home, Exile, Homeland* (London: Routledge), pp. 85–94.

Short, Robert (1997). 'Magritte and the Cinema', in Silvano Levy (ed.), *Surrealism: Surrealist Visuality* (Edinburgh: Keele University Press), pp. 95–108.

Skolimowski, Jerzy (1958). *Gdzieś blisko siebie* (Katowice: Śląsk).

───── (1959). *Siekiera i niebo* (Warsaw: Czytelnik).

Skwara, Janusz (1972). 'Nowa twarz znanego bohatera', *Kino*, 10, pp. 2–7.

Smader, Honorata and Krzysztof Demidowicz (2004). 'Bez walkowera', *Film*, 8, pp. 104–7.

Sobolewski, Tadeusz (1996). 'Outsider Skolimowski', *Kino*, 11, p. 53.

Sontag, Susan (1983). 'Under the Sign of Saturn', in *Under the Sign of Saturn* (London: Writers and Readers), pp. 109–34.

───── (1994). 'A Note on Novels and Films', in *Against Interpretation* (London: Vintage), pp. 242–45.

───── (2002). 'Gombrowicz's *Ferdydurke*', in *Where the Stress Falls* (London: Jonathan Cape), pp. 97–105.

Sowińska, Iwona (2006). *Polska muzyka filmowa 1945–1968* (Katowice: Wydawnictwo Uniwersytetu Śląskiego).

Stam, Robert (2000). 'Beyond Fidelity: The Dialogics of Adaptation', in James Naremore (ed.), *Film Adaptation* (London: Athlone), pp. 54–76.

Stanuch, Stanisław (1990). 'Kaskader uczuć', in Edward Kolbus (ed.), *Kaskaderzy Literatury* (Łódź: Wydawnictwo Łódzkie), pp. 9–25.

Strick, Philip (1978). 'Skolimowski's Cricket Match', *Sight and Sound*, Summer, pp. 146–47.

Thompson, David. (2007). '*Deep End*', in Nick James (ed.), '75 Hidden Gems', *Sight and Sound*, 8, pp. 18–32.

Thomsen, Christian Braad (1968). 'Skolimowski', *Sight and Sound*, Summer, pp. 142–44.

Tomasik, Wojciech (2004). 'All that Jazz! On Tyrmand's Challenge to Stalinism', *Blok*, 3, pp. 179–86.

Turgenev, Ivan (1980). *Spring Torrents*, trans. Leonard Schapiro (London: Penguin).

Uszyński, Jerzy (1989). 'Ousiderzy są zmęczeni?', *Kino*, 11, pp. 4–7.

───── (1990a). 'Jerzy Skolimowski o sobie: Całe życie jak na dłoni', *Film na świecie*, 379, pp. 3–47.

───── (1990b). 'Ładny numer – PH 232545', *Film*, 4, pp. 6–7.

Walker, Michael (1970). 'Jerzy Skolimowski', in Ian Cameron (ed.), *Second Wave* (London: Studio Vista), pp. 34–62.

Werner, Mateusz (1992). 'A kto widział – ten trąba', *Kino*, 7, pp. 8–9.

Wertenstein Wajda (ed.) (1991). *Wajda mówi o sobie: Wywiady i teksty* (Kraków: Wydawnictwo Literackie).

Willet, John (1970). *Expressionism* (London: Weidenfeld and Nicolson).

Wilson, Colin (1960). *The Outsider* (London: Victor Gollancz).

Wilson, David (1967). '*Barrier*', *Monthly Film Bulletin*, 12, p. 187.

Wojciechowski, Piotr (1992). 'Gęba przeciw Apokalipsie', *Film*, 10, pp. 12–13.

Woodward, Kath (2002). *Understanding Identity* (London: Arnold).

Wróbel, Szymon (2001). 'Biografia jako dzieło sztuki', *Sztuka i filozofia*, 19, pp. 140–63.

———— (2005). 'Polityka temporalna', in Piotr Nowak (ed.), *Wojna pokoleń* (Warsaw: Prószyński i S-ka), pp. 261–77.

Yakir, Dan (1982). 'Polestar', *Film Comment*, November–December, pp. 28–32.

Ziółkowski, Bohdan (1967). 'Rozmowa z Jerzym Skolimowskim', *Odgłosy*, 42, p. 8–9.

Žižek, Slavoj (1991). *Looking Awry: An Introduction to Jacques Lacan through Popular Culture* (Cambridge: MIT Press).

Index